MERGERS AND
ACQUISITIONS

Other books in the McGraw-Hill Executive MBA Series include:

SALES MANAGEMENT
FINANCE AND ACCOUNTING FOR NONFINANCIAL MANAGERS
CORPORATE STRATEGY

MERGERS AND ACQUISITIONS

THE McGRAW-HILL EXECUTIVE MBA SERIES

J. FRED WESTON

SAMUEL C. WEAVER

McGraw-Hill

New York   Chicago   San Francisco   Lisbon   London   Madrid
Mexico City   Milan   New Delhi   San Juan   Seoul
Singapore   Sydney   Toronto

1 2 3 4 5 6 7 8 9 0   DOC/DOC   0 9 8 7 6 5 4 (HC)
2 3 4 5 6 7 8 9 0   DOC/DOC   0 9 8 7 6 5 4 (PBK)

ISBN 0-07-136432-3 (HC)
ISBN 0-07-143537-9 (PBK)

This publication is designed to provide accurate and authoritative information in regard to the subject matter covered. It is sold with the understanding that neither the author nor the publisher is engaged in rendering legal, accounting, futures/securities trading, or other professional service. If legal advice or other expert assistance is required, the services of a competent professional person should be sought.
— From a Declaration of Principles jointly adopted by a Committee of the American Bar Association and a committee of Publishers.

McGraw-Hill books are available at special quantity discounts to use as premiums and sales promotions, or for use in corporate training programs. For more information, please write to the Director of Special Sales, Professional Publishing, McGraw-Hill, Two Penn Plaza, New York, NY 10121-2298. Or contact your local bookstore.

This book was printed on recycled, acid-free paper containing a minimum of 50% recycled, de-inked fiber.

Library of Congress Cataloging-in-Publication Data

Weston, J. Fred (John Fred), 1916-
    Mergers and acquisitions / by J. Fred Weston and
        Samuel C. Weaver.
        p.   cm.
    ISBN 0-07-136432-3
    1. Consolidation and merger of corporations.
    Consolidation and merger of corporations—
        United States. I. Title.
    HG4028.M4W468   2001
    658.1/6 21   12387665

CONTENTS

PREFACE

From 1992 to 2000, the pace of merger activity rose to unprecedented levels. An environment of sustained economic growth and rising stock prices facilitated transactions. Toward the end of 2000, the economic climate shifted and merger activity in the fourth quarter declined. The economy showed only small growth during the first quarter of 2001. Excess capacity in a number of industries had developed, and sales and profit disappointments began to widen. The business cycle had returned. Valuations in Internet companies and other high-tech industries have been sharply revised downward. The pooling method of accounting for mergers is scheduled to be abolished. New challenges face business firms large and small.

In this new economic environment, the nature of merger activity will change and the dollar volume may decline. But the economic role of mergers and related activities will expand. The term "mergers and acquisitions (M&As)" encompasses a widening range of activities, including joint ventures, licensing, spin-offs, equity carveouts, tracking stocks, restructuring, alliances, and other corporate interactions such as network relationships.

The fundamental role of M&A activities is to enable firms to adjust more effectively to new challenges and opportunities. If done efficiently, M&As can increase revenues and market share, improve profitability, and enhance enterprise values. The data show that mergers overall have increased market values. With excess capacity in a number of industries, mergers to facilitate the consolidation and reduction of capacity will be required. The new technologies will continue to impact industries and create opportunities for business firms of all sizes. There will continue to be opportunities for small firms to come into being and to establish substantial valuations. The venture capital industry and financial buyers will continue to represent important activities.

Earlier studies reported that two-thirds of mergers were failures in the sense that they did not earn the required cost of capital for the product-market activity involved. Later studies of strategic mergers of the 1990s suggest that the success rate is moving toward 50 percent. This book seeks to convey information that will help individual firms achieve successful M&A activities.

Thousands of articles and books have been written on the many aspects of M&As. Hundreds of new ones appear each year. In this small volume we seek to summarize the findings of the M&A literature without citations to the individual publications themselves. We seek to provide a framework for achieving M&A activities that add value to the firm.

We express our appreciation to Juan A. Siu and Brian A. Johnson, who had been our collaborators on many studies on M&As. We also benefited from our continuing interactions with Alexandra Reed Lajoux, who has written wisely and well on many aspects of M&As. We have long benefited from the contributions of Martin Sikora, the editor of the *Mergers & Acquisitions* magazine. We have also benefited from our UCLA colleagues who participate in the Anderson School's twice-a-year Merger Week executive programs. We have learned much from the executives that have participated in these merger programs. We received assistance also from our associates in our Takeovers and Restructuring Program at the Anderson School at UCLA. They include Cindy Chang and Laura Hougham. We also benefited from the continuous assistance from Brigitta Schumacher of the Anderson School finance area support staff.

Backup software related to the valuation materials and other topics are available at Weston's website: http://www. anderson.ucla.edu/faculty/john.weston

We invite comments and suggestions from our readers.

J. Fred Weston
Samuel C. Weaver

CHAPTER ONE

Change Forces and Mergers

Mergers and restructuring activities accelerated through the first quarter of 2000. The volume of deal activities declined quarter by quarter through the first quarter of 2001. But overcapacity in a number of industries will predictably result in consolidation mergers. The rules of the games are changing as well. The Hart-Scott-Rodino Act of 1976 was amended on December 21, 2000. The abolition of the pooling method of accounting appears to be likely. The rules for writing off goodwill and other intangibles are being changed. So while the pace of M&A activities may decline from the torrid levels of the late 1990s, they continue to represent a major force in the financial and economic environment.

Merger activity in the United States and worldwide rose to unprecedented levels in 1998 and 1999, as shown in Table 1.1. Merger activity leveled off in 2000. The stock market indexes reached their peak in March 2000, and stock prices continued to decline during the fourth quarter. This was associated with a decline in merger activity toward the end of the year. As shown in Table 1.1, the year 2000 represented a leveling off of worldwide M&A activity, but from unusually high levels. The average dollar volume of M&A activity in the United States for the years 1998 through 2000 was slightly more than $1.5 trillion; for the rest of the world the corresponding figure was somewhat more than $1.3 trillion. For both segments of the world, the percentage increases compared with average levels in 1995 to 1997 were approximately 157 percent.

The current merger activity is a part of what has been called the *fifth merger movement,* which began in 1993 and has been characterized by strategic megamergers. Table 1.2 lists the top 10 mergers in all history through January 2001. All these mergers are greater than $50 billion, and have occurred since 1998. The Vodafone–Air Touch transaction involved a foreign (United Kingdom) acquirer. The ninth largest transaction involved foreign

TABLE 1.1

Announced M&A Activity ($ Billion)

Year	U.S. Domestic		Worldwide		Rest of the World	
	$ Totals	% Change	$ Totals	% Change	$ Totals	% Change
1985	$201		$237		$36	
1986	205	2	260	10	55	53
1987	214	4	312	20	98	78
1988	356	66	503	61	147	50
1989	306	−14	556	11	250	70
1990	172	−44	430	−23	258	3
1991	133	−23	339	−21	206	−20
1992	132	−1	322	−5	190	−8
1993	219	66	435	35	216	14
1994	310	42	527	21	217	0
1995	404	30	825	57	421	94
1996	564	40	1003	22	439	4
1997	811	44	1497	49	686	56
1998	1480	82	2302	54	822	20
1999	1436	−3	3072	33	1636	99
2000	1661	16	3180	4	1519	−7
Average						
95–97	$593		$1108		$515	
98–00	1526	157.3	2851	157.3	1326	157.2

Source: Thomson Financial Securities Data.

T A B L E   1.2

Top 10 Mergers

Rank	Acquirer	Acquired	Announcement Date	Amount ($ Billion)	Industry
1	AOL	Time Warner	January 2000	$165.9	Internet/media
2	Exxon	Mobil	December 1998	78.9	Oil
3	Travelers Group	Citicorp	April 1998	72.6	Financial services
4	SBC Comm.	Ameritech	May 1998	62.6	Telecommunications
5	Nations Bank	BankAmerica	April 1998	61.6	Financial services
6	Vodafone Group	AirTouch Comm.	January 1999	60.3	Telecommunications
7	AT&T	MediaOne Group	April 1999	56.0	Telecommunications
8	AT&T	Tele-Communications	June 1998	53.6	Telecommunications
9	Total Fina	Elf Acquitaine	July 1999	53.5	Oil
10	Bell Atlantic	GTE	July 1998	53.4	Telecommunications

firms on both sides of the deal. Five of the ten were in telecommunications, two in oils and financial services. The largest of all was AOL and Time Warner, which will be placed in the Internet/media category, combining the new and old economies.

To understand the reasons for the strong growth of M&A activity worldwide in recent years and whether the slowing toward the end of 2000 will continue requires some historical perspective.

THE CHANGE FORCES

The increased pace of M&A activity in recent years has reflected powerful change forces in the world economy. Ten change forces are identified: (1) The pace of technological change has accelerated. (2) The costs of communication and transportation have been greatly reduced. (3) Hence markets have become international in scope. (4) The forms, sources, and intensity of competition have expanded. (5) New industries have emerged. (6) While regulations have increased in some areas, deregulation has taken place in other industries. (7) Favorable economic and financial environments have persisted from 1982 to 1990 and from 1992 to mid-2000. (8) Within a general environment of strong economic growth, problems have developed in individual economies and industries. (9) Inequalities in income and wealth have been widening. (10) Valuation relationships and equity returns for most of the 1990s have risen to levels significantly above long-term historical patterns.

Overriding all are technological changes, which include personal computers, computer services, software, servers, and the many advances in information systems, including the Internet. Improvements in communication and transportation have created a global economy. Nations have adopted international agreements such as the General Agreement on Tariffs and Trade (GATT) that have resulted in freer trade. The growing forces of competition have produced deregulation in major industries such as financial services, airlines, and medical services.

The next set of factors relates to efficiency of operations. Economies of scale spread the large fixed cost of investing in machinery or computer systems over a larger number of units. Economies of scope refer to cost reductions from operations in related activities. In the information industry, these would represent economies of activities in personal computer (PC) hardware, PC software, server hardware, server software, the Internet, and other related activities. Another efficiency gain is achieved by combining complementary activities, for example, combining a company strong in research with one strong in marketing. Mergers to catch up technologically are illustrated by the series of acquisitions by AT&T.

Another major force stimulating M&A and restructuring activities comprises changes in industry organization. An example is the shift in the computer industry from vertically integrated firms to a horizontal chain of independent activities. Dell Computers, for example, has been very successful concentrating on PC sales with only limited activities in the many other segments of the value chain of the information industry.

The economic and financial environments have also been favorable for deal making. Strong economic growth, rising stock prices, and relatively low interest rates have favored internal growth as well as a range of M&A activities. Individual entrepreneurship has responded to opportunities and, in turn, created further dynamism in industrial activities. Examples are Bill Gates at Microsoft, Andrew Grove at Intel, Jack Welch at General Electric, John Chambers at Cisco Systems, and Bernie Ebbers at MCI WorldCom, among the many.

CONSEQUENCES OF THE CHANGE FORCES

The change forces are having major impacts. The technological requirements for firms have increased. The requirements for human capital inputs have grown relative to physical assets. The knowledge and organizational capital components of firm value have increased. Growth opportunities among product areas are unequal. New industries have been created. The pace of product introductions has accelerated. Economic activity has shifted from manufacturing to services of increasing sophistication. Distribution and marketing methods have changed. The value chain has deconstructed in the sense that more activities are performed by specialist firms. Forces for vertical integration have diminished in some areas, but increased in others. Changes in the organization of industries have taken place. Industry boundaries have become increasingly blurred. The forms and number of competitors have been increasing. New growth opportunities have attracted such large flows of resources that unfavorable sales-to-capacity relationships have developed, even in new industries such as telecommunications and e-commerce. The decline and failure rates of firms in some sectors have accelerated. Strategy formulation and revisions are more important. Real-time financial planning and control information requirements have increased.

These impacts have expanded opportunities and risks. A wide range of adjustment processes have been used by firms in response to their increasingly changing environment. The characteristics of the many adjustment processes are briefly summarized in Table 1.3.

T A B L E 1.3

Forms of Adjustment Activities

I. Expansion and growth

   A. Mergers—any transaction that forms one economic unit from two or more previous units

   B. Tender offers—a method of making a takeover via a direct offer to target firm shareholders

   C. Joint ventures—a combination of subsets of assets contributed by two (or more) business entities for a specific business purpose and a limited duration

   D. Supplier networks—long-term cooperative relationships

   E. Alliances—more informal interbusiness relations

   F. Investments—a stake, but not control in another organization

   G. Franchising—contracts for the use of name, reputation, business format

II. Restructuring—changes in organizations and management systems

   A. Equity carve-outs—a public sale of a portion of a segment equity

   B. Spin-offs—distribution on a pro rata basis of segment equity to parent shareholders

   C. Divestitures—sale of a segment of a company to a third party

   D. Tracking stock—a separate class of common stock that tracks the performance of a segment

III. Financial engineering and changes in ownership structure

   A. Exchange offers—the right or option to exchange one class of a security for another, e.g., an exchange of common stock for debt

   B. Share repurchases—a public corporation buys its own shares (1) by tender offer, (2) on the open market, or (3) in negotiated buybacks

   C. Leveraged buyouts (LBOs, MBOs)—the purchase of a company by a small group of investors, financed largely by debt

   D. Leveraged recapitalizations—a large increase in the leverage ratio to finance the return of cash to shareholders

   E. Employee stock ownership plans (ESOPs)—a defined contribution pension plan designed to invest primarily in the stock of the employer firm

   F. Dual-class recapitalizations—creation of two classes of common stock, with the superior-vote stock concentrated in the hands of management

IV. Governance—control of decision powers

   A. Compensation arrangements—payment forms to align interests of managers, owners, and employees

   B. Proxy contest—an attempt by a dissident group of shareholders to gain representation on a firm's board of directors

   C. Premium buybacks (greenmail)—the repurchase of specified shares, usually from a party seeking to take over a firm

   D. Takeover defenses—methods employed by targets to prevent the success of bidders' efforts

By M&A activities, we refer to more than mergers and acquisitions. They include joint ventures and strategic alliances. Also included are restructuring activities such as divestitures, carve-outs, spin-offs, and tracking stocks. Changes in ownership structure have taken place through share repurchases, leveraged buyouts, dual-class recapitalizations, and leveraged recapitalizations. Corporate control and governance have changed through shareholder activism, proxy contests, and a wide range of merger defenses. But M&As, as broadly described, are an addition, not a substitution for internal improvements. Indeed, the most successful M&A activities are built on a base of a strong and efficient firm. Every firm must seek to improve strategic vision, efficiency of operations, and quality of products, through both internal efforts and external M&A activities.

MERGER MOVEMENTS

The foregoing describes M&A activities beginning in 1993, the fifth major merger movement—the era of strategic megamergers. This M&A activity exists worldwide, not just in the U.S. economy. The forces in Europe have been similar to the factors in the earlier merger movements in the United States. The four previous merger movements in the United States can be briefly summarized:

First Merger Movement—1893 to 1904

The merger movement at the turn of the century was associated with the completion of the transcontinental railroad system. It created the first common market. Europe is experiencing similar forces from its effort at integration. In relation to the gross domestic product (GDP), this merger movement in the United States has thus far been of greater magnitude than any others, so the merger forces in Europe are very strong. In the United States, major horizontal mergers took place in steel, oil, telephone, and the basic manufacturing industries at the time.

Second Merger Movement—1920s

This period was characterized by an increase in vertical mergers. These were associated with the development of the radio, which made national advertising possible, and the automobile, which permitted more effective geographic sales and distribution organizations. Vertical mergers enabled manufacturers to control distribution channels more effectively.

Third Merger Movement—1960s

The conglomerate mergers of the 1960s represented in part an adjustment to the slowdown in defense expenditures. In every sample of conglomerates, at least one-half of the companies were aerospace or natural resource–depleting companies (oil, forest). Also influencing this was the idea that a good manager, with the new planning literature, could manage anything. Also at this time, industries like the food industries, hoping to avoid their growth being tied down to population growth, diversified. Much of the diversification at this time was ill advised as companies moved away from their core competencies.

Fourth Merger Movement—1980s

Financial innovations, junk bonds, made all firms vulnerable to a takeover bid. Any company that was not performing up to its potential could be taken over. Chemical Bank and Disney were both almost taken over. So the availability of high-risk financing strongly propelled the 1980s and there was some dismantling of the diversification of the 1960s.

Each of the merger movements in the United States was driven by a different set of economic and development forces. But these movements did not occur randomly. A distinct group of change factors propelled each movement. In the fifth merger movement described above, more than 50 percent of the M&A activity in a given year has been accounted for by five or six industries. However, the identity of the industries has varied at different time periods. The industry characteristics related to strong M&A pressures can be summarized as follows:

1. *Telecommunications.* Technological change and deregulation in the United States and abroad (particularly
Europe) have stimulated efforts to develop a global
presence.

2. *Media (movies, records, magazines, newpapers).*
Technological changes have impacted the relationship
between the content and delivery segments. There is
potential overlap in the content of different media outlets. It is an attractive and glamorous industry
(attracted Japanese investors beginning in late 1980s).

3. *Financial (investment banks, commercial banks, insurance companies).* Globalization of industries and
firms requires financial services firms to go global to
serve their clients.

4. *Chemicals, pharmaceuticals.* Both require high
amounts of R&D, but suffer rapid imitation. Chemicals
become commodities. Pharmaceuticals enjoy a limited
period of patent protection, but this is eroded by "me,
too" drugs and generics. Changes in the technology of
basic research and increased risks due to competitive
pressures have created the stimulus for larger firms
through M&As.

5. *Autos, oil and gas, industrial machinery.* All face
unique difficulties that give advantages to size, stimulating M&As to achieve critical mass. Autos face global
excess capacity. Oil faces the uncertainty of price and
supply instability due to actions of the OPEC cartel.

6. *Utilities.* Deregulation has created opportunities for
economies from enlarging geographic areas. New kinds
of competitive forces have created needs for broadening
managerial capabilities.

7. *Food, retailing.* It is hampered by slow growth. Food
consumption will only grow at the rate of population
growth. Expanding internationally offers opportunities
to grow in new markets.

8. *Natural resources, timber.* Both face exhausting
sources of supply. Problems exist in matching raw
material supplies with manufacturing capacity.

It can be seen that the industry influences are somewhat different. However, they reflect the 10 strong change forces we identified at the beginning of this chapter.

ARBITRAGE ACTIVITIES

When a merger or takeover is announced, arbitrageurs sell short the stock of the acquiring company, and take a long position (buy) in the stock of the target company. Because of the risk that the transaction may not be completed, the price of the target stock may not immediately rise to the full offer price. So arbitrageurs may gain as the price of the target stock rises toward the offer price. Indeed, the target may resist, driving its price even above the initial offer price. Another possibility is that another firm may make a competing bid at a richer price.

An example will illustrate the arbitrage operation. When a tender is announced, the price will rise toward the offer price. For example, bidder B selling at $100 may offer $60 for target T, now selling at $40 (a 50 percent premium). After the offer is announced, the arbitrage firm (A) may short B and go long in T. The position of the hedge depends on price levels after the announcement. Suppose B goes to $90 and T to $55. If the arbitrage firm (A) shorts B and goes long on T, the outcome depends on a number of alternatives. If the tender succeeds at $60, the value of B may not change or may fall further, but the value of T will rise to $60, resulting in a profit of at least $5 per share of T for A. If the tender fails, T may fall in price but not much if other bids are made for T; the price of B may fall because it has "wasted" its search and bidding costs to acquire T. Thus, A may gain whether or not the bid succeeds. If the competition of other bidders causes B to raise its offer further, A will gain even more, because T will rise more and B will fall. (Remember that A is short on B and long on T.)

Information is the principal raw material in the arbitrage business. The vast majority of this information comes from careful analysis of publicly available documents, such as financial statements and filings with the Securities and Exchange Commission (SEC) and/or regulatory agencies. Arbitrageurs buy expert advice from lawyers and industry specialists. They may hire investment bankers to assist in their assessment of the offer.

In some cases, the investment bankers involved in the transaction may double-check their own assessment of valuation against that of the arbitrageurs. They attempt to get all available information from the investment bankers representing the target and bidding firms and from the participants themselves. This phase of information gathering may cross over the boundary into the gray area of inside trading if the pursuit is too vigorous.

With the increased pace of M&As in recent years, arbitrageurs in some cases have attempted to anticipate takeover bids to establish their stock positions in advance of any public announcement, thus increasing their potential return. To do so, they try to identify undervalued firms that would make attractive targets and to track down rumors of impending bids; they may monitor price increases that might signal someone is accumulating stock in a particular company to ferret out potential bidders before the 5 percent disclosure trigger at which the purchaser has to announce his or her intentions. The risk of taking a position based upon this type of activity is clearly greater. Also, if one firm in an industry is acquired, other firms in the industry may be expected to become targets.

Arbitrageurs perform another role in the merger process. Since they go long in the stock of the target and short the stock of the bidder, they are in a hedged position. A change in the price relationship between bidder and target is not a risk because they can cover their short position with their stock ownership in the target. The big risk to the arbitrageur is that the deal does not go through and the price relationship has shifted. When arbitrageurs have accumulated large positions in a target stock, they become a force pushing the deal to its completion. In addition, they may join activist institutional investors who identify underperforming companies and may even encourage well-managed companies to make an unsolicited bid that may lead to improvements in operation.

TERMINOLOGY

In mergers, the combining companies engage in prior negotiations which may ultimately lead to a transaction. In tender offers, the acquiring company may seek to hold preliminary discussions with the top officers of the target firm. If the two companies are not able to make progress toward a mutual agreement, the acquiring company may make an offer directly to the shareholders to tender their shares at a specified price. Mergers are mainly friendly. Tender offers may become hostile.

Types of Mergers

From an economic standpoint, mergers may be horizontal, vertical, or conglomerate. Horizontal mergers involve firms operating in similar businesses (e.g., Chevron and Texaco). Vertical mergers occur in different stages of production operations (e.g., AOL and Time Warner). In conglomerate mergers, the firms are in unrelated business activities (e.g., Tyco International has been acquiring companies in diverse activities). The degree of relatedness is somewhat subjective.

From a legal standpoint, the basic form of transaction is a statutory merger governed by the requirements of the state or states in which the major parties are chartered. The act of merger takes place by filing appropriate documents with those states. The law also makes provision for a short-form merger. When a small group has ownership control of 90 percent or more, the legal procedures can be streamlined.

The Tender Offer Process

In a tender offer process, approval by 50 percent or more of the shareholders of the target firm gives control to the bidder. After the bidder has obtained control, the terms of the transaction may be "crammed down" on the minority. If the acquirer does not complete the buyout, the minority holders are subject to the decisions of the control group—this is called a *freeze in*. The minority group may take legal actions if they feel they have been treated unfairly. A tender offer may be unconditional or conditional on obtaining some percentage of the shares. The tender offer may be unrestricted or restricted with respect to some classes of equity holders. An "any or all" offer is both unconditional and unrestricted. If a tender offer is restricted, an oversubscription may result in a prorationing of the number or percentage of shares taken. For example, if a bidder tenders for 70 percent of a target's 1000 shares and 80 percent are tendered, the bidder may accept all 800 or only seven-eighths of each share offered.

By law, shareholders of a target firm have a 20-day waiting period before they are required to vote. If another bidder competes with the first, the target shareholders must have an additional 10 business days to evaluate the new offer. In a two-tier tender offer, the first tier receives an offer with superior terms for 50 percent of the target firm's stock to obtain control. The second tier may receive a lower price or less favorable terms.

Acquisition Vehicles

The announcement of mergers in newspapers typically refers to a newly created subsidiary as the takeover vehicle. For example, in the AOL Time Warner merger, in their joint proxy statement dated May 19, 2000, the structure of the merger is described in page 7. America Online and Time Warner jointly formed a new company, AOL Time Warner, with two subsidiaries, America Online Merger Sub Inc. and Time Warner Merger Sub Inc. At the time the merger is completed, America Online Merger Sub will be merged into America Online, and America Online will be the surviving corporation; Time Warner Merger Sub will be merged into Time Warner, and Time Warner will be the surviving corporation. As a result, America Online and Time Warner will each become a wholly owned subsidiary of the new AOL Time Warner.

Generally companies use subsidiaries via a forward triangular merger or a reverse triangular merger. The nature of each is described in outline form.

A. The forward triangular three-party merger proceeds as follows:
    1. Requirements
        a. Consideration is limited to the parent company's stock.
        b. Controlled subsidiary must acquire "substantially all" of target's assets and liabilities [(*substantially all* is defined as 70 percent of fair market value (FMV) of the target's gross assets and 90 percent of FMV of the target's net assets)].

2. The parent forms a wholly owned subsidiary.

Parent			Subsidiary	
Assets	500	Liabilities 200 →		
		Common		
		stock 300		

3. The parent transfers the merger consideration (parent stock) to that subsidiary. The parent stock is the subsidiary's assets.

4. The subsidiary transfers all its stock to the parent. The two balance sheets are as follows:

Parent			Subsidiary (a)		
Assets	500	Liabilities 200	New parent		Subsidiary
		Common	stock 100		common
		stock *300* ←→			stock 100
Subsidiary		New common			
common		stock *100*			
stock	100				

5. The target's assets and liabilities are transferred to the subsidiary:

Subsidiary (b)			Target		
New parent		Subsidiary	Assets	400	Liabilities 300
stock 100		common			Target
Target		stock 100 ←			common
assets *400*		*Target*			stock *100*
		liabilities *300*			
		Target			
		common			
		stock *100*			

6. The merger consideration (parent stock) is paid to the target shareholders for all the target shares.

7. All the target shares are canceled.

8. All the target's assets and liabilities are now owned by the subsidiary. Since the subsidiary stock is wholly owned by the parent, the parent now indirectly owns all the target's assets and liabilities:

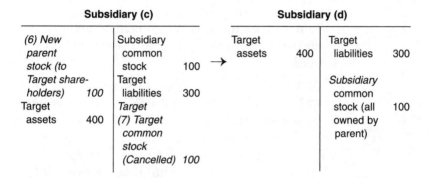

Subsidiary (c)		
(6) New parent stock (to Target shareholders) 100	Subsidiary common stock 100	
Target assets 400	*Target* liabilities 300	
	Target (7) Target common stock (Cancelled) 100	

→

Subsidiary (d)		
Target assets 400	Target liabilities 300	
	Subsidiary common stock (all owned by parent) 100	

9. Summary diagram of triangular forward three-party merger:

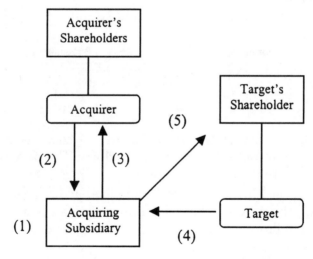

10. Advantages
   a. The shareholder of the acquiring corporation is the parent corporation. Parent shareholder approval is not necessary.

    b. The target's liabilities are isolated in a subsidiary corporation, avoiding the parent's exposure to target liabilities.

    c. If the acquisition were a statutory merger, the parent will incur recording fees and transfer taxes for its acquisition of the target's assets. If the assets go directly to the controlled subsidiary, recording fees and transfer taxes are avoided.

    d. Laws may prohibit a target from merging into the parent, but not into a controlled subsidiary.

    e. Since continuity of interest is the only restriction on consideration, there is a great deal of flexibility regarding the consideration. This is especially beneficial if there are a large group of dissenting shareholders.

B. The triangular reverse three-party merger proceeds as follows:

    1. The parent forms a wholly owned subsidiary:

Parent				Subsidiary
Assets	500	Liabilities	200 $\longrightarrow$	
		Common		
		stock	300	

    2. The parent transfers the merger consideration (parent stock) to that subsidiary. The parent stock is the subsidiary's assets.

    3. The subsidiary's common stock is owned by the parent. The two balance sheets are as follows:

Parent				Subsidiary (a)			
Assets	500	Liabilities	200	New parent		Subsidiary	
		Common		stock	100	common	
		stock	300 $\longleftrightarrow$			stock	100
Subsidiary		New common					
common		stock	100				
stock	100						

4. The subsidiary's assets and liabilities are transferred to the target:

Subsidiary (a)				Target (a)			
New parent stock	100	Subsidiary common stock	100 →	Assets New parent stock	400 100	Liabilities Target common stock Subsidiary common stock	300 100 100

5. The merger consideration (parent stock) is paid to the target shareholders for all the target shares.

6. All the target shares are canceled.

7. The target retains its original assets and liabilities. However, its original common stock is now canceled. The only stock outstanding is the subsidiary stock, which is wholly owned by the parent:

Target (b)				Target (c)			
Assets *(5) New parent stock (to target shareholders)*	400 *100*	Liabilities *(6) Target common stock (cancelled)* Subsidiary common stock	300 *100* 100 →	Assets	400	Liabilities Subsidiary common stock (all owned by parent)	300 100

8. The remaining subsidiary stock is transferred into new target stock. The parent, which owned all the subsidiary stock, now owns all the new target stock. The parent indirectly owns all the target's assets and liabilities.

Target (c)				Target (d)			
Assets	400	Liabilities Subsidiary common stock	300 100 →	Assets	400	Liabilities *New target common stock (all owned by parent)*	300 *100*

9. Summary diagram of a triangular reverse three-party merger:

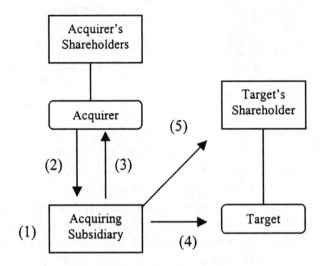

10. Requirements

   a. Target must hold "substantially all" of the subsidiaries' assets and liabilities.

   b. Substantially all the assets transferred from the parent to the subsidiary must be held by the surviving corporation, except parent stock distributed in the transaction and assets used to

     • Pay additional consideration to the surviving corporation's shareholders

     • Pay dissenting shareholders

     • Pay creditors of the surviving corporation

     • Pay reorganization expenses

   c. The assumption of the liabilities of the surviving corporation is treated as a contribution to capital by the controlling corporation to the surviving corporation.

   d. Target shareholders must exchange 80 percent of their stock for the parent's voting stock

11. Advantages
   a. Shareholder of the merged corporation is the parent, so shareholder approval of the merged corporation's shareholders is avoided.
   b. The target corporation remains in existence:
      • The target can retain any nonassignable franchise, lease, or other valuable contract rights.
      • Avoiding a transfer of the target's assets avoids a possible acceleration of a loan outstanding.
      • Regulatory rules (banks, public utilities, insurance companies) may require the target to remain in existence.

The concluding section of this chapter deal with the regulation of tender offers.

REGULATION OF TENDER OFFERS

The regulation of tender offers stems from the original Securities Acts of 1933 and 1934. The Securities Act of 1933 has primary responsibility for recording information. Section 5 prevents the public offering and sale of securities without a registration statement. Section 8 provides for registration and permits the statements to automatically become effective 20 days after it is filed with the SEC. However, the SEC has the power to request more information or to issue a stop order, which delays the operation of the 20-day waiting period.

It is the Securities Exchange Act of 1934 (SEA) that provides the basis for the amendments that were applicable to takeover activities. Section 12(j) empowers the SEC to revoke or suspend the registration of a security if the issuer has violated any provisions of the 1934 act. The SEC imposes periodic disclosure requirements under Section 13. The basic reports are (1) Form 10-K, the annual report; (2) Form 10-Q, the quarterly report; and (3) Form 8-K, the current report for any month in which specified events occur.

Section 14 governs proxy solicitation. Prior to every meeting of its security holders, they must be furnished with a proxy statement containing specified information. The SEC provides procedural requirements for proxy contests. Under SEA Rule 14a-8, any security holder may require management to include his or her proposal for action in the proxy statement. If management opposes the proposal, it must include in the proxy material a statement by the security holder not more than 200 words in length in support of his or her proposal.

Williams Act

The Williams Act, in the form of various amendments to the Securities Exchange Act of 1934, became law on July 29, 1968. Its stated purpose was to protect target shareholders from swift and secret takeovers in three ways: (1) by generating more information during the takeover process that target shareholders and management could use to evaluate outstanding offers; (2) by requiring a minimum period during which a tender offer must be held open, thus delaying the execution of the tender offer; and (3) by explicitly authorizing targets to sue bidding firms.

Section 13(d) of the Williams Act of 1968 required that any person who had acquired 10 percent or more of the stock of a public corporation file a Schedule 13D with the SEC within 10 days of crossing the 10 percent threshold. The act was amended in 1970 to increase the SEC powers and to reduce the trigger point for the reporting obligation under Section 13(d) from 10 to 5 percent. Basically, Section 13(d) provides management and the shareholders with an early warning system.

Section 14(d) applies only to public tender offers but applies whether the acquisition is small or large, so its coverage is broader. The 5 percent trigger rule also applies under Section 14(d). Thus, any group making solicitations or recommendations to a target group of shareholders that would result in owning more than 5 percent of a class of securities registered under Section 12 of the Securities Act must first file a Schedule 14D with the SEC. An acquiring firm must disclose in a Tender Offer Statement (Schedule 14D-1) its intentions and business plans for the target as well as any relationships or agreements between the two firms. SEA Section 14(c) prohibits misrepresentation, nondisclosure, or any fraudulent, deceptive, or manipulative acts or practices in connection with a tender offer.

Insider Trading

The SEC has three broad categories under which insider trading, fraud, or illegal profits can be attacked. Rule 10b-5 is a general prohibition against fraud or deceit in security transactions. Rule 14e-3 prohibits trading in nonpublic information in connection with tender offers. The Insider Trading Sanctions Act of 1984 applies to insider trading more generally. It states that those who trade on information not available to the general public can be made to give back their illegal profits and pay a penalty of 3 times as much as their illegal activities produced.

The traditional regulation of insider trading was provided for under SEA Sections 16(a) and 16(b). Section 16(a) applies to officers, directors, and any persons who own 10 percent or more of any class of securities of a company. Section 16(a) provides that these corporate insiders must report to the SEC all transactions involving their purchase or sale of the corporation's stock on a monthly basis. Section 16(a) is based on the premise that a corporate insider has an unfair advantage by virtue of his or her knowledge of information that is generated within the corporation. Section 16(b) provides that the corporation or any of its security holders may bring suit against the offending corporate insider to return the profits to the corporation because of insider trading completed within a 6-month period.

On April 4, 1988, the Supreme Court ruled by a 6–0 vote (three justices were not participating) that investors may claim damages from a company that falsely denied it was involved in negotiations that resulted in a subsequent merger. Such denials would represent misleading information about a pending merger, which would provide investors who sold stock during the period with a basis for winning damages from the company officers.

Regulation of Takeover Activity by the States

Early state laws regulating hostile takeovers were declared illegal by the courts. For example, in 1982 the U.S. Supreme Court declared illegal an antitakeover law passed by the state of

Illinois. The courts held that the Illinois law favored management over the interests of shareholders and bidders. The Illinois
law was also found to impose impediments on interstate commerce and was therefore unconstitutional.

The Supreme Court in April 1987 upheld the Indiana Act.
The Indiana Act provides that when an acquiring entity or bidder obtains shares that would cause its voting power to reach
specified threshold levels, the bidder does not automatically
obtain the voting rights associated with those shares. The transfer of voting rights must receive the approval of a majority of
shareholders, not including the shares held by the bidder or
insider directors and officers of the target company. A bidder can
request a special shareholders meeting that must be held within 50 days of the request, with the expenses of the meeting to be
borne by the bidder.

Critics of the Indiana Act regard it as a delaying tactic that
enables the target to delay the process by at least 50 days. The
special requirements in connection with voting make the outcome
of the tender offer much more uncertain. The Indiana Act was
tested in a case brought by Dynamics Corporation of America,
chartered in Connecticut. It announced a tender offer to increase
its holdings of CTS Corporation (incorporated in Indiana) from 9.6
to 27.5 percent. CTS invoked the Indiana Act. Dynamics would not
be able to vote either the additional shares or the initial 9.6 percent. Dynamics filed suit, arguing that the Indiana Act was pre-
empted by the Williams Act and violated the interstate commerce
clause. Dynamics won in the U.S. district court and in the appeals
court, but the decision was reversed in the U.S. Supreme Court.

Other states passed acts more moderate than the Indiana
Act. The New York–New Jersey pattern provides for a 5-year
moratorium preventing hostile bidders from doing a second-step
transaction such as merging a newly acquired company with
another. The Delaware law (enacted in 1988) moratorium on
second-step transactions is only for 3 years, and it does not
apply if the hostile bidder obtains the approval of the board of
the target company and two-thirds vote of the other stockholders for the transaction to proceed. The board of a Delaware corporation may also vote to "opt out" of the statute within 90 days
of its effective date.

Critics point out that the state antitakeover laws have hurt shareholders. Studies by the Office of the Chief Economist of the SEC found that when in 1986 New Jersey placed restrictions on takeovers, the prices for 87 affected companies fell by 11.5 percent. Similarly, an SEC study found that stock prices for 74 companies chartered in Ohio declined an average of 3.2 percent, a $1.5 billion loss, after that state passed restrictive legislation. Another study estimated that the New York antitakeover rules reduced equity values by 1 percent, costing shareholders $1.2 billion.

SUMMARY

Recent change forces driving mergers include globalization, technology, deregulation, a strong economic environment (high stock prices, low interest rates), and changes in industry organization. In tender offers, the bidder directly contacts shareholders, inviting them to sell (tender) their shares at an offer price. Mergers usually involve some mutuality of negotiations. In practice, the acquiring company may make a successful tender offer for the target followed by a formal merger of the two companies.

From an economic standpoint, different types of mergers or tender offers are grouped on the basis of the stage of economic activity and the degree of relatedness of the firms. Horizontal mergers involve firms operating in the same kind of business activity. Vertical mergers take place between firms in different stages of production operations. Pure conglomerate mergers involve firms engaged in unrelated types of business activity. Financial conglomerates develop financial planning and control systems for groups of segments that may be otherwise unrelated from a business standpoint.

Statutory mergers meet the formal legal requirements of the state or states in which the parties to the merger are chartered. After the approval of the tender offer followed by a merger agreement or the approval of a merger directly, the act of merger takes place upon the filing of appropriate documents with the state or states. Tender offers may have various types of conditions or restrictions.

Risk arbitrage in connection with M&As is the practice of making short-term gains from the relationship between the takeover bid price and the relative prices of the bidder's and target's stock. The announcement of a merger or tender offer causes the stock price of the target to rise because the bidder pays a premium. Arbitrageurs generally will take a long position in the target stock and a short position in the bidder stock, especially if they are out of line.

The Securities Act of 1933 and Securities Exchange Act of 1934 provided the framework for subsequent regulation. Most of the more recent legislation has been in the form of amendments to these two acts. The Williams Act of 1968 amended the 1934 act to regulate tender offers. Two main requirements were a filing with the SEC upon obtaining 5 percent ownership and a 20-day waiting period after making a tender offer. The disclosure requirements aim to give target shareholders information that will enable them to receive more of the gains associated with the rise in the share price of the takeover target. The 20-day waiting period gives the target more time to evaluate the offer and/or tailor a defense or seek multiple bids.

Historically, insider trading has little to do with M&A activity; it refers to the trading in their own companies' stock by corporate officers, directors, and other insiders. It is largely controlled by Section 16 of the Securities Exchange Act, which requires insiders to report such transactions to the SEC on a regular basis. However, the volatility of stock price changes in connection with M&As creates opportunities for gains by individuals who may not fit the traditional definition of insiders. Rule 10b-5 is a general prohibition of fraud and deceit in the purchase or sale of securities. Rule 14e-3 applies to insider trading, particularly in connection with tender offers. The Insider Trading Sanctions Act of 1984 provides for triple damage penalties in insider trading cases.

In addition to federal regulation of M&A activity, a number of states have enacted legislation to protect corporations headquartered within their boundaries. States are the primary regulators of corporate activities. However, there are problems in state regulation of takeovers. Securities markets represent interstate commerce, and state regulations that interfere with interstate commerce are, by definition, unconstitutional. Others argue that state regulations are not necessary, that federal reg-

ulations and corporate antitakeover amendments provide sufficient protection. There is evidence that shareholders are dam-
aged by restrictive state legislation that limits takeovers.

QUESTIONS AND PROBLEMS

1.1 What were the major change forces that contributed
to the high level of merger activity from 1993 through
2000?

1.2 What were the main factors associated with the previous four major merger movements?

1.3 What is the typical pattern of actions by arbitrageurs
when a merger is announced?

1.4 What is the basic nature of a triangular merger?

SOLUTIONS TO QUESTIONS AND PROBLEMS

1.1 Ten change forces are identified: (1) The pace of technological change has accelerated. (2) The costs of communication and transportation have been greatly
reduced. (3) Hence markets have become international in scope. (4) The forms, sources, and intensity of
competition have expanded. (5) New industries have
emerged. (6) While regulations have increased in
some areas, deregulation has taken place in other
industries. (7) Favorable economic and financial environments have persisted from 1982 to 1990 and from
1992 to mid-2000. (8) Within a general environment of
strong economic growth, problems have developed in
individual economies and industries. (9) Inequalities
in income and wealth have been widening. (10)
Valuation relationships and equity returns for most of
the 1990s have risen to levels significantly above
long-term historical patterns.

1.2 *First merger movement*—1893 to 1904.   The merger
movement at the turn of the century was associated
with the completion of the transcontinental railroad
system. It created the first common market.

Second merger movement—1920s.   This period was characterized by an increase in vertical mergers. These were associated with the development of the radio, which made national advertising possible, and the automobile, which permitted more effective geographic sales and distribution organizations.

Third merger movement—1960s.   The conglomerate mergers of the 1960s represented in part an adjustment to the slowdown in defense expenditures. Also influencing this was the idea that a good manager, with the new planning literature, could manage anything.

Fourth merger movement—1980s.   Financial innovations, junk bonds, made all firms vulnerable to a takeover bid. Any company that was not performing up to its potential could be taken over. There was also some dismantling of the diversification of the 1960s.

Each major merger movement was a response to some strong economic change forces which were different for each major merger movement.

1.3 Arbitrageurs sell short the stock of the acquiring company and take a long position (buy) in the stock of the target company.

1.4 An acquisition subsidiary is created as the transaction vehicle.

CHAPTER TWO

Antitrust Policies

Antitrust actions have increased along with the rise in merger activity. This can readily be documented from the annual reports of the Department of Justice (DOJ) and the Federal Trade Commission (FTC), available from their websites. The DOJ and the FTC have overlapping jurisdictions but manage to reach compromises on allocations of antitrust cases. In considering possible merger transactions, antitrust considerations are an important part of the planning process. For these reasons we review the relevant antitrust statutes and the policies promulgated by the DOJ and FTC.

SHERMAN ACT OF 1890

This law contains two sections. Section 1 prohibits mergers that would tend to create a monopoly or undue market control. This was the basis on which the DOJ stopped the merger between Staples and Office Depot. Section 2 is directed against firms that had already become dominant in their markets in the view of the government. This was the basis for actions against IBM and AT&T in the 1950s. Both firms were required to sign consent decrees in 1956 restricting AT&T from specified markets and requiring that IBM sell as well as lease computer equipment. Under Section 2, IBM and AT&T were sued again in the

1970s. The suit against IBM, which had gone on for 10 years, was dropped in 1983. The suit against AT&T resulted in divestiture of the operating companies effective in 1984. The Microsoft case illustrates the policies of the Department of Justice under Section 2 of the Sherman Act. Parallel to DOJ's suits against IBM during the 1970s, the DOJ turned its attention to Microsoft during the decade of the 1990s.

CLAYTON ACT OF 1914

The Clayton Act created the Federal Trade Commission for the purpose of regulating the behavior of business firms. Among its sections, two are of particular interest. Section 5 gives the FTC power to prevent firms from engaging in harmful business practices. Section 7 involves mergers. As enacted in 1914, Section 7 made it illegal for a company to acquire the stock of another company if competition could be adversely affected. Companies made asset acquisitions to avoid the prohibition against acquiring stock. The 1950 amendment gave the FTC the power to block asset purchases as well as stock purchases. The amendment also added an incipiency doctrine. The FTC can block mergers if it perceives a tendency toward increased concentration—that the share of industry sales of the largest firms appeared to be increasing.

HART-SCOTT-RODINO ACT OF 1976

The Hart-Scott-Rodino Act of 1976 (HSR) consists of three major parts. Its objective was to strengthen the powers of the DOJ and FTC by requiring approval before a merger could take place. Before HSR, antitrust actions were usually taken after completion of a transaction. By the time a court decision was made, the merged firms had been operating for several years, so it was difficult to "unscramble the omelet."

Under Title I, the DOJ has the power to issue civil investigative demands in an antitrust investigation. The idea here is that if the DOJ suspects a firm of antitrust violations, it can require firms to provide internal records that can be searched for evidence. We have seen cases in which firms were required to provide literally boxcar loads of internal files for review by the DOJ under Title I.

Title II is a premerger notification provision. On December 21, 2000, an amendment to Title II was signed into law by President Clinton. The amendment was designed to reduce the number of transactions that require HSR notification and to increases the fees for large transactions. The HSR amendment increases the amount of time the reviewing agency has from 20 to 30 days. It became effective February 1, 2001.

The amendment increases the minimum threshold that requires filing from $15 million to $50 million and eliminates the alternative 15 percent of target voting stock threshold. The transaction threshold will be annually adjusted to follow GNP. Some deals that currently are not covered would become reportable (firms with assets below the $10 million threshold that have an acquisition price over $200 million would become reportable). It is expected that the amendment will cut the number of reportable transactions in half.

In the interest of maintaining the same HSR revenue levels, the amendment increases the filing fees. There will now be a three-tier fee system in place of the old $45,000 fee. For transactions under $100 million, the fee is $45,000. From $100 million to $500 million, the fee will increase to $125,000. For transactions that are valued at more than $500 million, the fee will become $280,000.

Title III is the Parens Patriae Act—each state is the parent or protector of consumers and competitors. It expands the powers of state attorneys general to initiate triple damage suits on behalf of persons (in their states) injured by violations of the antitrust laws. The state itself does not need to be injured by the violation. This gives the individual states the incentive to increase the budgets of their state attorneys general. A successful suit with triple damages can augment the revenues of the states. In the Microsoft case, the attorneys general of 22 states joined in the suit filed by the DOJ.

Companies should follow a proactive strategy during the 30-day review period. The HSR process should be viewed as an educational endeavor to provide the necessary information to the government staff attorneys. The staff attorneys should be contacted with an offer to voluntarily provide additional information. A briefing package should fully develop the business reasons for the merger. Under the guidance of attorneys, high-level business executives should be made available for informal presentations or staff interviews.

The overriding approach should be for the lawyers and executives to convey a factual, logical story, emphasizing the industry dynamics that make the transaction imperative for the preservation of the client as a viable entity for providing high-quality products to its customers at fair prices. The presentation should demonstrate how the industry dynamics require the transaction to enable the firm to fulfill its responsibilities to consumers, employees, the communities in which it has its plants and offices, and its owners and creditors.

THE ANTITRUST GUIDELINES

In the merger guidelines of 1982, and successively in 1987, 1992, and 1996, the spirit of the regulatory authorities was altered. In the merger guidelines of 1968, concentration tests were applied somewhat mechanically. With the recognition of the internationalization of competition and other economic realities, the courts and the antitrust agencies began to be less rigid in their approach to antitrust. In addition to the concentration measures, the economics of the industry were taken into account.

Beginning in the 1982 guidelines the quantitative test shifted to the Herfindahl-Hirschman Index (HHI), which is a concentration measure based on the market shares of all firms in the industry. It is simply the sum of the squares of market shares of each firm in the industry. For example, if there were 10 firms in the industry and each held a 10 percent market share, the HHI would be 1000. If one firm held a 90 percent market share, and the nine others held a 1 percent market share, the HHI would be 8109 ($90^2 + 9 \times 1$). Notice how having a dominant firm greatly increases the HHI. The HHI is applied as indicated in Table 2.1.

A merger in an industry with a resulting HHI of less than 1000 is unlikely to be investigated or challenged by the antitrust

TABLE 2.1

Critical Concentration Levels

Postmerger HHI	Antitrust Challenge to a Merger?
Less than 1000	No challenge—industry is unconcentrated.
Between 1000 and 1800	If HHI increased by 100, investigate.
More than 1800	If HHI increased by 50, challenge.

authorities. An HHI between 1000 and 1800 is considered to represent moderate concentration. Investigation and challenge depend on the amount by which the HHI increased over its premerger level. An increase of 100 or more may invite an investigation. An industry with a postmerger HHI above 1800 is considered a concentrated market. Even a moderate increase over the premerger HHI is likely to result in an investigation by the antitrust authorities.

Beginning in 1982, the guidelines had begun to recognize the role of market characteristics. Particularly important is the ability of existing and potential competitors to expand the supply of a product if one firm tries to restrict output. On the demand side, it is recognized that there are usually close substitutes for any product, so a high market share of the sales of one product does not give the ability to elevate price. Quality differences, the introduction of new products, and technological change result in product proliferation and close substitutes. The result is usually fluctuating market shares. For these reasons, concentration measures alone are not a reliable guide to measure the competitiveness of an industry.

Most important is whether entry is easy or difficult. If output can be increased by expansion of noncooperating firms already in the market or if new firms can construct new facilities or convert existing ones, an effort by some firms to increase price would not be profitable. The expansion of supply would drive prices down. Conditions of entry or other supply expansion potentials determine whether firms can successfully collude regardless of market structure numbers.

Next considered is the ease and profitability of collusion, because there is less likelihood that firms will attempt to coordinate price increases if collusion is difficult or impossible. Here the factors to consider are product differences (heterogeneity), frequent quality changes, frequent new products, technological changes, contracts that involve complicated terms in addition to price, cost differences among suppliers, and so on. Also, DOJ challenges are more likely when firms in an industry have colluded in the past or use practices such as exchanging price or output information.

PRIVATE ANTITRUST SUITS

Actions by government agencies such as the FTC or the DOJ have usually resulted from complaints received from business competitors. For example, Sun Microsystems and others filed complaints about the behavior of Microsoft.

The ability to file private antitrust lawsuits creates undesirable incentives for lawyers. The cost of litigating private antitrust lawsuits is high. So just the threat of such a suit can be used by a company and its lawyers to pressure the prospective defendant to make a cash settlement. Most private antitrust cases are brought under the Sherman Act in which the plaintiff alleges abuse of power by a dominant firm or cartel behavior. If the plaintiff wins, it receives triple damages.

REGULATORY BODIES

Proposed mergers in regulated industries require approval of antitrust agencies as well as the regulatory agencies. For example, the AOL–Time Warner merger first received approval from the FTC and then the Federal Communications Commission (FCC). The process took approximately 1 year. The FCC has primary responsibility for the radio and television industries. It defers to the FTC and DOJ on antitrust issues. The Federal Communications Act of 1996 called for partial deregulation of the telephone and related industries. But partial deregulation involved complicated provisions requiring involvement by the FCC.

The banking industry is subject to regulation by three agencies. The Board of Governors of the Federal Reserve System (Fed) has broad powers over economic matters as well as antitrust. The Comptroller of the Currency has jurisdiction when national banks are involved. The Fed makes decisions for state banks that are members of the Federal Reserve System. The Federal Deposit Insurance Corporation (FDIC) reviews mergers for state-chartered banks that are not members of the Fed, but are insured by the FDIC. In conducting its reviews, each agency takes into account a review provided by the Department of Justice.

Bank mergers have long been subject to Section 7 of the Clayton act of 1914. Modifications were enacted by the Bank Merger Act of 1966. Past bank mergers were legalized. Any merger approved by one of the three regulatory agencies had to be challenged within 30 days by the Attorney General. The Act of 1966 provided that anticompetitive effects could be outweighed by a finding that the transaction served the "convenience and needs" of the community to be served. The convenience and needs defense is not applicable to the acquisition by banks of nonbanking businesses. The review by one of the three agencies substitutes for filing under Hart-Scott-Rodino of 1976.

The Interstate Commerce Commission, established in 1887, had long regulated the railroad industry. Under the ICC Termination Act of 1995, it was replaced by the Surface Transportation Board (STB). The STB has final authority on antitrust matters, but must file notices with the Justice Department, which may file objections at STB hearings. Among the tests the STB is required to consider are (1) the effect on adequacy of transportation, (2) the effect on competition among rail carriers, and (3) the interests of rail carrier employees affected by the proposed transaction.

INTERNATIONAL ANTITRUST

Most of the developed countries of the world have some form of merger control. Cross border transactions will be subject to the multiple jurisdictions of the home countries of bidders and targets. At the end of February 2000, the International Competition Policy Advisory Committee released its two-year study. It recommended that the more than 80 nations conducting antitrust enforcement make more explicit what their antitrust policies are. It proposed faster approval of transactions that do not present obvious problems. It recommended that the U.S. "second-request" process, in which the U.S. antitrust agencies ask for more information about a merger, should be streamlined. The report noted that about one-half of the mergers reviewed by the U.S. Federal Trade Commission or Justice Department have an international component.

The European Union Merger Regulation grants the European Commission (EC) exclusive authority to review the antitrust implications of transactions which affect the economy of the European Community. Transactions have a community impact if total sales of the combined firm are greater than $4.5 billion annually and the EU sales of each party are greater than $250 million. However, if two-thirds of the revenues of each firm are achieved in a single EU country, the EC will defer to that country's antitrust authorities.

Premerger notification is required. The Minister of Competition of the EU requires a three-week waiting period, but can extend it. The commission is required to decide upon further investigation within the waiting period and must render an approval decision within five months. The critical issue is whether the combination will create or strengthen a dominant position.

One problem with international antitrust is the growth of regulatory agencies with different standards and different filing fees for regulatory approval. The chairman of the International Bar Association's Global Forum for Competition Policy, J. W. Rowley, stated that the differences in policies have become aggravated (*The New York Times*, January 28, 2001, sec. 3, p. 4). From 6 or 7 jurisdictions 10 years ago, antitrust regulatory commissions have grown to more than 80 with an additional 24 expected shortly. Coca-Cola's 1999 acquisition of the Cadbury Schweppes beverage brands, including Schweppes, Dr. Pepper, and Canada Dry, involved activities in more than 160 countries. Antitrust approval was required in more than 40 jurisdictions around the world. Fees for seeking approval ranged from $77 in Austria to $300,000 in Russia to $2.5 billion in Argentina according to the International Bar Association. The U.S. fee is $280,000 for transactions valued over $500 million.

SUMMARY

Antitrust policies in the United States continue to be suspicious of large firms and merger activity. Yet the increasing dynamism of the economy has intensified the forces of market competition. Some fundamental economic factors have changed.

1. International competition has clearly increased, and many of our important industries are now international in scope. Concentration ratios must take into account international markets and will be much lower than when measured on the assumption of purely domestic markets.
2. The pace of technological change has increased, and the pace of industrial change has increased substantially. This requires more frequent adjustments by business firms, including many aspects of restructuring that include acquisitions and divestitures.
3. Deregulation in a number of major industries requires industrial realignment and readjustments. These require greater flexibility in government policy.
4. New institutions, particularly among financial intermediaries, represent new mechanisms for facilitating the restructuring processes that are likely to continue.

Some see merger activity as a natural expression of strong change forces. Mergers during the 1980s and 1990s were associated with extraordinary growth in employment and in gross domestic product. Through mergers and restructuring, firms all over the world have become more efficient. In light of the increased dynamism of their environments and the greater intensity of competitive forces, firms should not be restricted by antitrust policies from making required adjustments to economic turbulence.

QUESTIONS AND PROBLEMS

2.1 The market shares of the top 5 firms in a particular industry are: 15 percent, 10 percent, 6 percent, 5 percent, and 4 percent. The remaining 60 firms in the industry each have a 1 percent market share.

a. What is the HHI?

b. If the largest two firms merge, what is the new HHI?

2.2 Why would it be difficult for the firms in the automobile industry to collude on prices?

2.3 What are the implications of the globalization of markets for antitrust policies?

2.4 What was the nature of the Febuary 1, 2001, amendment to Title II of the Hart-Scott-Rodino Act of 1976?

SOLUTIONS TO QUESTIONS AND PROBLEMS

2.1

a. 225 + 100 + 36 + 25 + 16 + 60(1) = 462

This is well under the 1000 HHI critical level.

b. 625 + 36 + 25 + 16 + 60 = 762

This is still under the 1000 critical value.

2.2 With overcapacity in the industry, there will always be downward pressure on prices. To collude, agreements would have to be reached on the quality of products, the number and type of models, fuel economy performance, financing deals, warranty policies, recall policies, support of dealer advertising, pace of technological change, etc. Each of these has virtually infinite gradations so agreements would be difficult. Furthermore, each firm feels that if it made a significant breakthrough on product design and style or on fuel economy, it could increase its market share and profitability.

2.3 Globalization has brought an increased number of competitors into national markets. Competition has intensified. Antitrust authorities should use, for their initial appraisal of market concentration, shares based on world markets rather than shares of U.S. firms alone in the domestic U.S. market.

2.4 The minimum threshold that requires filing is raised from $15 million to $50 million, to be adjusted annually to follow GNP changes. It is expected that the amendment will reduce the number of reportable transactions by 50 percent.

CHAPTER THREE

Strategy*

A central principle deserves great emphasis. It is the proposition that all M&A policies and decisions should take place within the general framework of the firm's strategic planning processes.

NATURE OF STRATEGY

Strategies define the plans, policies, and cultures of an organization in a long-range horizon. Strategies cannot be static. Strategies must be related to the firm's changing environments. Strategic planning is a way of thinking and must involve all segments of the organization. But it is the chief executive or executive committee who must take ultimate responsibility for formulating the strategic vision of the firm.

For example, in the early 1980s, Hershey Foods' senior management defined a long-term gap between their desired performance of the firm and what its strategic plan projected. The gap was in terms of size: sales and income. Acquisitions could fill the gap. One of the staff's major undertakings was to highlight a list of the top 50 acquisition candidates. The analysis was

---

* This chapter benefited from the presentations on Strategy by Jeffrey H. Dyer, William G. Ouchi, and Richard P. Rumelt to the Anderson School–UCLA Merger Week Programs.

carefully crafted and utilized a scan of the entire Compustat data set. First companies that were too large or too small were eliminated. The next set of parameters related to historical profitability, sales growth, leverage, and stock price performance. Management participated in setting the parameters of the screening process, every step along the way. The effort was completed, a list of the top 50-acquisition candidates was compiled and presented to senior management. At the top of the list, the number one acquisition candidate for Hershey Foods was Cross (as in Cross pens). Management sat in silence, until someone asked the question, "What does Hershey know about running a pen company?" The answer of course was nothing. Forty-eight of the fifty companies were outside the food industry and outside of Hershey's area of expertise.

Although, at the time, it seemed like a wasted effort, that exercise helped senior management focus on strategy, not just filling a "gap" in a strategic plan. It began a keen self-assessment by senior management that culminated in understanding that Hershey's key strengths and core competencies center around manufacturing a quality confectionery product, selling that product, and delivering the product anywhere in the United States and Canada. From these core competencies, Hershey's general acquisition strategy was formed.

Strategy involves continued reassessment of the firm's political, economic, financial, and technological environments. These must be related to the changing characteristics of the firm's industry and its competitive environment. The purpose of environmental reassessment is to reassess the broad forces for change. In this framework, the firm must determine whether its current policies and performance are appropriate in relation to its opportunities and threats. The firm then formulates strategic alternatives to achieve its goals. The firm must judge whether the managerial, technological, and financial resources it possesses are sufficient to achieve a competitive superiority. The goal is to develop a bundle of capabilities that will enable the firm to achieve an advantage over its competitors. The advantages should be reflected in superior growth and superior returns to shareholders. The literature of strategy emphasizes that these capabilities cannot be readily imitated by competitors.

M&A activities can perform an important contribution in developing an organizational system with superior performance.

EFFECTIVE STRATEGIES

To illuminate the preceding, examples of effective strategies may be summarized. Michael Dell formulated the vision of selling made-to-order computers by mail. From this basic concept, the vision expanded to a broad supplier system to maximize choice and quality, minimizing investment in inventory and warehouses to achieve cost and prices that competitors could not match.

Amazon early recognized the potential of e-commerce for providing convenience in the purchase of books. Warehousing and other inventory costs were reduced. Investments in retail facilities and receivables were avoided. Much information about the books was provided using the potential of the Internet. From books, Amazon has expanded into a wide range of products such as music CDs and electronics.

Starbucks reflected the concept that the consumption of premium coffee could take place in an attractive setting with facilities for relaxing, reading, and perhaps socializing. Mergers facilitated expanding nationally and internationally.

Borders provided a superstore in which to browse for books in a pleasant environment including coffee. Its strategic vision has to be adjusted to meet the competition of the Internet bookstores.

McDonald's formulated the concept of supply of high-quality beef for its hamburgers sold in a clean environment at low prices. The Golden Arches symbolize its quality assurance.

Wal-Mart began with the concept that less populated areas made it possible to establish department stores within a broader geographic business operation that could achieve economies of inventory control, warehousing, and logistical support. Greater variety at lower prices could be achieved. Sam Walton implemented a friendly welcome back to shoppers by helpful employees. From regional beginnings Wal-Mart has moved worldwide, expanding into a broader range of products including groceries.

In 1984, Intel found that Japanese companies were producing higher-quality memory chips at lower costs and prices.

Memories were key to Intel's early strategy. Intel developed and refined new technologies on memory products where they were easier to test. But it shifted its strategy from memory to processors. Its mix of employees shifted from hardware to software programmers.

Cisco began selling basic network routers to corporate customers. From a single-product company, Cisco evolved into a complete data networking solution provider. Between 1993 and 1999, Cisco engaged in more than 50 acquisitions. Its underlying strategy was to acquire the technology and people to provide Cisco with the capabilities to perform an expanded role in the data networking industry.

The above represents a small sample of strategic visions that guided firms to success. They represent important innovations in thinking and implementation. There are no simple formulas for innovation and creativity, but the strategy literature has developed a number of approaches for achieving competitive superiority.

STRATEGY FORMULATIONS

The strategic challenges a firm faces cannot be solved by mathematical formulas. A deep understanding of the firm and its industry is the foundation for strategic planning. Some generalizations are possible, but strategic planning processes make considerable use of checklists. Much analysis is required to formulate checklists in an effort to arrive at insights and new visions. In his seminal work *Competitive Strategy* (1980), Michael Porter has 134 checklists, one every three pages. More studies seem to lead to more checklists. In his *Competitive Advantage* (Porter, 1985), the number of checklists increases to 187, one every 2.5 pages. Stryker (1986) has one checklist every 1.5 pages.

Thus the strategic planning process makes heavy use of checklists to stimulate discussion and evaluation of alternatives. Guided by the firm's strategic vision, the exchange of ideas leads to insights in sound strategies, policies, and decisions. Computer analysis helps develop decision support systems.

A diagram, which is a checklist in spirit, is developed from five-forces analysis of Porter (1979). We expand his framework into Fig. 3.1. A firm's competitive position can be evaluated by an analysis of 11 factors reflecting demand and supply conditions. On the demand side, what is critical is the degree of feasible product substitutability. On the supply side, the nature and structure of costs are critical. Of particular importance is the ability to switch among suppliers of inputs. This may be critically affected by switching costs—the costs involved in shifting from one supplier to another. Supply competition from existing firms including their potentials for capacity expansion is also a major influence on the competitive position of the firm. Complementary firms are important. Is there a threat that your business could be carried out in another way by other firms?

In addition to checklists, considerable use is made of matrix diagrams. One is the product-market matrix presented in Fig. 3.2. This framework analyzes products and markets with respect to their degree of relatedness to the firm's existing product-market pattern. Reflecting one view of strategy, this

FIGURE 3.1

Competitive Analysis

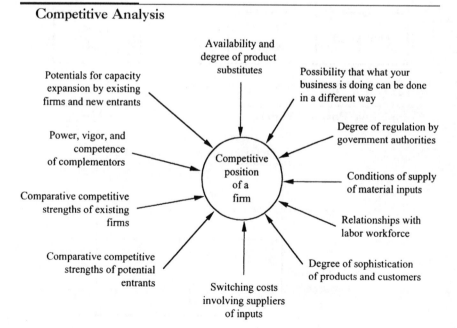

matrix is based on the proposition that the more related the
new activities of a firm, the smaller the degree of risk.

Figure 3.3 provides a matrix for analyzing combinations of
degree of product differentiation over a small range of products
versus a proliferation of products and markets. For example, Cisco
Systems seeks to meet the needs of customers for networking systems. The 3M Corporation, in contrast, draws on 37 different technology platforms with which the company has expertise.

FIGURE 3.2

Product-Market Matrix

Product / Market	Present	Related	Unrelated
Present	Low Risk		High Risk
Related			
Unrelated	High Risk		Highest Risk

FIGURE 3.3

Competitive Position Matrix

	Product Differentiation	Cost Leadership
Narrow Focus		
Broad Range of Markets		

The product growth-share matrix in Fig. 3.4 is associated with an early approach by Boston Consulting Group. Products for which the firm has a high market share in an industry with favorable growth rates are potential "stars" with high profitability. As an industry matures, its growth slows; so if a firm continues to have high market share, the attractive profits are available for investments in markets with more favorable growth rates, and the products become "cash cows." Products and markets with low growth where the firm has a small market share are "dogs," and the firm should discontinue such products, according to the simple product portfolio approach.

A variant of the growth-share matrix is the strength-market attractiveness matrix shown in Fig. 3.5. The greatest opportunities for investment and growth occur where the outlook for an industry is attractive and the firm has high capabilities for performance in that industry. Where the industry outlook is unfavorable and the firm has weakness in such markets, the firm should divest or close down such businesses.

Figure 3.6 moves the analysis to an international basis. In the international setting the most attractive countries, in terms of growth or political stability, in which the firm has competitive strengths offer the most favorable growth opportunities. The

FIGURE 3.4

Growth-Share Matrix

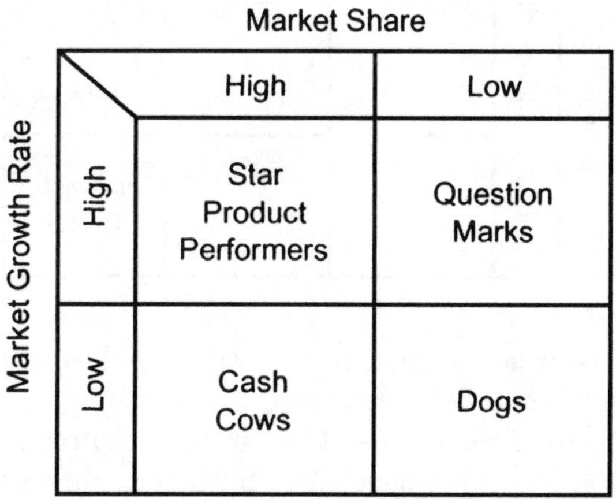

Market Share

		High	Low
Market Growth Rate	**High**	Star Product Performers	Question Marks
	Low	Cash Cows	Dogs

F I G U R E   3.5

Strength-Market Attractiveness Matrix

		Industry Attractiveness		
		High	Medium	Low
Business Strengths	High	Invest / Grow		
	Medium			
	Low			Harvest / Divest

F I G U R E   3.6

Strength-Country Attractiveness Matrix

		Country Attractiveness		
		High	Medium	Low
Business Strengths	High	Invest / Grow		
	Medium			
	Low			Harvest / Divest

opposite, of course, occurs in countries of low attractiveness where the firm's competitive strengths are low.

The preceding examples of the matrix approach to strategy represent in spirit the checklist approach to formulating alternatives. They are useful devices for suggesting factors to take into account in formulating strategies. The different analytical frameworks are not mutually exclusive. In strategic planning a wide range of analytical approaches may usefully be employed. Their use is facilitated by a checklist and an adaptive approach to strategic planning. Practicing consultants as well as individual firms have employed a combination of methodologies and analytical approaches with considerable success.

Another view is that the increasing complexity of business operations requires simple rules for making timely decisions (Eisenhardt and Sull, 2001). We summarize their five basic rules with some modifications to their terminology. (1) What they call "how-to rules" is really defining the central strategic vision of the firm. Their example of Akamai's requirement that its customer service function be staffed by persons with the technical capability to answer any questions is as much a key strategy as a how-to rule. (2) Boundary rules define the areas in which opportunities can be pursued. They illustrate with Cisco's early acquisition rule that acquisition targets should be relatively small in size with highly qualified engineers. (3) Priority rules are used to rank opportunities; the example is Intel's rule to allocate manufacturing capacity on the basis of a product gross margin (are potential growth and risk not considered?). (4) Timing rules synchronize managers with the pace of emerging opportunities; they refer to Nortel's requirements that product development teams know the critical dates for new product deliveries. (5) Exit rules are obviously "knowing when to fold them." They refer to Oticon's rule of stopping a project if a key team member seeks to move to another project.

Many writers view strategy more as an adaptive process or a way of thinking (see, for example, Ansoff, 1965; Bogue and Buffa, 1986; Quinn, Mintzberg, and James, 1988; Steiner, 1979; Steiner, Miner, and Gray, 1986). The adaptive processes orientation involves matching resources to investment opportunities under environmental uncertainty compounded with uncertain competitors' actions and reactions. The methodology for dealing with these kinds of "ill-structured problems" requires an iterative solution process. Most managers in an organization have responsibilities for the inputs and studies required for the repeated "going around the loop" in the strategic planning processes outlined in Table 3.1. Although different approaches

T A B L E   3.1

Essential Elements in Strategic Planning

---

1. Assessment of changes in the environments.
2. Evaluation of company capabilities and limitations.
3. Assessment of expectations of stakeholders.
4. Analysis of company, competitors, industry, domestic economy, and international economies.
5. Formulation of the missions, goals, and policies for the master strategy.
6. Development of sensitivity to critical environmental changes.
7. Formulation of internal organization performance measurements.
8. Formulation of long-range strategy programs.
9. Formulation of midrange programs and short-run plans.
10. Organization, funding, and other methods to implement all the preceding elements.
11. Information flow and feedback system for continued repetition of all essential elements and for adjustments and changes at each stage.
12. Review and evaluation of all processes.

---

to strategic planning may be found, they all include the steps set forth in Table 3.1, which lists the critical activities involved in strategic planning processes.

In performing the iterated checklist procedures, difficult questions are encountered. For example, is the firm maximizing its potential in relation to its feasible environment? Is there a gap between the firm's goals and prospects, based on its present capabilities? Should the firm attempt to alter its environment or capabilities or both? Should the firm change its mission? What will be the cost of each alternative? What are the risks and unknowns? What are the rewards for success and penalties for failure? The methodology involves not closed-form mathematics, but management processes. It involves ways of thinking that assess competitors' actions and reactions in relation to the changing environments. The process approach is especially applicable to merger analysis because it is difficult to find out all that is needed when combining with another entity.

FORMULATING A MERGER STRATEGY

The literature on long-range strategic planning indicates that one of the most important elements in planning is the continual reassessment of the firm's environment. To determine what is happening in the environment, the firm should analyze its industry, competitors, and social and political factors.

Industry analysis allows the firm to recognize the key factors required for competitive success in the industry as well as the opportunities and threats present in the industry. From competitor analysis, the firm determines the capabilities and limitations of existing and potential competitors and their probable future moves. Through these analyses and with additional consideration of societal factors, the firm's strengths and weaknesses relative to present and future competitors can be ascertained.

The purpose of the environmental reassessment is to provide the firm with a choice among strategic alternatives. For this choice, the firm then considers whether its current goals and policies are appropriate to exploit industry opportunities and to deal with industry threats. At the same time, it is necessary for the firm to examine whether the goals and policies match the managerial, technological, and financial resources available to the firm, and whether the timing of the goals and policies appropriately reflects the ability of the organization to change.

The firm then works out feasible strategic alternatives, given the results of the analyses. The current strategy (represented by its goals and policies) may or may not be included in the set of feasible alternatives. A strategic choice is made from this set such that the chosen strategy best relates the firm's situation to external opportunities and threats. Mergers represent one set of alternatives.

When it is necessary to take action to close a prospective gap between the firm's objectives and its potential based on its present capabilities, difficult choices must be made. For example, should the firm attempt to change its environment or capabilities? What will be the costs of such changes? What are the risks and unknowns? What are the rewards of success? What are the penalties of failure? Because the stakes are large, an iterative process is employed. A tentative decision is made. The process is repeated, perhaps from a different management function orientation, and at some point, the total-enterprise point of view is brought to bear on the problem. At some point, decisions are made and must involve entrepreneurial judgments. Mergers may help or hurt.

The emphasis is on the effective alignment of the firm with its environments and constituencies. Different approaches may be emphasized. One approach seeks to choose products related to the needs or wants of the customer that will provide large markets. A second approach focuses on technological bottlenecks or barriers, the solution of which may be to create new markets. A third strategy chooses to be at the frontiers of technological capabilities on the theory that some attractive product fallout will result from such competence. A fourth approach emphasizes economic criteria including attractive growth prospects and appropriate stability.

If it is necessary for the firm to alter its product-market mix or range of capabilities to reduce or close the strategic gap, a diversification strategy may be formulated. Thus, the key connection between planning and diversification or mergers lies in the evaluation of current managerial and technological capabilities relative to capabilities required to reach objectives.

Thus far in the chapter, we have focused on strategy as the vision that guides the firm. We also reviewed alternative approaches of strategy. We next turn to the relationships between strategy and structure and their implications for merger decisions.

STRATEGY AND STRUCTURE

A substantial literature discusses the relationship between strategy and structure. Some authors hold that structure determines strategy—the firm can only access those strategies which it is organized to undertake. Our view is that there is a feedback relationship between structure and strategy. The focus of our analysis here is on organizational architecture. We describe alternative organizational structures with emphasis on their implications for acquisition strategies. First we describe the advantages and disadvantages of different types of organization structures.

The unitary form, or U form (Fig. 3.7), is highly centralized under the president. It is broken into functional departments, and no department can stand alone. The president must stay close to the departments to know what needs to be improved, because there is no easy way to measure each as a profit center. A long-term vision is often left solely to the president. Although this form allows rapid decision making, it is usually only successful in small organizations. It is difficult for the U form to handle multiple products. Acquired firms have to fit into the limited span of control of the top executive group. Acquisitions are likely to be horizontal or very closely related activities. The new units are likely to be consolidated fully into the unitary organization.

The holding company, or H form, is arranged, as shown in Fig. 3.8, around various unrelated operating businesses. The leadership of the firm is able to evaluate each unit individually, and can allocate resources according to projected returns. The firm has superior knowledge of the situation of each unit, allowing it to act as an "inside investor."

The holding company arrangement makes it possible for firms to acquire relatively unrelated activities. Each of the dissimilar operations is permitted to function almost as an independent company. The risk is that the H form may be less than fully effective because of the requirement to guide activities that are widely diverse.

The multidivisional organization, or M form, lies between the centralization of the U form and the decentralization of the H form. Each division is autonomous enough to be judged as a

FIGURE 3.7

The Unitary Form of Organization

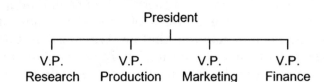

F I G U R E   3.8

The Holding Company Form of Organization

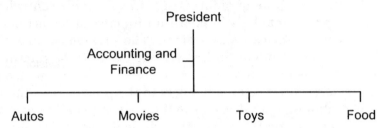

profit center, but all divisions share some endowments such as production or marketing. Hewlett-Packard, before it restructured in 1999, was arranged along product lines such as computers and measurement products. While these divisions were largely separate, they shared electrical engineering technology, as well as some facets of production (see Ouchi, 1984, for insights and extensions).

The multidivisional firm can handle related product and geographic market extensions. Its structure is represented in Fig. 3.9. The acquisition of a firm with a related product line might result in designating it as a separate division. Since the products are related, the same functional staff groups may be able to serve the new division effectively. At some point, groups of divisions may have elements in common and require their own thrust with support staff groups having the required specialized knowledge. This appeared to be what developed at Hewlett-Packard when it restructured in 1999, separating the computer-related activities from the non-computer-related products. The latter group of activities was placed in the new company called Agilent. The new company had its own stock, a portion of which was sold to the public and was well received.

The matrix form of organization, as shown in Fig. 3.10, consists of functional departments such as finance, manufacturing, and development. The employees of these functional departments are assigned to subunits that are organized around products, geography, or some other criterion. In such an organization, employees report to a functional manager as well as a product

FIGURE 3.9

The Multidivisional Form of Organization

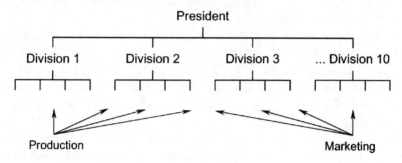

FIGURE 3.10

The Matrix Form of Organization

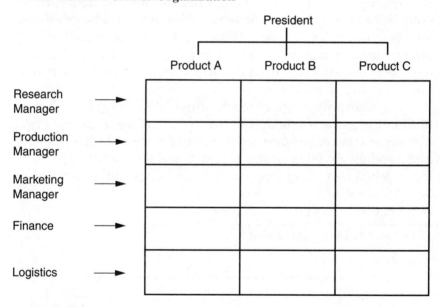

manager. The matrix form is most effective in firms character-ized by many new products or projects. Intel, as of 1992, was structured around five major product groups.

The matrix form represents another way to handle the acquisition of related products or to engage in geographic market expansion. However, as new product groups are added, a heavier burden is placed on the communication system. The possibility of disputes and conflicts arising from multiple lines of authority is likely to be increased.

The impact of structure on strategy is especially important in multinational organizations. Two alternative approaches are illustrated. In Fig. 3.11, a product division basis is dominant. Matsushita Electric Industrial Company is representative. Product groups such as radios or tape recorders report directly to the executive level. Each product has its own functional activities such as R&D and manufacturing. Matsushita Electric Trading Company is organized geographically, representing the sales arm of the product segments. The diagram shows a third group of overseas management activities also organized geographically. The advantage of this form of organization is that since production is centralized, economies of scale can be achieved. Products can be developed and get to market quickly. With tight budgetary control, top management can impose fiscal discipline. The drawback to this approach is that individual country's product preferences may not be matched effectively.

An alternative approach is illustrated by Fig. 3.12 with national organizations dominant; N.V. Philips is an example. The organization has two major groups: national organizations and product divisions. The product divisions are responsible for development, production, and global distribution. In theory,

F I G U R E 3.11

Product Division Dominant

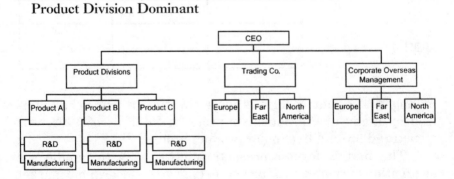

F I G U R E   3.12

National Organizations Dominant

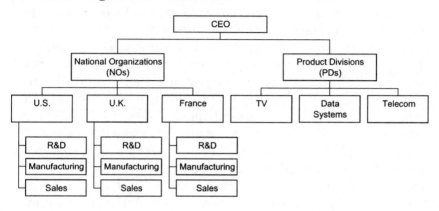

product divisions coordinate across national organizations. A potential problem with this organizational structure is that economies of scale may be lost by geographic dispersion of manufacturing activities. A strength is greater responsiveness to individual country's preferences. But a danger is that because of the autonomy of national organizations, brands developed by the product divisions may be rejected in favor of those of competitors.

So there is a tension in each form of organizational structure. In addition, the organizational structure may influence the kind of strategies that may be feasible. Certainly a central question of merger integration concerns the decision of how to fit an acquired entity into the organizational structure and philosophy of the acquiring firm. The M form structure appears to have considerable flexibility for handling acquisitions, small relative to the acquiring firm. The acquired entity should be placed in a group with related business activities. The interactions between the existing support group and the new entity should provide opportunities for adoption of the best practices and reciprocal learning experience over time. Both the top executives and the staff support for the group should have sufficient knowledge and experience with the operations of the new segment to help it achieve performance improvements.

VIRTUAL INTEGRATION

A new form of organization has been developed by firms, such as Dell, which are pursuing *virtual integration*. Under such a system, the links of the value chain are brought together by informal arrangements among suppliers and customers. Dell establishes close ties with suppliers, enjoying many of the benefits of vertical integration. Shipments of the components that Dell needs can be easily arranged through the Internet or a networked computer system. This same type of arrangement allows Dell to fully serve customers in ordering, services, or any other needs.

A qualification to such an arrangement being considered a "form of organization" is that it involves multiple firms, with a variety of organizational forms. This form of virtual integration represents a blurring of company boundaries. As communication strengthens the ties between different firms in a value chain, it is easier to envision grouping them as an "organization." Indeed, a firm's networks help create "inimitable" value in the resource-based view of the firm (Gulati, Nohria, and Zaheer, 2000; Lippman and Rumelt, 1982).

SUMMARY

In the process approach to strategy, each firm has a set of capabilities and opportunities. The firm must seek to exploit these effectively in relation to its changing environments. It must recognize that the dynamics of competition and economic change will require continuous reassessment of its position and realignment to its new challenges and opportunities. In this view the firm is required to make strategic decisions in the face of great uncertainty and considerable risk, especially with respect to mergers.

In this process view of strategy, divestitures represent a form of strategic adjustment process. Numerous case studies demonstrate that many divestitures were planned in advance in order to retain the desired parts of an acquisition. Or divestitures can represent a method of making acquisitions and paying them off in part or sometimes entirely by the segments sold off. At a minimum this may help make the diversification effort a low-cost one. Hence, it is erroneous to conclude that divestitures represent management mistakes.

Internal and external investment programs may be successful or unsuccessful. Firms may try either or both approaches in their efforts to increase shareholder value. The generalizations of writers on strategic planning contain valuable insights for helping firms carry out strategies with a higher degree of efficiency than they otherwise would have been able to attain. The critical need is a rapid information feedback system in the firm to improve its capabilities for adapting to change, correcting errors, and seizing new opportunities. It is in this framework that merger and takeover decisions are made.

A substantial literature develops the relationship between strategy and the structure of firms. Organizational form can be critical to implementing strategy. Our view is that there is a feedback relationship between strategy and structure. The unitary form is highly centralized under the president. The holding company form is very decentralized and usually includes unrelated businesses. The multidivisional form has different units that share some common functions. The matrix form is organized around various products or projects. Virtual integration is a developing method of blurring the lines between organizations.

REFERENCES

Ansoff, H. Igor, *Corporate Strategy*, New York: McGraw-Hill, 1965.

Bogue, Marcus C., III, and Elwood S. Buffa, *Corporate Strategic Analysis*, New York: Free Press, 1986.

Boston Consulting Group, *The Strategy Development Process*, Boston: Boston Consulting Group, 1985.

Eisenhardt, Kathleen M., and Donald N. Sull, "Strategy as Simple Rules," *Harvard Business Review*, 79, January 2001, pp. 106–116.

Gulati, R., N. Nohria, and A. Zaheer, "Strategic Networks," *Strategic Management Journal*, March 2000, pp. 203–215.

Lippman, S., and R. Rumelt, "Uncertain Imitability: An Analysis of Interfirm Differences in Efficiency under Competition," *The Bell Journal of Economics*, 13, 1982, pp. 418–438.

Ouchi, William, *The M-Form Society: How American Teamwork Can Recapture the Competitive Edge*, Reading, MA: Addison-Wesley, 1984.

Porter, Michael E., "How Competitive Forces Shape Strategy," *Harvard Business Review*, 57, March–April 1979, pp. 137–145.

_____, *Competitive Strategy*, New York: Free Press, 1980.

_____, *Competitive Advantage*, New York: Free Press, 1985.

Quinn, James Brian, Henry Mintzberg, and Robert M. James, *The Strategy Process*, Englewood Cliffs, NJ: Prentice-Hall, 1988.

Steiner, George A., *Strategic Planning*, New York: Free Press, 1979.

_____, John B. Miner, and Edmund R. Gray, *Management Policy and Strategy*, 3d ed., New York: Macmillan, 1986.

Stryker, Steven C., *Plan to Succeed: A Guide to Strategic Planning*, Princeton, NJ: Petrocelli Books, 1986.

QUESTIONS AND PROBLEMS

3.1 Why is strategy important for M&A planning?

3.2 Give some examples of strategic visions that guided the success of individual firms.

3.3 What is the nature of strategy as an adaptive learning process?

3.4 Why is the organizational structure of a firm important in international operations?

3.5 What is meant by virtual integration?

SOLUTIONS TO QUESTIONS AND PROBLEMS

3.1 Mergers are only one of many paths to growth for a firm. Mergers and other methods of growth (joint ventures, alliances, investments, licensing, etc.) must be formulated within the general framework of the firm's long-range strategic planning processes.

3.2 Starbucks reflected the concept that the consumption of premium coffee could take place in an attractive setting with facilities for relaxing, reading, and perhaps socializing. Mergers facilitated expanding nationally and internationally.

McDonald's formulated the concept of supply of high-quality beef for its hamburgers sold in a clean environment at low prices. The Golden Arches symbolize its quality assurance.

Michael Dell formulated the vision of selling made-to-order computers by mail. From this basic concept, the vision expanded to a broad supplier system to maximize choice and quality, minimizing investment in inventory and warehouses to achieve cost and prices that competitors could not match.

Wal-Mart began with the concept that less populated areas made it possible to establish department stores within a broader geographic business operation that could achieve economies of inventory control, warehousing, and logistical support. Greater variety at lower prices could be achieved.

3.3 It is the iterative going-around-the-loop of the 12 steps listed in Table 3.1 of the text.

3.4 The Matsushita example shows the advantages of being organized geographically. The advantage of this form of organization is that since production is centralized, economies of scale can be achieved. Products can be developed and get to the market quickly. With tight budgetary control, top management can impose fiscal discipline. The drawback to this approach is that individual country's product preferences may not be matched effectively.

An alternative approach is illustrated by N.V. Philips. The organization has two major groups: national organizations and product divisions. The product divisions are responsible for development, production, and global distribution. In theory, product divisions coordinate across national organizations. A potential problem with this organizational structure is that economies of scale may be lost by geographic dispersion of manufacturing activities. A strength is the greater responsiveness to individual country's preferences.

3.5 Virtual integration is created by a web of arrangements between suppliers and customers. Firms such as Dell have used relatively new communications technologies to closely bind their production operations with their suppliers and customers. Dell's suppliers are networked with the firm to allow very precise shipping of the exact products that Dell needs. Dell's customers have easy access to ordering, services, and other needs.

The use of new technology is bringing firms closer together to the point that organizational forms may have to be reevaluated to include multiple firms.

CHAPTER FOUR
Deal Structuring

Deal structuring involves the choice of accounting method, taxability, methods of payment, premiums, contingent payouts, and the use of collars in designing the terms of a transaction. Clearly what the buyers and sellers actually receive in a merger deal is defined by these factors. We will discuss each in the sequence listed.

ACCOUNTING ASPECTS

Two methods of accounting for mergers and other combinations were permitted by the accounting standards boards. The pooling of interests method of accounting provides that historical cost data be used in combining the accounts of the combining entities. The purchase method of accounting requires that actual transaction prices be reflected in the financial statements of the combined firm. The two methods were originally adopted in 1972, and despite studies and recommendations for amendments, no fundamental changes were put in motion until 2000. In 2000, the Financial Accounting Standards Board (FASB) announced that the pooling method would be eliminated by the end of 2001.

Pooling of Interests Accounting

To understand the arguments for its elimination, we first describe the pooling method and then discuss the pros and cons of its use. We illustrate the method by an actual case. Table 4.1 presents a summary of the pro forma balance sheet taken from the proxy to shareholders in the Dow Chemical / Union Carbide merger. Pooling of interests accounting was used. The methodology is basically simple. All asset and liability items of the two companies are added. In Table 4.1, total assets of the combined firm pro forma are the addition of the total assets of the individual firms. It works similarly for total liabilities. For stockholders' equity, the common stock of the acquired firm is eliminated by a debit to the common stock account of Union Carbide. Union Carbide had 133 million shares outstanding prior to the merger. The terms of the deal gave 0.537 share of Dow for 1 share of Union Carbide. Hence, 71 million shares of Dow were issued to Union Carbide shareholders. The par value of the Dow common stock was $2.50. So a total of $177 par value was paid to Union Carbide. This is the credit entry. A balancing debit of $20 million is made to the paid-in capital account, representing a "plug" entry. If the par value paid by the acquirer were less than the debit to eliminate the common stock of the acquired firm, the plug entry would have been a credit to the paid-in capital account. If the debit to the paid-in capital account were greater than the pro forma combined amount, the excess would be debited to retained earnings.

Pooling of interests accounting was therefore quite simple. It was attractive because no goodwill was created that would subsequently have to be written off as a charge against reported net income. Twelve conditions had to be met to qualify for pooling of interests accounting. For example, none of the combining companies could change the equity interest of its voting common stock for two years before the plan to combine is initiated or between the dates when the combination is initiated and consummated. In 1996, when the First Bank System (FBS) of Minneapolis, Minnesota, was competing with Wells Fargo Bank to take over First Interstate Bank Corporation, the SEC ruled that FBS would not be able to use pooling of interests accounting

TABLE 4.1

Completed Pro Forma Balance Sheet

	Dow Chemical	Union Carbide	Pro Forma Adjustments	Combined Pro Forma
Total Assets	$23,105	$7,465		$30,570
Total Liabilities	$15,411	$5,024		$20,435
Stockholders' Equity:				
Common stock (Dow par value = $2.50)	818	157	(157)*	818
Additional paid-in capital	891	114	(20)†	985
Retained earnings	13,242	3,404		16,646
Unearned employee compensation—ESOP and other equity adjustments		(58)		(58)
Accumulated other comprehensive loss	(300)	(157)		(457)
Treasury stock, at cost	(6,957)	(1,019)	177‡	(7,799)
Net stockholders' equity	7,694	2,441		10,135
Total Liabilities and Stockholders' Equity	$23,105	$7,465		$30,570

Adjustments:
*Debit of $157 to eliminate Union Carbide common stock.
†Balancing entry of $20 debit to additional paid-in capital.
‡Credit of 177 for Dow stock being given to Union Carbide shareholders
(71 million Union Carbide shares * $2.50 par Dow stock = $177).

because of its stock buyback activities and plans. FBS dropped out of the bidding.

The main reason given by FASB for abolishing pooling accounting was that an actual transaction had taken place. But pooling accounting simply added historical numbers without reflecting the current realities that had been revealed by a marketplace transaction.

Purchase Accounting

In purchase accounting the excess of the market value of the consideration paid over the book value of target equity is assigned first to depreciable assets and the remainder to good-will. The goodwill created was required to be written off over a period no longer than 40 years. We illustrate the methodology by use of the pro forma accounting statements contained in the proxy to shareholders in connection with the AOL Time Warner (TWX) transaction.

The merger was announced on January 10, 2000. Before the merger announcement, AOL had been trading at about $74 per share and TWX at $65. The basic purchase accounting entries without nonrelevant other adjustments were:

Debit ($ billion)

Goodwill	$132.5
Time Warner book equity	10.3
	$142.8

Credit ($ billion)

AOL common stock issued to pay for TWX (1.93B times $.01 par)	$0.0193
Paid-in capital ($142.8 − $0.0193)	142.78
	$142.8

The effects on the asset structures of AOL and TWX are shown in Table 4.2. Only 4 percent of AOL's assets were good-will. For TWX the ratio of tangible assets to intangibles was slightly more than 1. AOL paid about $150 billion for the Time Warner book equity of $10.3 billion. So the goodwill account of the combined firm was greatly increased. As a consequence, the ratio of tangible assets to total assets in the combined company dropped to about 15 percent.

The effects on leverage are summarized in Table 4.3. Before the transaction, AOL had only about $68 in liabilities for every $100 of shareholders' equity. For TWX, liabilities were $389 to $100. With the huge increase in the equity of the combined firm as a consequence of the roughly $90 per share paid for TWX in relation to the penny per share par value of the AOL shares used in payment, the paid-in capital account of the combined company increased by a huge amount. Consequently, the leverage ratio for the combined firm was reduced, especially for TWX.

T A B L E 4.2

Asset Structure Changes in AOL and TWX ($ Million)

	AOL		TWX		Combined	
	Amount	Percent	Amount	Percent	Amount	Percent
Total assets	$10,789	100.0	$50,213	100.0	$235,388	100.0
Goodwill + other intangibles	$432	4.0	$24,507	48.8	$199,325	84.7
Tangible assets	$10,357	96.0	$25,706	51.2	$36,063	15.3

T A B L E 4.3

Leverage Changes in the AOL and TWX Merger

	AOL		TWX		Combined	
	Amount	Percent	Amount	Percent	Amount	Percent
Total liabilities	$4,370	40.5	$39,949	79.6	$79,095	33.6
Shareholders' equity	$6,419	59.5	$10,264	20.4	$156,293	66.4
Total claims	$10,789	100.0	$50,213	100.0	$235,388	100.0
Liabilities/equity		68.1%		389.2%		50.6%

Implications for the FASB Proposal to Eliminate Pooling of Interests

The AOL/TWX example demonstrates that the use of purchase accounting has some strange results. The higher the ratio of the price paid to the book equity acquired, the greater the degree to which a high book leverage company will become a lower book leverage company. The result is somewhat misleading.

Another problem is the FASB proposal to require a 20-year non tax-deductible write-off of goodwill. There are some logical inconsistencies involved. Many companies engaged in M&A programs have had records of sustained growth in market values over at least a decade. Why should their goodwill be written off when the investment in that goodwill has increased company value? There is some logic to not writing off goodwill since increases in value demonstrate that the goodwill is not being "used up."

Alternatively, if goodwill is to be written off, why shouldn't the write-off be tax-deductible to reflect the using up of the investment which purchased the goodwill? In Switzerland, for example, total goodwill in an acquisition can be written off in the first year and is tax-deductible. In 1993, goodwill in taxable asset purchases became tax deductible in the United States. Such goodwill is amortized and deductible over a 15-year period for tax purposes. One reason FASB offered for the elimination of pooling was to make U.S. accounting policy and practice consistent with international standards. Using international standards as a criterion argues for relating the design of purchase accounting to practices used by other countries, such as Switzerland.

FASB Further Modifications of Goodwill Proposals

In December 2000, the Financial Accounting Standard Board issued further clarifications with respect to the treatment of goodwill and intangible assets in purchase transactions. The modifications were made in response to the type of criticisms in the preceding section. FASB announced that goodwill arising from merger transactions would be accounted for under an impairment approach. Goodwill will be reviewed for impairment, requiring that it be written down and expensed against earnings, in periods in which the recorded value of goodwill is greater than its "fair market value."

Acquired intangible assets (other than goodwill) will continue to be subject to amortization over their useful economic life and reviewed for impairment in accordance with FASB Statement No. 121, *Accounting for the Impairment of Long-Lived Assets and for Long-Lived Assets to Be Disposed of.* FASB will eliminate the presumption proposed in the initial Exposure Draft that such acquired intangible assets have a useful economic life of 20 years or less. FASB proposes that until the life of acquired intangible assets is determined to be finite, it should be carried at the lower of its carrying amount or fair value. FASB has not spelled out the criteria for determining which intangible assets are deemed to be recognizable separately from goodwill and which of these assets are deemed to have a finite versus indefinite useful economic life.

Taxable versus Nontaxable Transactions

The basic tax rule is simple. If the merger or tender offer involves exchanging the stock of one company for the stock of the other, it is a nontaxable transaction. If cash or debt is used, it is a taxable transaction. In practice, however, many complications exist.

The Internal Revenue Code makes a technical distinction between three types of *acquisitive tax-free reorganizations*, which are defined in Section 368 of the code. They are referred to as type A, B, and C reorganizations. A type A reorganization is a statutory merger or consolidation (under state laws). In a merger, target firm shareholders exchange their target stock for shares in the acquiring firm; in a consolidation, both target and acquiring firm shareholders turn in their shares and receive stock in the newly created company.

Type B reorganizations are also stock-for-stock exchanges. Following a type B reorganization, the target may be liquidated into the acquiring firm or maintained as an independent operating entity.

Type C reorganizations are stock-for-asset transactions with the requirement that at least 80 percent of the fair market value of the target's property be acquired. Typically, the target firm "sells" its assets to the acquiring firm in exchange for voting stock in the acquiring firm; the target then dissolves, distributing the acquiring firm's stock to its shareholders in return for its own (now-canceled) stock.

In practice, a three-party acquisition technique is employed as described in Chapter 2. The parent creates a shell subsidiary. The shell issues stock, all of which is bought by the parent with cash or its own stock. The target as the third party is bought with the cash or stock of the parent held by the subsidiary. The advantage of creating the subsidiary as an intermediary is that the parent acquires control of the target through the subsidiary without incurring responsibilities for the known and possibly unknown liabilities of the target. The transaction still qualifies as an A reorganization. The target firm may remain in existence if the stock of the parent is used in the acquisition. Because the parent-acquirer shareholders are not directly involved, they are denied voting and appraisal rights in the transaction. In a reverse three-party merger, the subsidiary is merged into the target. The parent stock held by the subsidiary is distributed to the target's shareholders in exchange for their target stock. This is equivalent to a B reorganization.

The "tax-free" reorganization actually represents only tax deferral for the target firm shareholders. If the target shareholder subsequently sells the acquiring firm's stock received in the transaction, a capital gains tax becomes payable. The basis for the capital gains tax is the original basis of the target stock held by the target shareholder. If the former target shareholder dies without selling the acquiring firm's stock, the estate tax laws establish the tax basis as the value at the time of death.

In a nontaxable (tax-deferred) reorganization, the acquiring firm can generally use the net operating loss (NOL) carryover and unused tax credits of the acquired firm. However, even though the value of the shares paid may be greater than the net book value of the assets acquired, no write-up or step-up of the depreciable values of the assets acquired can be made. For the shareholders of the target firm, taxes are deferred until the common shares received in the transaction are sold. Thus, the shareholders can defer the taxes.

In taxable acquisitions, the acquiring firm may assign the excess of purchase price over the book value of equity acquired to depreciable assets, as described under purchase accounting. The acquiring firm, however, is unable to carry over the NOLs and tax credits. The shareholders of the target firm in a taxable acquisition must recognize the gain over their tax basis in the shares. If, in addition, the target firm has used accelerated depreciation, a portion of any gain that is attributable to excess depreciation deductions will be recaptured to be taxed as ordinary income rather than capital gains, the amount of recapture depending on the nature of the property involved.

Stock versus Asset Purchases

Tax considerations are part of the general topic of structuring the deal. One issue is the effects on buyers and sellers of a stock versus asset purchase in a taxable transaction. We use a specific example to illustrate the factors involved.* The selling company in this example is a regular C corporation, not a limited liability corporation (LLC) or S corporation. The other data assumed are listed below:

Purchase price, stock	$100 million
Purchase price, assets	$100 million
Liabilities of seller	$25 million
Basis in assets (seller)	$60 million
Basis in shares (of seller)	$50 million
Corporate tax rate (federal and state)	40 percent
Individual tax rate (federal and state)	25 percent
Applicable discount factor	10 percent

Based on the above data the net proceeds to the shareholders of the selling firm are compared in Table 4.4.

The explanation for the acquisition of stock alternative is straightforward. The assumed purchase price is $100. The tax basis for the shareholders of the seller is $50. Their capital gain is $50. With an assumed federal plus state capital gains tax of 25 percent, the tax to the shareholders would be $12.50. The net proceeds to the seller shareholders would be $87.50.

If the transaction is an acquisition of assets, the seller corporation must be included in the analysis. If the buyer pays $100 for the assets, its assumption of the liabilities ($25) of the corporation is added to the purchase price ($125). We postulate that the seller corporation has a tax basis of $60 in the assets sold. Its gain is therefore $65. With a combined state and federal corporate income tax rate of 40 percent, the tax on the sale of the assets would be $26. The amount available to the target shareholders would be $74. Their tax basis was postulated to be $50, so the capital gain would be $24. With the same individual

---

* Our presentation is based on the booklet "Tax Considerations—Mergers & Acquisitions," used in a presentation by Deloitte & Touche LLP, March 24, 1999 to the UCLA Mergers and Acquisition Program, Los Angeles, California.

T A B L E 4.4

Stock versus Asset Purchases

	(1) Acquisition of Stock	(2) Acquisition of Assets
Assumed purchase price	$100	$100
Assumed liabilities	—	25
Total purchase price	$100	$125
Basis in assets		(60)
Gain		65
Corporate tax rate		40%
Tax on sale of assets		26
Net to shareholders (SH)	$100	74
Basis in shares	(50)	(50)
Capital gain	50	24
Tax rate on individual	25%	25%
Tax on individual on sale	12.50	6
Net proceeds to seller SH	$87.50	$68

tax rate of 25 percent (as above), the net proceeds to the seller shareholders would be $68.

The buyer may prefer the acquisition of assets to avoid unknown liabilities of the seller for which the buyer would otherwise be liable. In this asset acquisition with purchase accounting, the buyer is able to step up the tax basis of the assets acquired. The excess of the purchase price of $125 over the seller's original basis in assets can be allocated first to tangible assets and the remainder to goodwill. The purchaser will have a step-up for both book and tax purposes. In the present example it is assumed that all the differential is assigned to goodwill, depreciable for tax purposes over 15 years.

The tax benefits of the step-up may influence the purchase price in a competitive corporate control market. The present value of the tax benefit may be added to the purchase price. The calculation of the present value of the tax benefit is as follows.

Purchase price	$100
Assumed liabilities	25
Total purchase price	$125
Basis in assets	(60)
Goodwill	65
Life of tax benefit, years	15
Annual tax benefit	$4.333
Expected future tax rate	40%
Actual cash savings	$1.733
Discount rate	10%
PV of tax benefit	**$13.18**

The goodwill of $65 spread over 15 years results in an annual tax benefit of $4.333. Using an expected future tax rate of 40 percent, the annual tax benefits would be $1.733. With a 10 percent discount factor, the present value of an annuity of $1 for 15 years would be 7.6061, to be multiplied by $1.733. The result is a present value of tax benefits of $13.18. If competition forces the buyer to pay this additional amount, the purchase price of assets becomes $113. The total purchase price becomes $138. The net proceeds to the selling shareholders would rise from $68 to $74.

Even if the tax benefits to the buyer of the asset step-up in the purchase of assets are passed on to the selling shareholders, they still receive less than they would have in the sale of stock. For relatively small firms the major shareholders are likely to be the founding executives. Tax and legal advisers usually counsel the closely held small corporations to be formed as limited liability corporations (LLCs) or S corporations. For both LLCs and S corporations, income from the entity flows directly to the shareholders. This avoids the double taxation that otherwise occurs when the business is sold as an asset acquisition.

DO TAX GAINS CAUSE ACQUISITIONS?

Empirical studies of tax effects find that tax factors are of significant magnitude in less than 10 percent of merger transactions. Individual case studies yield similar results. Even when tax effects are significant, they are not the main motivation for merger transactions (Hayn, 1989).

A possible qualification of the role of taxes is in *going private* transactions, such as leveraged buyouts (LBOs) and management

buyouts (MBOs). The initial financial structures of LBOs and
MBOs can be as high as 90 percent debt. Although the tax savings from such high debt ratios can be substantial, systematic
studies show that debt is paid down as rapidly as possible. The
main objective is to achieve value increases so that the companies
can be taken public again within 3 to 5 years. The proceeds from
such public offerings are usually applied to pay down debt even
further. All this is evidence that tax savings from high leverage
are not the dominant influence.

Furthermore, there are more dimensions to the analysis.
Jensen, Kaplan, and Stiglin (1989) considered a broader range of
effects of LBOs on tax revenues of the U.S. Treasury. They listed
five sources of incremental tax revenues. First, capital gains
taxes are paid on the realized capital gains of shareholders.
Second, the LBO may sell off assets, realizing taxable capital
gains. Third, the interest income from the LBO debt payments is
subject to tax. Fourth, the LBO increases operating income,
which gives rise to incremental taxes. Fifth, by using capital
more efficiently, additional taxable revenues are generated in
the economy. The negative effects are the increased tax deductions from the additional debt and the lower personal tax revenues because LBOs pay little or no dividends.

Jensen, Kaplan, and Stiglin (1989) drew on the data in
Kaplan (1989), which covered 48 of the 76 LBOs greater than
$50 million in size announced during the years 1979 to 1985.
They developed the tax revenue implications of the average
LBO based on Kaplan's study. They concluded that, on average, LBOs generated tax increases that were almost twice the
size of the tax losses they created. The authors estimated that
the average LBO involved a purchase of $500 million, which
generated $227 million in present value (using a 10 percent
discount factor) of tax revenue increases versus $117 million in
present value of tax losses to the Treasury.

They made similar estimates for the R.J. Reynolds/Nabisco
leveraged buyout. They estimated that in present-value terms
the increased revenue to the Treasury was $3.76 billion. They
observed that these payments were more than eight times the
$370 million in federal taxes paid by RJR Nabisco in 1987
(Jensen, Kaplan, and Stiglin, 1989, p. 733). A *Fortune* magazine

article (Newport, 1988) obtained similar results from its analysis of the tax effects of LBOs.

METHOD OF PAYMENT

The method of payment in a merger or takeover transaction is mainly cash, stock, debt, or some combination of the three. The Mergerstat data (*Mergerstat Review 2000*, p. 15) show cash accounting for about 46 percent of merger transactions, stock about 30 percent, debt and other about 1 percent, with some combination at about 23 percent. However, these data are misleading. The method of payments in the largest transactions ($500 million or more) is predominantly stock for stock. For transactions in which a larger buyer buys a smaller firm, cash is more likely to be used. Table 4.5 presents a distribution of merger transactions by purchase price since 1990. The median percent of transactions of $5 million and under is about 16.3

TABLE 4.5

Purchase Price Distribution, 1990–1999 (Percent)

Year	$5 Million and under	$5 Million to $25 Million	$25 Million to $100 Million	$100 Million to $500 Million	$500 Million to $1 Billion	$1 Billion and over
1990	19.4	34.3	25.1	15.8	2.9	2.5
1991	19.4	32.4	27.4	16.6	2.4	1.8
1992	20.7	31.4	26.8	16.6	2.5	1.9
1993	17.8	31.6	28.2	18.3	1.6	2.5
1994	13.7	30.5	27.4	21.5	3.1	3.8
1995	13.1	31.9	28.4	19.2	3.2	4.3
1996	17.5	32.3	26.1	17.6	3.0	3.5
1997	15.2	31.7	24.1	20.7	4.3	4.0
1998	14.5	29.8	26.5	20.4	3.8	5.1
1999	14.4	26.6	26.7	21.7	4.9	5.8
Mean	16.6	31.2	26.7	18.9	3.2	3.5
Median	16.3	31.7	26.7	18.8	3.0	3.7

Source: *Mergerstat Review.*

percent of all transactions. The $5 million to $25 million category accounts for another 31.7 percent. These relatively small transactions account for almost 50 percent of the deals and would be likely to be bought by cash. Transactions at $500 million and above account for less than 10 percent of the deals by number but close to 50 percent by total dollar value. These are mostly stock-for-stock transactions. The median purchase price in recent years has been $40 million. The generalization that we can draw is that large transactions are mostly stock for stock, while small acquisitions are likely to be paid for in cash.

PREMIUMS

As shown in Table 4.6, the mean premium offered since 1990 has been 40 percent. The arithmetic mean gives higher weights to higher values, so the median figure of 31 percent is a better measure. Thus, in one-half of the transactions, the premium paid is less than 31 percent. Thus the frequent comment that premiums of 60 percent or more make it difficult for the acquiring firm

T A B L E 4.6

Percent Premium Offered, 1990–1999

Year	Average	Median
1990	42.0	32.0
1991	35.1	29.4
1992	41.0	34.7
1993	38.7	33.0
1994	41.9	35.0
1995	44.7	29.2
1996	36.6	27.3
1997	35.7	27.5
1998	40.7	30.1
1999	43.3	34.6
Mean	40.0	31.3
Median	40.9	31.1

Source: *Mergerstat Review.*

to earn a return higher than its cost of capital is an exaggeration. As Table 4.7 shows, the median percentage of premiums greater than 60 percent is only 17 percent of total transactions.

CONTINGENT PAYOUTS

Contingent payouts provide for additional payments to acquired firms based on their future performance. As shown in Table 4.8, both the mean and median contingent payout transactions accounted for 2.4 percent of total deals. Most acquired companies in such transactions are small, privately held firms. They are often in service-oriented establishments. Valuations of small, privately held companies are difficult because the future role of the owner-manager is uncertain. Contingent payouts may be employed to provide incentives for the owner-manager to stay with the firm after she or he has been made rich.

However, contingent payouts are not observed in almost 98 percent of transactions. To measure performance, the acquired

TABLE 4.7

Distributions of Premium Offered, 1990–1999 (Percent)

Year	20% and Less	Over 20% through 40%	Over 40% through 60%	Over 60% through 80%	Over 80% through 99.9%	100.0% and over
1990	34.9	25.1	19.4	8.0	4.0	8.6
1991	36.5	30.7	20.4	5.1	2.9	4.4
1992	29.6	29.6	14.8	13.4	9.9	2.8
1993	27.2	36.4	19.7	8.1	5.2	3.5
1994	25.4	34.2	20.0	10.8	2.7	6.9
1995	32.7	33.3	17.0	6.8	1.9	8.3
1996	35.7	30.7	18.4	8.9	2.6	3.7
1997	35.1	34.7	17.2	7.2	3.1	2.7
1998	34.2	30.5	16.2	9.0	3.3	6.8
1999	24.8	34.7	20.3	10.2	3.6	6.4
Mean	31.6	32.0	18.3	8.7	3.9	5.4
Median	33.4	32.0	18.9	8.5	3.2	5.4

Source: *Mergerstat Review.*

T A B L E   4.8

Contingent Payouts, 1990–1999

Year	Number	Percent of Total Deals
1990	55	2.65
1991	40	2.13
1992	55	2.14
1993	73	2.74
1994	63	2.10
1995	99	2.82
1996	95	1.62
1997	180	2.31
1998	215	2.75
1999	230	2.48
Mean	110.5	2.37
Median	84	2.40

Source: *Mergerstat Review.*

firm would have to operate autonomously. But this will interfere with the measurement of its future performance. If the firms are combined, it is difficult to separate the contributions. Another issue is, Who measures the future performance? If the acquired firm does the measurement, it may defer maintenance or otherwise understate costs and overstate revenues. If the acquiring firm takes over the accounting activities, it may take write-offs of receivables, inventories, and fixed assets to avoid the additional payouts. This somewhat cynical appraisal is supported by the frequency of lawsuits encountered in contingent payout transactions.

These predications are confirmed by empirical studies on earn-outs (Kohers and Ang, 2000). Their empirical study of completed takeovers using earn-outs covered the period from January 1, 1984 to June 30, 1996. Their sample consisted of 844 cases. Their median size of target measured by total assets was $5.9 million. The median size of acquirer total assets was $54.25 million, a multiple of 9.2 times the median size of targets. The median of the value of the merger transaction was $7.7 million of which the value of the earn-out was $0.7 million, or 9.1 percent. The authors observe that the earn-out mergers were mostly privately held targets in high-technology and business-related service activities. The acquirers and targets were mostly from different industries with little integration between bidder and target after the merger. In the earn-out sample, bidders experienced positive excess returns that are highly significant and more than 50 percent higher than in the non-earn-out sample. Earn-outs succeed in retaining target managers beyond the earn-out period. So earn-outs do have the value of providing incentives for valuable human capital to stay with the target firm.

USE OF COLLARS

Another method of dealing with the uncertainty of valuations is the use of collars in stock-for-stock transactions. Collars are found in about 10 percent of stock-for-stock transactions. Three main types of collar are used. The most widely used collars consist of a variable exchange ratio between a maximum and a minimum. For example, suppose the market price of the bidder's stock when the price is set is $50 compared with $20 paid for the target. Thus the initial terms are 0.4 share of the bidder for each share of the target. If the price of the bidder fell to $40, the target would be receiving $16 of market value, a decline of 20 percent. A collar might provide that for a price of the bidder between $60 and $40, the exchange ratio would fluctuate between 0.33 and 0.5 so that the target would always receive $20. But if the bidder stock rose above $60, the target would receive more than $20 in value; at a bidder stock price below $40, the target would receive less than $20 in value. An alternative type of collar would be unrestricted. It would provide that regardless of the market price of the bidder stock, the exchange ratio would be adjusted so that the target would receive $20 in value.

Market prices can fluctuate between the announcement of the deal and its closing date. The AOL Time Warner (TWX) deal terms were announced January 10, 2000. Their respective closing prices on Friday, January 7, were $74 for AOL and $65 for TWX. The merger terms called for TWX shareholders to receive 1.5 AOL shares per 1 TWX share. This valued TWX at 1.5 times $74, or $111. The TWX shares initially moved to over $100. However, the general stock market declined after March 2000. The deal received final approval from the FCC on January 11, 2001, a year and a day after it was announced. When the deal was announced, the market cap of the two companies added together was $266 billion. The total paid for TWX was $143 billion. The market value of TWX had declined to $99 billion on January 11, 2001, or approximately $71 per share, and AOL was around $47 per share.

The AOL/TWX example illustrates some of the issues in the use of a collar. In the year after the announcement date, the general stock market declined and particularly the Internet companies. Several possibilities are suggested. The relative prices in a merger transaction can change because the outlook of one of the companies or its industry has changed up or down. Another possible factor is the stock market reaction to the merger announcement. If the market judgment is that the deal makes no sense, the prices of both bidder and target are likely to fall. If the market feels that the bidder overpaid, the price of the bidder would fall relative to the price of the target. The price of the target would fall because it is being paid in bidder's stock.

So a number of factors can influence both the absolute and the relative market prices of the bidder and target. Research in this area has not yet settled on what the systematic relationships are.

SUMMARY

Deal structures established the terms of merger agreements. The method of accounting has a considerable influence on subsequent earnings reports. FASB is in the process of eliminating pooling of interests accounting. Pooling is criticized for simply adding the balance sheets and income statements at their historical book values. It ignores the actual market prices paid in a merger transaction.

The use of the purchase method in financial accounting results in lower reported net income. When the excess of the price paid over the target net worth is assigned to depreciable assets or to deductible amortization of goodwill, cash flows will be higher by the tax shelter effects of the increased depreciation or amortization of goodwill. When all the excess paid in purchase accounting is assigned to goodwill whose amortization is not tax-deductible, the cash flows are the same under both pooling and purchase accounting.

FASB is currently discussing the treatment of goodwill and intangible assets in purchase transactions. Its tentative proposal was that goodwill be reviewed for impairments which would require it to be written down and expensed against earnings. Acquired intangible assets (other than goodwill) would continue to be subject to amortization over their useful economic life and would be reviewed for impairments on the basis of FASB Statement No. 121.

Tax considerations affect the planning and structuring of corporate combinations. Even in M&As undertaken for other motives, transactions are structured to maximize tax benefits while complying with Internal Revenue Code regulations. In some individual instances, the tax benefits may have been substantial and may have had a major impact. Unfavorable tax rulings by the IRS have also led to the abandonment of some proposed M&As. But tax effects are not the dominant influence in merger and acquisition decisions.

In LBOs, taxes could have a significant influence because of the greater leverage employed. However, such leverage increases could also have been accomplished without LBOs. Furthermore, LBOs reduce leverage from cash flows and from subsequent public offerings of equity, so high leverage is not the major motive. Also improvements in operating performance and in higher profits result in increased tax payments.

REFERENCES

Applied Financial Information LP, *Mergerstat*, Los Angeles, California, 2000.

Hayn, C., "Tax Attributes as Determinants of Shareholder Gains in Corporate Acquisitions," *Journal of Financial Economics*, 23, 1989, pp. 121–153.

Jensen, M., S. Kaplan, and L. Stiglin, "The Effects of LBO's on Tax Revenues," *Tax Notes*, February 6, 1989, pp. 727–733.

Kaplan, S., "Management Buyouts: Evidence on Taxes as a Source of Value," *Journal of Finance*, 44, July 1989, pp. 611–632.

Kohers, Ninon, and James Ang, "Earnouts in Mergers: Agreeing to Disagree and Agreeing to Stay," *Journal of Business*, 73, 2000, pp. 445–476.

Newport, J. P., Jr., "Why the IRS Might Love Those LBOs," *Fortune*, December 5, 1988, pp. 145–152.

QUESTIONS AND PROBLEMS

4.1 What is the range of factors involved in deal structuring?

4.2 The basic purchase accounting entries for the AOL/Time Warner merger were as follows:

Debit ($ billion)

Goodwill	$132.5
Time Warner book equity	10.3
	$142.8

Credit ($ billion)

AOL common stock issued to pay for TWX (1.93B times $.01 par)	$0.0193
Paid-in capital ($142.8 − $0.0193)	142.78
	$142.8

What are the rules reflected in these accounting entries for purchase accounting?

4.3 What are the effects of paying for a company with stock on the behavior of the selling firm?

4.4 Summarize briefly what determines whether a merger transaction is taxable.

SOLUTIONS TO QUESTIONS AND PROBLEMS

4.1 Deal structuring involves the choice of accounting method, taxability, methods of payment, premiums, contingent payouts, and the use of collars in designing the terms of a transaction.

4.2 The merger was announced on January 10, 2000, when AOL had been trading at $74 and TWX at $65. The merger terms provided for 1.5 AOL shares per 1

TWX share. The number of TWX shares outstanding had been 1.287 billion multiplied by 1.5, which gives 1.93 billion. At the AOL $74 value this represented a total payment of $142.8 billion. This is the key figure. The book equity of TWX was $10.3 billion. The total debit is the purchase price. One debit is to eliminate the TWX book equity of $10.3 billion. The difference between the purchase price and the debit for the book equity of the acquired firm is assigned to depreciable assets to the degree possible. The remainder is charged to goodwill.

On the credit side, the book value of common stock issued by AOL of 1.93 billion shares is multiplied by the $0.01 par value to obtain $0.0193 billion. This is subtracted from the purchase price of $142.8 billion to obtain the $142.78 billion credit to the AOL paid-in capital account.

4.3 Since the seller receives the stock of the buyer, any losses in value from misleading the buyer with respect to the characteristic of the seller will be partially borne by the seller. The seller might try to sell the stock received immediately, but this would put downward pressure on the price of the stock.

4.4 In general, if stock is the method of payment, the transaction is nontaxable. If cash or equivalent is the method of payment, the transaction is taxable. The logic is that if stock is used, there is continuity of ownership by the seller. If the seller receives cash, he or she no longer has an ownership interest.

Mergers and Takeovers— Theory and Practice

This chapter focuses on the role of mergers in enhancing the value of the firm. Many writers express the view that about 70 percent of mergers fail in the sense that they do not earn the cost of capital for acquiring firms. This estimate is somewhat misleading since it includes many small transactions where the level of sophistication is not high. Our own studies of the largest mergers suggest that the probability of success is closer to 50 percent than 30 percent. In this chapter we begin with a review of the theories and reasons for mergers. This is followed by a summary of empirical studies on mergers.

THEORIES AND REASONS

The theories of mergers can be summarized into three major explanations, as summarized in Table 5.1. The first category is synergy or efficiency, in which total value from the combination is greater than the sum of the values of the component firms operating independently. Hubris (the second category) is the result of the winner's curse, causing bidders to overpay; it postulates that value is unchanged. Of course, in a synergistic merger, it would be possible for the bidder to overpay as well. The third class of mergers comprises those in which total value is decreased as a result of mistakes or managers who put their

T A B L E 5.1

Pattern of Gains Related to Takeover Theories

Type	(1) Total Value	(2) Gains to Target	(3) Gains to Acquirer
I. Efficiency or synergy	+	+	+
II. Hubris (winner's curse, overpay)	0	+	−
III. Agency problems or mistakes	−	+	−

Source: Berkovitch and Narayanan, 1993.

own preferences above the well-being of the firm, the agency problem.

As column 2 indicates, gains to targets are always positive. The acquired firm is usually paid a premium, so there are pluses under each type of takeover theory. Next, we consider gains to acquirers, shown in column 3. With synergy or efficiency, total value can be increased sufficiently to provide gains to acquirers. With hubris, by definition, total value is not increased, so acquirers lose. With mistakes or agency problems, total value is decreased, so that the gains to targets imply severe loses in value for acquirers.

So within this framework, the main source of value increases is efficiency gains. Detailed within the broad category of synergy or efficiency gains are many individual items. They are listed in Table 5.2. They include a wide range of items.

Additional insights on the role of mergers are provided by Table 5.3, which lists the industries in which a high-level takeover has occurred. The factors include the major change forces described earlier. Excess capacity in oil and steel has led to consolidation mergers to reduce capacity. In Europe, movements toward a common market provide opportunities for economies of scale, similar to those that produced the major merger movement in the United States at the turn of the century.

Illustrative examples of high M&A activity companies are shown in Table 5.4. General Electric has followed the philosophy of making acquisitions of strong companies in attractive areas. If

T A B L E 5.2

Sources of Gains in M&As

A. Strategy
1. Develop a new strategic vision
2. Achieve long-run strategic goals
3. Acquire capabilities in new industry
4. Obtain talent for fast-moving industries
5. Add capabilities to expand role in a technologically advancing industry
6. Quickly move into new products, markets
7. Apply a broad range of capabilities and managerial skills in new areas
B. Economies of scale
1. Cut production costs due to large volume
2. Combine R&D operations
3. Increased R&D at controlled risk
4. Increased sales force
5. Cut overhead costs
6. Strengthen distributions systems
C. Economies of scope
1. Broaden product line
2. Provide one-stop shopping for all services
3. Obtain complementary products
D. Extend advantages in differentiated products
E. Advantages of size
1. Large size can afford high-tech equipment
2. Spread the investments in the use of expensive equipment over more units
3. Ability to get quantity discounts
4. Better terms in deals
F. Best practices
1. Operating efficiencies (improve management of receivables, inventories, fixed assets, etc.)
2. Faster tactical implementation
3. Incentives for workers—rewards
4. Better utilization of resources
G. Market expansion
1. Increased market shares
2. Obtain access to new markets
H. New capabilities, managerial skills
1. Apply a broad range of capabilities and managerial skills in new areas
2. Acquire capabilities in new industry
3. Obtain talent for fast-moving industries
I. Competition
1. Achieve critical mass early before rivals
2. Preempt acquisitions by competitor
3. Compete on EBIT growth for high valuations
J. Customers
1. Develop new key customer relationships
2. Follow clients
3. Combined company can meet customers' demand for a wide range of services

T A B L E 5.2 (Continued)

K. Technology
    1. Enter technologically dynamic industries
    2. Seize opportunities in industries with developing technologies
    3. Exploit technological advantage
    4. Add new R&D capabilities
    5. Add key complementary technological capabilities
    6. Add key technological capabilities
    7. Add new key patent or technology
    8. Acquire technology for lagging areas
L. Shift in industry organization
    1. Adjust to deregulation—relaxing of government barriers to geographic and product market extensions
    2. Change in strategic scientific industry segment
M. Adjust to industry consolidation activities
    1. Eliminate industry excess capacity
    2. Need to cut costs
N. Shift in product strategy
    1. Shift from overcapacity area to area with more favorable sales capacity
    2. Exit a product area that has become commoditized to area of specialty
O. Industry roll-ups—taking fragmented industries, and because of improvements in communication and transportation, rolling up many individual firms into larger firms, obtaining the benefits of strong and experienced management teams over a large number of smaller units
P. Globalization
    1. International competition—to establish presence in foreign markets and to strengthen position in domestic market
    2. Size and economies of scale required for effective global competition
    3. Growth opportunities outside domestic market
    4. Diversification
        a. Product line
        b. Geographically—enlarge market
        c. Reduce systematic risk
        d. Reduce dependence on exports
    5. Favorable product inputs
        a. Obtain assured sources of supply—sources of raw materials
        b. Labor (inexpensive, well-trained, etc.)
        c. Need for local manufacturing
    6. Improve distribution in other countries
    7. Political/regulatory policies
        a. Circumvent protective tariffs, etc.
        b. Political/economic stability
        c. Government policy
        d. Invest in a safe, predictable environment
        e. Take advantage of common markets
    8. Relative exchange rate conditions
Q. Investment – acquire company, improve it, sell it
R. Prevent competitor from acquiring target company
S. Create antitrust problem to deter potential acquirers of our firm

T A B L E 5.3

The High Takeover Industries

The industry characteristics related to M&A pressures can be summarized as follows:

1. *Telecommunications*—Technological change, deregulation in the United States and abroad (particularly Europe) have stimulated efforts to develop a global presence.

2. *Media* (movies, records, magazines, newpapers)—Technological changes have impacted the relationship between the content and delivery segments. Potential overlap in content of different media outlets. Attractive and glamorous industry (attracted Japanese investors beginning in late 1980s).

3. *Financial* (investment banks, commercial banks, insurance companies)—Globalization of industries and firms requires financial services firms to go global to serve their clients.

4. Chemicals, pharmaceuticals—Both require high amounts of R&D, but suffer rapid imitation. Chemicals become commodities. Pharmaceuticals enjoy a limited period of patent protection, but are eroded by "me too" drugs and generics. Changes in the technology of basic research and increased risks due to competitive pressures have created the stimulus for larger firms through M&As.

5. *Autos, oil & gas, industrial machinery*—All face unique difficulties that give advantages to size, stimulating M&As to achieve critical mass. Autos face global excess capacity. Oil faces the uncertainty of price and supply instability due to actions of the OPEC cartel.

6. *Utilities*—Deregulation has created opportunities for economies from enlarging geographic areas. New kinds of competitive forces have created needs for broadening managerial capabilities.

7. *Food, retailing*—These are hampered by slow growth. Food consumption will only grow at the rate of population growth. Expanding internationally offers opportunities to grow in new markets.

8. *Natural resources, timber*—Both face exhausting sources of supply. Problems of matching raw material supplies with manufacturing capacity.

they become number one or two, they are developed further; otherwise, they are divested. Cisco Systems has made a series of acquisitions to broaden its role in networking for the Internet. Tyco International has placed acquisitions in four groups, described as related. After a bump related to accounting questions raised, it appears to have resumed its progress. Microsoft, despite its alleged dominant position, has been concerned about protecting against the changing nature of the computing industry

TABLE 5.4

Illustrative M&A Activity

Fifty largest U.S. companies: 4190 deals from 1/3/94 to 2/10/99 (market caps as of 7/31/99)

1. General Electric [market cap $380 billion] (Jack Welch)
   1981–1997 Acquisitions: 617 of $74 billion.; Divestitures: 310 of $16 billion.
2. Cisco Systems [market cap $210 billion] (John Chambers)
   1993–1998 thirty major acquisitions—networking for the Internet
3. Tyco International [market cap $82 billion] (Dennis Kozlowski)
   Conglomerate, four groups of "related" companies, tops list of cumulative acquisitions, 24 major acquisitions since 1986
4. Microsoft [market cap $403 billion] (Bill Gates) 1994–1998 fifty deals
5. Intel [market cap $225 billion] (Andrew Grove) 75 to 100 deals per year

---

in general and the role of software in relation to emerging developments, such as the Internet. Intel has sought to maintain its growth by expanding the applications of the memory devices it sells. It, too, has been concerned about the pace of change and the rise of strong competitors in its product market areas.

Another influence in mergers is differential price/earnings (P/E) ratios of companies. When an acquiring firm with a high P/E ratio combines with a firm with a lower P/E ratio, the earnings per share (EPS) of the buyer will rise. Table 5.5 illustrates this generalization. The first three rows present assumed data for a buyer in column 1 and a seller in column 2 on P/E ratios, net income, and shares outstanding. Row 4 is calculated as net income divided by shares outstanding to obtain EPS. The final row is the indicated market value per share obtained by multiplying the P/E by the EPS.

The results in column 3 for the combined firms are explained briefly in column 4. The P/E ratio of the buyer is assumed to continue for the combined firm. The net income of $200 million is a simple addition. We postulate that the buyer pays a 20 percent premium for the seller, or $60 per share. Hence, the buyer pays the seller 0.6 of its $100 stock, so the buyer issues 12 million shares to replace the 20 million shares of the seller. The total shares in the combined column are 32

T A B L E 5.5

Playing the Relative *P/E* Game

	(1) Buyer	(2) Seller	(3) Combined	(4) Explanation for Column 3
Price-earnings ratio (*P/E*)	20 times	10 times	20 times	Assumed
Net income	$100 million	$100 million	$200 million	(1) + (2)
Shares outstanding	20 million	20 million	32 million	(1) + 0.6 (20 million)
Earnings per share (EPS)	$5	$5	$6.25	$200/32
Market value per share	$100	$50	$125	20 × $6.25

million. Dividing this number into the combined net income of $200 million gives $6.25 as the new EPS. Applying the *P/E* of 20 gives a market price per share of $125.

In Table 5.6, the effects on buyers and sellers are summarized. The postmerger EPS for the buyer increases by $1.25, or 25 percent. Its market price per share also increases by 25 percent to $125. The EPS of the seller is 0.6 of the postmerger price of $6.25, which is $3.75. It suffers dilution in EPS. But the seller now owns 0.6 share of stock worth $125. So postmerger, for each share the seller owned premerger, the seller holds a value of $75. This represents an increase in market value of 50 percent. This is the nature of *P/E* magic.

The key assumption in the above is that the *P/E* ratio of the buyer will carry over to the combined firm. Since the buyer could announce that its earnings per share had increased by 25 percent, its actual postmerger *P/E* ratio was likely to increase even further. While *P/E* magic works in the short run, in the longer run it is likely to come apart. The lower *P/E* ratio of the seller company must reflect lower growth and/or higher risk. In the longer term, the lower growth of the seller will depress the earnings growth of the buyer. The higher risk implies the occurrence of unfavorable events, also depressing earnings. So *P/E*

T A B L E 5.6

Effects on Buyer and Seller (Dollars)

	Buyer		Seller	
	Premerger	**Postmerger**	**Premerger**	**Postmerger**
Earnings per share	5	6.25	5	3.75
Market price per share	100	125	50	75
Total market value	2 billion	2.5 billion	1 billion	1.5 billion

magic works only if the new acquisitions are sufficient to offset the depressing influences of the older acquisitions.

An alternative possibility is that the market has overvalued the price of the high *P/E* firm and undervalued the low *P/E* firm. If so, the high *P/E* firm is gaining an advantage from mispricing by the market. We are skeptical that such pricing mistakes are a general explanation of differential *P/E* ratios.

MAJOR CHALLENGES TO MERGER SUCCESS

While there are many potential gains from merger activity, they can fail for weaknesses in three particularly important areas: due diligence, cultural factors, and implementation difficulties.

Due Diligence

Due diligence may begin with legal aspects, but it must be extended to business and management considerations. It involves all the following. An examination of all aspects of prospective partners should be performed. Firms should be sure there are no legal problems, such as pension funding, environmental problems, or product liabilities. Inspection should determine important factors such as the relevance of accounting records, the maintenance and quality of equipment, and the possibility of maintaining cost controls. It should also be determined whether the firm has potential for product improvements or superiority.

Broader business aspects also need to be taken into account. In particular, management relationships must be analyzed. A business combination should fill gaps in managerial capabilities and also extend capabilities. The firm's resources should be extended in multiple dimensions. Consideration must be given to how the two management systems will fit together, and whether managers will have to be hired or fired. Firms should be aware of new developments that will benefit the firm or require adjustments. Ultimately, the acquired unit should be worth more as a part of the acquiring firm than alone or with any other firm.

Cultural Factors

Corporate culture is defined by an organization's values, traditions, norms, beliefs, and behavior patterns. Corporate culture may be articulated in formal statements of organization values and aspirations. It also is expressed in informal relationships and networks. Corporate cultures may be reflected in a company's operating style, including both formal and informal influences. More concretely, corporate culture may be conveyed by the kinds of behavior that are rewarded in an organization.

We argue that a firm must manage its own corporate culture effectively before engaging in merger activity. If its organizational culture house is not in order, combining companies and their cultures will aggravate problems. The firm must be consistent in its formal statements of values and the kinds of actions that are rewarded. The firm must already have a program of proactive employee training and communications systems that convey the importance of the value of individual development and recognition of contributions to organizational effectiveness.

The foregoing emphasizes that in planning for external growth through mergers, alliances, and other relationships, the firm must recognize cultural factors in addition to products, plant and equipment, and financial factors. The firm must be sensitized to recognizing the requirement for pulling together all the systems, informal processes, and cultures required for organizational effectiveness. Due diligence must include coverage of cultural factors in all their dimensions. A wise acquirer puts culture on the table at the earliest planning sessions.

Cultural differences have caused mergers to fail or prevented them from achieving their potentials. Cultural differences are almost certain to be involved when companies are combined. Cultural differences are increasingly important in the rising number of cross-border transactions.

Pitfalls begin with simply ignoring the problem. Another is to promise equal treatment and respect but to impose the culture from one firm onto another. Problems inherent in inconsistent cultures can escalate to conflict. Information on how the acquiring firm has handled cultural factors in the past or how the firm has handled organizational change can be developed. Formal tools are available for assessing cultural problems and prospects. Potential partners may be asked to complete a questionnaire describing the cultural dimensions of the prospective merger partners. Focus groups may be employed to conduct sessions with senior officers and directors of the combining firms.

End solutions may take various forms. One is to recognize cultural differences and to respect them. This may occur in firms with vertical relationships in which required management styles may vary at different levels of activity such as research, production, marketing, and finance. Another practice is to exchange executives across the organizations that have been brought together.

Ultimately, the cultures may move toward similarity. Or differences may even be valued as sources of increased efficiency. Diversity of patterns may be the result in different types of industrial activities or between firms with different histories. A general recommendation is to involve the human resources managers in the process so that modern concepts and tools can be used.

Implementation

A key challenge in doing M&As is implementation. Some discussions propose that implementation starts when the merger agreement has been signed. Our view is that implementation starts as a condition for thinking about M&As. The firm must have implemented all aspects of efficient operations before it can effectively combine organizations. This means that the firm must have a shareholder value orientation. It must have strategies and organizational structures compatible with its multiple business units.

Companies should pursue only mergers that further their corporate strategy: strengthening weaknesses, filling gaps, developing new growth opportunities, and extending capabilities. Integration leadership is required. The demands of regular business operations and integration are too much for one person to handle. The integration leader should have management leadership qualities, experience with external constituencies, and credibility with the various integration participants.

Poor communication distresses employees; good integrators use communication plans that provide early, frequent, and clear integration messages. The company should maintain ongoing communication that clearly addresses the concerns of employees.

M&As may fail because of slow integration. Firms should create cross-functional teams to devote attention to the issues of integration. But the firm should also be sensitive to the need for balance between speed and disruption. Day-to-day operations should not be sacrificed for rapidity of integration. The key is to formulate in advance integration plans that can effectively accomplish the goals of the M&A processes.

EMPIRICAL STUDIES OF MERGER PERFORMANCE

We next consider factual studies of the returns to mergers.

Returns to Bidders and Targets

Using mainly the market model adjusted for beta risk, the broad patterns of returns are shown in Table 5.7. Other evidence shows that the returns to target firms increased over the decades as government regulation increased and as sophisticated defensive tactics were developed by targets. The returns to bidding firms decreased over the decades because of the same influences operating in the reverse direction. But even for the 1980s it appears that the total wealth increase from M&A activity is positive.

The mean returns cover up the wide diversity in experience for both target and bidder companies. Although bidder companies experience negative returns for some time period, there are

T A B L E 5.7

Pattern of Event Returns

	Mergers	Tender Offers
Targets	Positive 20–25%	Positive 30–40%
Buyers	Positive 1–2%	Negative 1–2%

always a substantial fraction of the bidder companies that experience positive returns. This may provide motivation for bidder firms to continue to engage in M&A activity even though average results may be unfavorable. Each firm, based on the evidence, may formulate the judgment that its own results can be positive.

The results presented in Table 5.7 are measured net of general market movements. These are calculated by careful statistical procedures described next.

Calculation of Returns

The first step in measuring the effect of an *event* (announcement of a tender offer, share repurchase, and so on) on stock value is to define an event period. Usually this is centered on the announcement date, which is designated date 0 in event time. The purpose of the event period is to capture all the effects on stock price of the event. Longer periods will make sure that all the effects are captured, but the estimate is subject to more noise in the data. Many studies choose a period such as days −40 to +40, that is, from 40 days before the announcement to 40 days after the announcement. Note, day 0 is the date the announcement is made for a particular firm and will denote different calendar dates for different firms.

The next step is to calculate a predicted (or normal) return $\hat{R}_{jt}$ for each day t in the event period for each firm j. The predicted return represents the return that would be expected if no event took place. Next the residual r_{jt} is calculated for each day for each firm. The residual is the actual return for that day for the firm minus the predicted return, or $r_{jt} = R_{jt} - \hat{R}_{jt}$. The residual represents the abnormal return, that is, the part of the return that is not predicted and is therefore an estimate of the change in firm value on that day, which is caused by the event. For each day in event time the residuals are averaged across firms to produce the average residual for that day, AR_t, where

$$AR_t = \frac{\sum_j r_{jt}}{N}$$

and N is the number of firms in the sample. The reason for averaging across firms is that stock returns are "noisy," but the noise tends to cancel out when averaged across a large number of firms. Therefore, the more firms in the sample, the better the ability to distinguish the effect of an event. The final step is to cumulate the average residual for each day over the entire event period to produce the cumulative average residual or return, CAR, where

$$CAR = \sum_{t=-40}^{40} AR_t$$

The cumulative average residual represents the average total effect of the event across all firms over a specified time interval.

There are two main methods of calculating predicted returns. These are the market model method and the market-adjusted return method. For most cases the two methods yield similar results.

To use the market model, a clean period is chosen and the market model is estimated by running a regression for the days in this period. The clean period may be before the event period, after the event period, or both, but it never includes the event period. The clean period includes days on which no information related to the event is released. The market model is

$$R_{jt} = \alpha_j + \beta_j R_{mt} + \epsilon_{jt}$$

where R_{mt} is the return on a market index (for example, the S&P 500) for day t, β_j measures the sensitivity of firm j to the market (this is a measure of risk), α_j measures the mean return over the period not explained by the market, and ϵ_{jt} is a statistical error term $\Sigma \epsilon_{jt} = 0$. The regression produces estimates of α_j and β_j; call these $\hat{\alpha}_j$ and $\hat{\beta}_j$. The predicted return for a firm for a day in the event period is the return given by the market model on that day using these estimates. That is,

$$\hat{R}_{jt} = \hat{\alpha}_j + \hat{\beta}_j R_{mt}$$

where now R_{mt} is the return on the market index for the actual day in the event period. Because the market model takes explicit account of both the risk associated with the market and mean returns, it is the most widely used method.

The market-adjusted return method is the simplest of the methods. The predicted return for a firm for a day in the event period is just the return on the market index for that day. That is:

$$\hat{R}_{jt} = R_{mt}$$

The market-adjusted return method can be thought of as an approximation to the market model where $\hat{\alpha}_j = 0$ and $\hat{\beta}_j = 1$ for all firms. Because $\hat{\alpha}_j$ is usually small and the average $\hat{\beta}_j$ over all firms is 1, this approximation usually produces acceptable results.

Single Bids versus Multiple Bids

We have summarized the pattern of returns with single bidders versus multiple bidders for target firms in Fig. 5.1 and for acquiring firms in Fig. 5.2. In Fig. 5.1, the returns to target firms begin to rise about 20 days before the announcement date. On the announcement date, a further increase moves the abnormal returns of single-bidder target firms to about 30 percent. Shortly after the announcement date, the returns to target firms drift down slightly. In multiple-bidder contest, the event returns to targets continue to rise after the announcement date. As subsequent bids take place, the event returns continue to rise. About 40 days after the announcement date for the first bidder, the event returns to the target firms level off at about 45 percent.

In Fig. 5.2, we see that the event returns for acquiring firms that are single bidders rise to more than 2 percent at the

F I G U R E 5.1

Cumulative Abnormal Returns of Target Firms

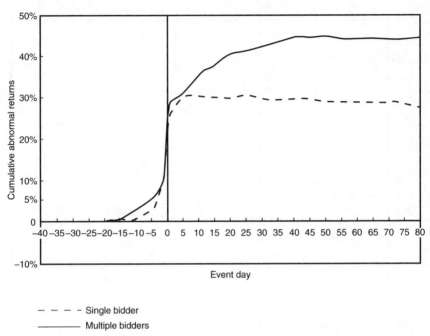

– – – – Single bidder
————— Multiple bidders

announcement date. Subsequently, the event returns drift down but only slightly. For acquiring firms that are competing in multiple-bidder contests, the event returns are slightly positive. But shortly after the announcement date, as new bidders come onto the scene, the event returns drop to negative levels.

Positive Total Returns versus Negative Total Returns

Of critical importance is whether the total event returns are positive or negative—whether value is created or destroyed. Berkovitch and Narayanan (1993) tested alternative theories of takeovers by grouping the results for positive total gains versus negative returns. Of their sample of 330 transactions, 250, or 76 percent, achieved positive total gains.

For the sample of negative total gains, the correlation between target gains and total gains was negative and significant.

F I G U R E 5.2

Cumulative Abnormal Returns of Acquiring Firms

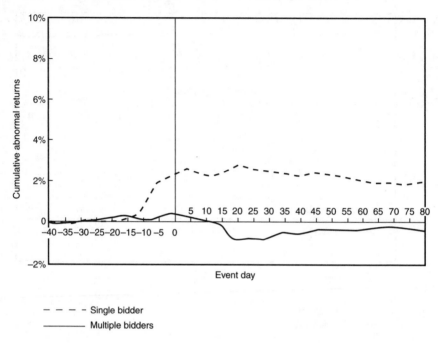

− − − − Single bidder
─────── Multiple bidders

This could result because target gains are always positive, so that when total gains are negative, target gains would be negatively correlated with the nonpositive total gains. When target gains were related to bidder gains for the negative total gains sample, the correlation was again negative and highly significant. This implies that agency problems cause total gains to be negative and hubris still provides positive gains to targets, which implies that bidders will have negative returns.

Berkovitch and Narayanan also analyzed the influence of competition among bidders as reflected in multiple-bid contests. For positive total gains, the correlation between target returns and total gains was strongly positive. It appears that the synergy influence was reinforced. When total gains were negative, however, the correlation between target returns and total gains was negative. Multiple bidding appears to aggravate the agency problem and to stimulate hubris as well.

Berkovitch and Narayanan conclude that total gains are mostly positive and that synergy appears to be the dominant driving force in mergers and takeovers. They suggest that the empirical data convey that agency and hubris play some role as well. They observe that in more than three-fourths of the cases in the sample they employed, total gains are positive. It is likely, therefore, that value is created by M&As. This reinforces the conclusions of other studies as well.

Houston and Ryngaert (1994) studied gains from large bank mergers using a sample of 131 completed mergers and 22 uncompleted for the period 1985 to 1991. They focused on the total return measured by the return to a value-weighted portfolio of the bidder and target. The average total return to a completed bank merger was slightly positive but not significantly different from zero. However, in the later years covered by their sample, the total merger returns were positive and significant.

Bidding banks were more profitable than target banks. Total returns were significantly higher when acquiring banks had been more profitable. Banks with good track records were considered more likely to engage in value-increasing acquisitions.

Houston and Ryngaert point out that most bank takeover bids are financed with stock. When a bidding bank announces an acquisition, this may be interpreted as a signal that its stock is overvalued. This may partially account for the negative returns to bidder banks. Houston and Ryngaert find that the market responds most favorably when acquisition announcements are made by bidders that have a historical record of superior operating performance. Bank merger transactions in which there is a high degree of market overlap earn higher positive returns, presumably because of a greater potential for cost savings.

Methods of Payment

A study by Huang and Walkling (1987) combined the analysis of method of payment with acquisition form and managerial resistance. Whereas previous studies found higher abnormal returns (30 to 35 percent) for tender offers than for mergers (15 to 20 percent) for target shareholders, such studies did not consider the effect of payment method and target management resistance. Huang and Walkling found that when method of payment and degree of resistance were taken into account statistically, abnormal returns were no higher in tender offers than in mergers.

Managerial resistance carried somewhat higher abnormal returns, but the results were not statistically significant. These results were not affected after controlling for form of payment and form of acquisition. The most powerful influence they found was the method of payment. After controlling for type of acquisition and for managerial resistance, cash offers had much higher abnormal returns than stock offers. The average return for cash offers was 29.3 percent compared with 14.4 percent for stock offers. For mixed payments, the average return was 23.3 percent, which fell between the values reported for stock and cash offers.

Runup versus Markup Returns

An in-depth study was made of the relationship between the CAR for the preannouncement period (the runup) and the CAR for the postannouncement period (the markup) (Schwert, 1996). On average, for 1174 successful deals, the runup and markup were about the same at 15 percent each. In the 564 tender offers, the runup was about 16 percent and the markup about 20 percent, approximating the 35 percent gain to targets in tender offers found in previous studies. In the 959 mergers, their runup was 12 percent and the markup 5 percent. The total premium of 17 percent was slightly below the average 20 percent found in earlier studies.

With regard to returns to acquirers, Schwert found, as did earlier studies, that in establishing parameters for measuring CARs, the market model had a positive slope during the preannouncement test period. Schwert calculated the market model regression for trading days −253 to −127 in relation to the announcement date. As in earlier studies, Schwert found that bidder firms had unusual stock price increases prior to their decisions to make takeover bids. Schwert sought to adjust for this by setting the intercepts of the market model regression to zero. The consequence is that the negative CAR for bidders found in other studies that did not make such adjustments becomes zero. Our interpretation is that the abnormal returns to bidders on average are zero. This is consistent with a takeover market that is highly competitive so that bidders earn only normal returns on average.

Bad Bidders Become Good Targets

Mitchell and Lehn (1990) studied stock price reactions to acquisitions during the period 1982 to 1986. One sample was composed of firms that became targets of takeovers after they had made acquisitions. A control group consisted of acquiring firms that did not subsequently become targets of takeover bids. The stock prices of acquirers that became targets declined significantly when they announced acquisitions. The stock prices of acquiring firms that did not become subsequent targets increased significantly when they announced acquisitions.

Furthermore, Mitchell and Lehn found that for the entire sample of acquisitions, those that were subsequently divested had significantly negative event returns. Acquisitions that were not subsequently divested had significantly positive event returns. This suggests that when companies announce acquisitions, the event returns forecast the likelihood that the assets will ultimately be divested. Mitchell and Lehn point out that in the aggregate the returns to acquiring firms were approximately zero. But when acquiring firms experienced negative event returns, they were subsequently likely to become takeover targets. Bidders that experienced positive event returns were less likely to become targets. Event returns were able to discriminate between "bad" bidders and "good" bidders.

Postmerger Performance

The studies of event returns described in the preceding section report the stock market reactions to announcements of mergers and tender offers. We now turn to studies of longer-term effects.

The seminal study of postmerger performance is that of Healy, Palepu, and Ruback (HPR) (1992). They studied the postacquisition performance of the 50 largest U.S. mergers between 1979 and 1984. They used accounting data primarily but tested their results by using market valuation measures as well. They analyzed both operating characteristics and investment characteristics.

They looked at the results for the firms themselves and then made a further adjustment. They made an industry adjustment to test whether the changes in the variables occurred because of industry effects as distinguished from the effects of the mergers on the individual firms. For example, the merged firms may have reduced employment. But if employment reduction in nonmerging firms in the same industry was even greater, then industry-adjusted employment in the merged firms would have increased.

Their data show that industry-adjusted employment decreased. This implies that the merging firms did more restructuring and reorganization than other firms in the industry. But the cash flow margin on sales did not significantly change. However, asset turnover significantly improved. The return on the market value of assets also improved significantly. However, the fact that the cash flow margin on sales had not changed implies that the improvement in the return on assets did not come from the reduction of employment costs, which would have increased the cash flow margin on sales. It was better asset management that increased the return on assets. Pension expense per employee was reduced somewhat but not by a statistically significant degree; none of the investment characteristics were significantly changed on the basis of industry-adjusted performance, except asset sales measured at book value.

These results imply that industry-adjusted performance of the merging firms had improved. The improvement came not at the expense of labor income but by improving the management of assets. The investments in capital equipment and investments in research and development were not significantly changed.

One of the important findings in the HPR study related to the event returns calculated as described in connection with the previous studies summarized in this chapter: The event returns for the firms are significantly correlated with the subsequent accounting returns during the postmerger period. This is evidence that on average, for their sample, event returns correctly forecast postmerger performance.

Agrawal, Jaffe, and Mandelker (AJM) (1992) also studied postmerger performance. They developed a larger sample of 937 mergers and 227 tender offers. Their sample included firms smaller than those of the HPR study, which focused on the 50 largest mergers. They adjusted for size effect and beta-weighted market returns. They found that shareholders of acquiring firms experienced a wealth loss of about 10 percent over the 5 years following the merger completion.

This finding has some interesting implications. First, it represents an anomaly in the sense that it provides an opportunity for a positive abnormal investment return. If acquiring firms always lose after a merger, this suggests that investors short the acquiring firm on a long-term basis at the time of a merger announcement. Of course, over time this anomaly should be wiped out.

Another implication may be explored. Healy, Palepu, and Ruback (1992) found that industry-adjusted postmerger performance was positive. Agrawal, Jaffe, and Mandelker (1992) found that marketwide or economywide adjustments result in negative returns. These two results together imply that merger activity took place mainly in industries where performance was subpar compared to the market or the economy as a whole.

Loughran and Vijh (1997) studied 947 acquisitions during the period 1970 to 1989. Their overall sample had an average 5-year buy-and-hold return of 88.2 percent compared to 94.7 percent for their matching firms. The difference had a t statistic of 0.96, which was not significant. The compound annual return was 13.5 percent for their sample; 14.2 percent for the matching firms. Over the 20-year time period covered by their study, the Standard & Poor's 500 experienced a compound annual return of 6.15 percent—less than one-half the returns for their two samples. The returns to acquirers in cash tender offers for the 5-year period were 145.6 percent, as compared with 83.9 percent for their matching firm sample—statistically significant. For cash mergers, the difference was not statistically significant. In stock-for-stock mergers, the acquisition sample underperformed the matching firms; they also underperformed in tender offers, but the sample size was only eight observations over the 20-year period.

When we consider these findings and counterfindings and the many variables discussed at the beginning of this chapter that influence event returns as well as postmerger performance, it is clear that results are sensitive to sample selection and measurement methodology. Some mergers perform well; others do not. Also, it is probable that industry conditions influence merger results.

MERGER PERFORMANCE DURING THE 1990s

Another study used a sample of 364 transactions that accounted for almost one-half of the total M&A values between 1992 and mid-1998 (Weston and Johnson, 1999). The information was obtained from the *Mergerstat* database, supplemented by proxy statements to shareholders soliciting approval of transactions. The study summarized deal structure patterns and calculated event returns. The results reflect large transactions whose patterns are different from those of smaller transactions; the event return results could differ also.

The selection criteria began with all M&As in which the price paid for the target exceeded $500 million. By 1997, this annual number became so large that the cutoff was raised to $1 billion or more. The study ended with transactions announced through June 1998. The stock market adjustment that began in July 1998 dampened new M&A deal announcements. For completed transactions, however, the third quarter of 1998 was still high because of deals initiated earlier. The stock market began to recover in mid-October and was associated with a resumption in an active M&A market, with 11 major deals totaling $65 billion announced on "Merger Monday," November 23, 1998. Thus, the study captures a distinctive cycle of M&A activity. The sample accounted for about 40 to 45 percent of total deal value in most years, increasing to almost 69 percent for the first half of 1998. The exploding number of blockbuster transactions is consistent with these data.

Pooling versus Purchase Accounting

Transactions that use purchase accounting involve a larger firm buying a smaller firm. Since one of the 12 requirements for pooling accounting is that the firms be of approximately equal size, the acquisition of smaller firms by larger firms would have to receive the accounting treatment of a purchase transaction. The sample of the 364 largest transactions between 1992 and June 30, 1998, accounted for 44 percent of total transaction value over the entire period and 69 percent for the first half of 1998. The number of total transactions in 1998 was 9149 in the *M&A Almanac* and 7759 for *Mergerstat*. Thus, most of the 8000 to 9000 annual transactions in the broader compilations represent purchase accounting.

For the sample of 364 transactions, pooling accounted for slightly more than 52 percent of the transactions, as shown in Table 5.8. However, 75 of the 364 transactions (20.6 percent) involved banks. As shown by Table 5.8, for banks, 80 percent of the transactions were pooling, only 20 percent purchase. For our nonbank sample, purchases predominated at 55 percent of the total. The data indicate that banks had a very strong preference for pooling. One possible explanation is that the banks are strongly averse to the negative impact of goodwill write-offs on reported net income. In contrast, in nonbank transactions, the strong avoidance of nonpooling transactions does not manifest itself. One possible explanation is that in general the economies or synergies in the nonbank transactions are sufficiently strong that the negative effect of the goodwill write-off is overcome by the increase in earnings that the new combined firm will be able to achieve. Firms in highly synergistic transactions would be less averse to the negative impact of the goodwill write-off because the increase in earnings of the combination would more

TABLE 5.8

Accounting Treatment, 1992 to 1998

Method	Bank Number	Bank Percent	Nonbank Number	Nonbank Percent	Combined Number	Combined Percent
Pooling	60	80.0	130	45.0	190	52.2
Purchase	15	20.0	159	55.0	174	47.8
Total	75	100.0	289	100.0	364	100.0

than offset the negative effects. This also leads to the prediction that highly synergistic mergers will not be deterred after 2001 when the use of pooling accounting may no longer be available in merger transactions.

Method of Payment

The 1980s are referred to as the decade of mergers propelled by junk bond financing. The debt sold raised cash that was used in takeovers, often hostile. Data compilations showed these deals as cash transactions, but the underlying source was debt. The data show that in the 364 largest deals during the 1990s, summarized in Table 5.9, stock accounted for 60 percent of the number of transactions, with combinations of stock and cash moving the proportion up to 80 percent. Stock-for-stock transactions are generally nontaxable. In bank mergers, stock is involved in more than 90 percent of the deals. In nonbank mergers, the proportion drops to about 75 percent.

In large compilations of transactions, most would be smaller deals. These smaller transactions are typically made for cash. Thus, in broader compilations we find that stock is involved in about one-third of the transactions. A brief generalization is that big deals in the 1990s were mainly stock for stock. In the smaller deals, the seller was likely to be paid off in cash.

T A B L E 5.9

Method of Payment in Largest Mergers, 1992 to 1998

Method	Bank		Nonbank		Combined	
	Number	Percent	Number	Percent	Number	Percent
Cash	7	9.3	72	24.9	79	21.7
Stock	61	81.3	159	55.0	220	60.4
Cash and stock	7	9.3	57	19.7	64	17.6
Debt	0	0.0	1	0.3	1	0.3
Total	75	100.0	289	100.0	364	100.0

Taxability

Table 5.10 shows that for nonbank transactions in 1992 to 1998, 60 percent were nontaxable. Table 5.8 showed that 45 percent of nonbank deals in this period were accorded pooling of interests accounting treatment. Pooling deals are generally not taxable. Hence the additional 15 percent of nontaxable, nonbank transactions used purchase accounting but still qualified for nontaxable treatment. The reason for this is that some stock-for-stock transactions may not have met all 12 rules required to qualify for pooling of interests accounting. For example, if one of the participants in a merger had engaged in stock buybacks during the 2 years preceding the year of the deal, it would fail to qualify for pooling of interests treatment. However, since it was a stock-for-stock transaction, it could still qualify for nontaxability.

Table 5.11 shows that about 54 percent of all nonbank transactions in which purchase accounting was used were taxable transactions. In another 19 percent, taxability depended on whether the seller chose to take cash or stock when this election option was provided by the buyer.

More than 85 percent of bank transactions are nontaxable. This reflects the predominance of pooling in bank deals. If we add the 6.7 percent of bank deals in which the buyer offers the seller the option to take cash or stock, we find that probably more than 90 percent of the bank deals qualified for nontaxability.

T A B L E 5.10

Taxability, 1992 to 1998

Method	Bank		Nonbank		Combined	
	Number	Percent	Number	Percent	Number	Percent
Taxable	6	8.0	85	29.4	91	25.0
Nontaxable	64	85.3	174	60.2	238	65.4
Election	5	6.7	30	10.4	35	9.6
Total	75	100.0	289	100.0	364	100.0

T A B L E 5.11

Purchase Accounting and Taxability, 1992 to 1998

	Bank		Nonbank		Combined	
Method	Number	Percent	Number	Percent	Number	Percent
Taxable	6	40.0	85	53.5	91	52.3
Nontaxable	4	26.7	44	27.7	48	27.6
Election	5	33.3	30	18.9	35	20.1
Total	15	100.0	159	100.0	174	100.0

Premiums Paid

The premium measured was based on the market price of the seller stock 30 days before the public announcement of the deal. This was done to avoid the runup in price of the seller stock in response to the leaks that occur predominantly in the 5 to 10 days before the formal public announcement date.

As shown in Table 5.12, the 30-day premium was about 40 percent for the seller in nonbank transactions when an arithmetic mean is used to average over the deals. In an arithmetic average, the larger numbers receive a higher implicit weighting. To avoid this, the median firm was used as a measure of the average (one-half of the sample is above and one-half below the median). This gives less weight to the larger numbers, so the median falls to 33 percent for pooling transactions and 37 percent for purchase transactions.

When the purchase accounting nonbank transactions are grouped by taxability, the target received a 42 percent premium as compared with a 34 percent premium in nontaxable transactions. This implies that the buyer pays more when the seller is in a taxable transaction.

As a general guideline, for the big deals the pattern has been that premiums paid over the seller market price 30 days before the formal announcement date ranged from about 33 to 40 percent for nontaxable, nonbank deals. For taxable nonbank deals, the premiums to sellers appear to jump by 3 to 4 percentage points.

T A B L E 5.12

30-Day Percent Premium

Accounting Method	Tax Treatment	Bank		Nonbank		Combined	
		Mean	Median	Mean	Median	Mean	Median
Pooling	Nontaxable	44	35	40	33	41	34
Purchase	Total purchase	36	34	41	37	40	37
	Taxable	23	12	42	37	41	37
	Nontaxable	48	41	34	36	35	36
	Election	34	45	52	49	47	46

Analysis of Event Returns

Empirical studies have found that the initial market reactions to merger announcements are good predictors of subsequent performance (Healy, Palepu, and Ruback, 1992). Stock price data were not available for all transactions, so for this analysis, the sample size dropped from 364 to 309. The positive or negative net percentage gains or losses times the market value of equity for the acquirer and the target 20 trading days before through 10 trading days after the announcement date [− 20, +10] gives the results in absolute dollar terms. The dollar returns to targets, measured over the 30-day window, are almost always positive. The event returns for the acquiring firm will be positive or negative depending on the market's judgment of whether the premium paid to the seller by the buyer will be recovered in the subsequent performance of the combined firm.

Table 5.13 presents the overall results for the event return analysis. For the total bank plus nonbank sample, about two-thirds of the deals had positive returns. This provides one measure of whether M&As are successful in some sense. These results suggest that two out of three large mergers are likely to add value to shareholders. Looking at the bank subsample alone, the percentage of predicted success drops somewhat. Without banks, the success ratio is slightly higher.

Table 5.14 presents the absolute dollar amounts involved. In the nonbank sample, when one adds the dollar amount of

T A B L E 5.13

Percentage of Positive and Negative Total Gains

		Buyer		Seller		Combined	
		Number	Percent	Number	Percent	Number	Percent
Banks	Positive	27	38.0	63	88.7	41	57.7
	Negative	44	62.0	8	11.3	30	42.3
Nonbanks	Positive	124	52.1	213	89.5	161	67.6
	Negative	114	47.9	25	10.5	77	32.4
Total sample	Positive	151	48.9	276	89.3	202	65.4
	Negative	158	51.1	33	10.7	107	34.6

T A B L E 5.14

Summation of Positive and Negative Total Gains ($ Million)

		Buyer	Seller	Combined
Banks	Positives	12,782	26,006	26,812
	Negatives	(28,191)	(3,946)	(20,162)
	Sum	(15,409)	22,060	6,650
Nonbanks	Positives	129,675	108,880	213,947
	Negatives	(81,641)	(9,723)	(66,756)
	Sum	48,034	99,157	147,191
Total sample	Positives	142,457	134,886	240,759
	Negatives	(109,832)	(13,669)	(86,918)
	Sum	32,625	121,217	153,841

increases in the market cap of the buyer over the 30-day window of 20 days before and 10 days after the formal announcement date, the positive gains of $130 billion exceed the deals in which the buyer suffered stock price losses of $82 billion, for a net gain to buyers of $48 billion. The stock market response for sellers is usually positive. So the total of plus event returns of market cap increases of $109 billion for sellers less negatives of $10 billion leaves a net of plus $99 billion for sellers. Bank buyers had net losses of $15 billion, while bank sellers had net gains of $22 billion. So even for bank transactions the gains of sellers did not simply represent a shift based on the loss in market value of the buyers.

Stock market gains and losses are also stratified by method of accounting, taxability, etc. However, the differences are not statistically significant. If the market judges the deal will work out well in the future, the initial market response is likely to be favorable. If the market judges the deal to be illconceived and to not have a sound business foundation, it will react negatively. Whether the deal is soundly conceived or not determines whether the stock prices of the sellers and/or buyers will increase. The method of accounting used and taxability are of secondary importance. The important lesson is that good deals will assuredly increase market prices for the sellers and even for the buyers despite some initial shorting by risk arbitrage traders. Bad deals will be bad news for shareholders, both for the acquiring firms and ultimately for the selling firms.

The preliminary evidence on merger performance in the 1990s suggests that large buyers increased their ability to make value-increasing mergers. Studies of individual companies in the high-technology sector reveal spectacular successes. Cisco Systems grew in considerable measure by acquisitions. Its return to shareholders was remarkable. The Internet companies made considerable use of acquisitions to expand their customer coverage; their shareholder returns were high. Mergers continue to be high-risk investments. Bad mergers and failures will continue to occur. But the odds for success in the 1990s appear to have significantly improved over those of the previous two decades.

INDUSTRY INFLUENCES ON M&A ACTIVITY

In an in-depth analysis of industry effects, Mitchell and Mulherin (1996) studied industry-level patterns of takeover and restructuring activity during the 1982 to 1989 period. They found that in their sample of 1064 firms, 57 percent were the object of a takeover attempt or experienced a major restructuring during the 1980s. Of the firms involved in takeovers or restructuring, 40 percent were hostile takeover targets. Somewhat more—47 percent of the firms—were targets of friendly takeovers. The remaining 13 percent of the firms engaged in defensive asset restructuring or financial recapitalization.

Among their 51 sample industries, they found significant differences in the rate of M&A activity as well as in the timing of the activity. Most of the M&A activity occurred in relatively few industries, owing to identifiable major shocks defined as factors causing a marked change in overall industry structure and corporate control activity. One major force was deregulation, which had a major impact on the air transport, broadcasting, entertainment, natural gas, and trucking industries.

A second major factor was the oil price shocks that occurred in 1973 and 1979. These shocks affected not only the oil industry but also the structure of industries in which energy represented 10 percent or more of input costs. The industries most directly affected were integrated petroleum, natural gas, air transport, coal, and trucking.

A third major factor was foreign competition. This is measured by changes in the import penetration ratio, the ratio of imports to total industry supply. The industries with the largest change in import penetration ratios were shoes, machine tools, apparel, construction equipment, office equipment and supplies, autos and auto parts, tires and rubber, and steel.

A fourth major influence was innovations. The ability to use public markets for leveraged financing increased both the rate of takeovers and the size of takeover targets.

Mitchell and Mulherin conclude that the interindustry patterns in takeovers and restructuring reflect the relative economic shocks to the industries. Their results support the view that a major influence on the takeover activity of the 1980s was a combination of broad underlying economic and financial forces.

Andrade and Stafford (1999) extend the Mitchell and Mulherin results. Their data set is based on Value Line companies and industry groupings covering the period 1970 to 1994. Their evidence supports an impact of industry shocks. Their broader framework also measures the role of other influences—synergy, diversification, agency costs, and market power. Their basic economic finding is that mergers, like internal investment, are a response to favorable growth potentials. They find a dual role in that own-industry mergers are used in industries with excess capacity to achieve consolidation. In contracting industries, acquiring firms appear to be those with better performance, lower capacity utilization, and lower leverage. The asset reallocation results in improved efficiency.

RETURNS FOR UNRELATED ACQUISITIONS

Anslinger and Copeland (1996) studied returns to shareholders covering the 1985 to 1994 period for seemingly unrelated acquisitions. They studied in depth 21 successful acquirers of two types: diversified corporate acquirers and financial buyers such as leveraged buyout firms. These companies made a total of 829 acquisitions.

Anslinger and Copeland were consultants at McKinsey and Company at the time of their study. Their findings are in contrast to widely cited earlier studies for the 1970s and 1980s attributed to McKinsey and Company, which found that two-thirds of all mergers and takeovers were failures in that they did not earn their cost of capital. In this later study, merger performance was subjected to a particularly challenging test, because the sample covered only unrelated mergers. The Anslinger and Copeland study found that 80 percent of the 829 transactions (611) earned their cost of capital. Indeed, the corporate acquirers averaged more than 18 percent per year in total returns to shareholders over a 10-year period, exceeding Standard & Poor's 500 benchmark by a substantial margin. The financial buyers estimated that they averaged returns of 35 percent per year over a corresponding period.

Anslinger and Copeland note that although many of the acquisitions seem to be unrelated in some respects, successful acquirers focused on a common theme. Clayton, Dubilier & Rice stockpiled management capabilities used to make turnarounds. Another financial buyer, Desai Capital Management, focused on retail-related industries. Emerson Electric Company looked for companies with a core competence in component manufacturing to exploit cost control capabilities. Sara Lee used branding and retailing as its common thread.

The evidence on both stock market reactions to mergers and long-term performance demonstrates that mergers can contribute to value improvement.

HOSTILE TAKEOVERS

When the management and the board of directors resist the takeover attempt by bidders, we have hostile takeovers. The bidder in hostile takeovers is often referred to as a raider. Many large and well-publicized hostile episodes have taken place. Table 5.15 shows that as a percent of total value of transactions, hostile M&A activity is relatively small. The median level of hostile M&A activity to the total worldwide value of transactions is 3.3 percent. The number rises to 3.7 percent for the

TABLE 5.15

Percent of Hostile M&A Activity to Total Value of Transactions

Year	U.S. Domestic	Worldwide	Rest of the World
1985	11.9	14.3	27.8
1986	4.4	6.2	12.7
1987	3.7	3.5	3.1
1988	22.2	17.9	7.5
1989	3.6	6.1	9.2
1990	4.7	3.0	1.9
1991	2.3	2.1	1.9
1992	0.8	0.3	0.0
1993	0.0	0.5	0.9
1994	5.2	4.6	3.7
1995	5.9	6.4	6.9
1996	1.1	1.2	1.4
1997	0.5	0.8	1.2
1998	0.2	0.5	1.1
1999	7.0	15.1	22.2
2000	2.3	1.6	0.8
Mean	4.7	5.3	6.4
Median	3.7	3.3	2.5

Source: Thomson Financial Securities Data.

United States, and drops to 2.5 percent for the rest of the world. Schwert (2000) shows the difficulty of distinguishing between hostility versus strategic efforts to increase bidder or target gains from a potential transaction.

The outcome of hostile bids is shown in Table 5.16. The hostile bids succeed in somewhat more than one-third of the attempts. In somewhat less than one-third of the efforts, the target company is sold to a third party. In somewhat under 40 percent of the cases, the company remains independent.

At best, combining companies is difficult. As noted, differences in cultural factors, differences in information systems, and problems in implementing the combination of two different organizations are formidable. All these challenges are magnified in hostile mergers. The target will not cooperate in providing information. Considerable animosity is likely to be encountered in combining the two organizations. All empirical studies find that the returns to bidders in hostile takeovers are negative. The probability of success of a hostile bid is low. Given the evidence, a bidder needs to understand the difficulties likely to be encountered and have a well-formulated plan that has a reasonable probability of success.

T A B L E 5.16

Outcome of Hostile Bids (Percent)

Year	Sold to Raider	Sold to Third Party	Remained Independent
1994	38	25	37
1995	41	29	29
1996	36	23	41
1997	12	44	44
1998	27	33	40
1999	39	44	17
2000	36	14	50
Mean	32.7	30.3	36.9
Median	36.0	29.0	40.0

Source: J.P. Morgan M&A Research.

SUMMARY

Many theories have been advanced to explain why mergers and takeovers take place. The operating synergy theory postulates that economies of scale and/or scope help merging firms to achieve levels of efficiency in excess of the sum of the combining parts. Mergers have also been explained as a rapid means for firms to deal with powerful change forces. Some attribute mergers to the agency problem of management; managers put their own priorities above those of the firm. Managers may also be guilty of hubris, which can cause overpayment.

Mergers face significant challenges. The combination of organizations is a difficult undertaking. Due diligence is critical. Firms should use a careful due diligence process to discover not only legal factors, but also potential cultural and business problems that may emerge when firms combine. Slow and ineffective integration has destroyed value in combining firms.

Event studies of merger announcements show that returns to targets are always positive; the positive returns to targets are even higher with multiple bidders. Returns to bidders tend to be around zero and negative with multiple bidders. Event studies have been shown to be relatively good predictors of subsequent performance. Industry-adjusted postmerger performance of merging firms shows that they perform better than nonmerging firms in their same industries.

REFERENCES

Agrawal, Anup, Jeffrey F. Jaffe, and Gershon N. Mandelker, "The Post-Merger Performance of Acquiring Firms: A Re-examination of an Anomaly," *Journal of Finance*, 47, September 1992, pp. 1605–1621.

Andrade, Gregor, and Erik Stafford, "Investigating the Economic Role of Mergers," working paper, August 1999.

Anslinger, Patricia L., and Thomas E. Copeland, "Growth through Acquisitions: A Fresh Look," *Harvard Business Review*, 74, January–February 1996, pp. 126–135.

Berkovitch, Elazar, and M. P. Narayanan, "Motives for Takeovers: An Empirical Investigation," *Journal of Financial and Quantitative Analysis*, 28, September 1993, pp. 347–362.

Healy, Paul M., Krishna G. Palepu, and Richard S. Ruback, "Does Corporate Performance Improve after Mergers?" *Journal of Financial Economics*, 31, 1992, pp. 135–175.

Houston, Joel F., and Michel D. Ryngaert, "The Overall Gains from Large Bank Mergers," *Journal of Banking & Finance*, 18, December 1994, pp. 1155–1176.

Huang, Yen-Sheng, and Ralph A. Walkling, "Target Abnormal Returns Associated with Acquisition Announcements," *Journal of Financial Economics*, 19, 1987, pp. 329–349.

Loughran, Tim, and Anand M. Vijh, "Do Long-Term Shareholders Benefit from Corporate Acquisitions?" *Journal of Finance*, 52, December 1997, pp. 1765–1790.

Mitchell, Mark L., and Kenneth Lehn, "Do Bad Bidders Become Good Targets?" *Journal of Political Economy*, 98, 1990, pp. 372–398.

———, and J. Harold Mulherin, "The Impact of Industry Shocks on Takeover and Restructuring Activity," *Journal of Financial Economics*, 41, June 1996, pp. 193–229.

Schwert, G. William, "Markup Pricing in Mergers and Acquisitions," *Journal of Financial Economics*, 41, 1996, pp. 153–192.

———, "Hostility in Takeovers: In the Eyes of the Beholder?," *Journal of Finance*, 55, December 2000, pp. 2599-2640.

Weston, J. Fred, and Brian Johnson, "What It Takes for a Deal to Win Stock Market Approval," *Mergers & Acquisitions*, 34, September/October 1999, pp. 43–48.

QUESTIONS AND PROBLEMS

5.1 Give some examples of synergies from mergers.

5.2 Explain the central forces in the high-level merger activity industries of (*a*) telecommunications, (*b*) financial services, and (*c*) pharmaceuticals.

5.3 One factor involved in mergers has been "playing the differential *P/E* game." Given the following information, calculate the effects on earnings per share and market price per share on buyer and seller.

	(1) Buyer	(2) Seller	(3) Combined	(4) Explanation for Col. 3
Price-earnings ratio (P/E)	30 times	10 times	25 times	Assumed
Net income	$100 million	$100 million	$200 million	(1) + (2)
Shares Outstanding	20 million	20 million	30 million	(1) + 0.5 (20 million)
Earnings per share	$5	$5	$6.67	$200/30
Market value per share	$150	$50	$166.75	25 × $6.67

SOLUTIONS TO QUESTIONS AND PROBLEMS

5.1 In industry consolidation mergers, efficiency is gained by shutting down the least efficient plants and thereby improving sales to capacity as well.

In industry rollup mergers, fragmented operations are combined into a firm that has capable and experienced staff executives who can provide valuable guidance to operating units in areas such as research, production, and marketing.

Larger size may enable the combined firm to finance high-technology equipment to produce better-quality products at lower cost.

Combining two firms in different geographic areas may change a firm from a local or regional operation to national or international scope.

5.2

 a. Technological change in the form of the substitution of microwave and fiber-optics systems for hardwire transmission has lowered investment cost and multiplied the number of competitors. The increased competition led to deregulation in the United States and abroad.

 b. In financial services, technological change provided new types of services to customers. Increased investments were required to buy the equipment and systems to meet these new needs. Specialized financial institutions began to take on multiple activities to become department stores of financial products. The relaxing of government barriers to geographic expansion and to product expansion by commercial banks has led to the convergence of commercial banking, investment banking, investment management, and insurance. Mergers combined banks in different geographic areas. Mergers enabled firms to expand the financial sectors in which they operated.

 c. Changes in the technology in basic research and increased risk due to competitive pressure have created the need for larger firms. When one firm falls behind in research capabilities, merger is one way to maintain the flow of new product offerings. Pharmaceutical firms may merge to broaden their range of therapeutic product classes.

5.3 The example uses a price-earnings (P/E) ratio of 25 for the combined company. This is a judgment matter. The large earning accretion for the high ratio P/E buyer may actually increase its P/E multiple in the short range. Earnings per share (EPS) for the buyer has increased from $5 to $6.67, a 33.4 percent increase. The market price per share of the buyer has increased from $150 to $166.75, an increase of 11.2 percent. For the seller, the EPS for the 0.5 new share it owns is $3.335, a dilution of 33.3 percent. But the market price of the 0.5 share increases from $50 to $83.375, an increase of 66.8 percent.

	Buyer		**Seller**	
	Premerger	**Postmerger**	**Premerger**	**Postmerger**
Earnings per share	$ 5	$ 6.67	$ 5	$ 3.335
Market price per share	$150	$166.75	$50	$83.375

CHAPTER SIX

Alternative Paths to Growth

Growth opportunities can be achieved through both internal and external strategies. Both should be mutually reinforcing. So initially the firm reviews its core strategy and related business model or plan. It formulates the scope of its product (services)-market activities. It reviews the managerial capabilities and resources required. These include the research personnel and programs, technological capabilities, plant and equipment, human resources, and financing requirements. Organizational structures must be related to the requirements of product-market characteristics. Organizational structures involve the relationship between the general management functions and the specific functional activities. The general management functions involve research, planning, organizing, legal issues, and development. The specific management activities include applied research, production, marketing, human resources, accounting, and finance. All these activities are integrated with a particular system defined by corporate culture. Corporate culture is developed by the behavior which is rewarded in the firm's compensation systems, and defines the firm's values and norms.

The entire organization system of a firm must be continuously reassessed to determine the contributions to corporate goals and objectives that can be achieved from internal resources, capabilities, and organizational systems. Simultaneously, the potential complementary roles of external strategies must be continuously monitored. The external expansion strategies include mergers, takeovers, joint ventures, and alliances—both domestic and international.

Acquired firms achieve substantial gains. Acquiring firms on balance have small gains in mergers and small losses in tender offers. Mergers involve negotiations and probably some sharing of prospective synergistic gains. Since acquiring firms are on average much larger, their percentage gains would be smaller than those for acquired firms. For example, if an acquiring firm is 10 times as large as the acquired and gains are shared equally, then the acquired firm gains 20 percent, and the acquiring firm would gain 2 percent.

These overall statistics cover large samples, different time periods, and transactions of widely different characteristics. They include firms in troubled industries as well as attractive industries. The inherent potentials for merger success vary widely. Some firms such as Cisco Systems and WorldCom have grown spectacularly through acquisitions. So the potentials for augmenting growth opportunities from external investments through mergers and takeovers can be substantial.

We next analyze how the different forms of external relationships with other firms can contribute to value growth. Multiple growth strategies are available. We list eight major types below:

1. Internal base or core growth
2. Mergers and takeovers
3. Joint ventures
4. Alliances and partnerships
5. Investments
6. Exclusive agreements
7. Licensing
8. Franchising

INTERNAL PLUS EXTERNAL GROWTH

Internal growth and external growth through M&A activities are not mutually exclusive. Indeed, M&A activities are likely to have the highest returns if they are built on successful existing operations. An advantage of internal growth is that it avoids the problems of mergers where combining different cultures and integrating two separate organizations can be formidable.

M&As or external growth may have advantages for several reasons. An organization is already in place with a track record. The cost of acquiring a company may be determined in advance. Historically, 35 to 45 percent of all acquisitions represent divestitures by other firms. The economic rationale would be that acquiring firms can create greater value from the operation than the divesting firm. For example, at Hershey Foods, growth through new products was expensive and took a long time to yield positive results. Although new products were designed to enhance growth by taking away competitors' market share, inevitably new product introductions would dampen existing product sales and result in cannibalization of Hershey's own products. The acquisition route provided Hershey tremendous "new" products that were to varying degrees already established in the marketplace. Most acquisitions were the result of Hershey buying another company's division or family-owned business. In all cases, improvement in operating efficiency provided the catalyst to consummate the transaction, thus increasing Hershey's shareholder value. Such efficiencies included the use and rationalization of plant capacity, the leveraging of a highly skilled marketing and sales force, minor augmentation of logistics, etc. Sometimes the main motivation for external acquisitions is to acquire highly capable executive talent or to round out executive capabilities.

In addition, the economic circumstances of industries may favor M&As. Horizontal mergers in industries with excess capacity may be used to close plants to bring capacities and sales into better balance. Firms in fragmented industries may become more effective when joined in consolidation rollups.

THE USE OF JOINT VENTURES

A joint venture is a separate business entity that usually involves only a fraction of the activities of the participating organizations. The participants in a joint venture continue as separate firms, but create a new corporation, partnership, or other business form. Joint ventures are limited in scope and duration.

There are several objectives that may be achieved by a joint venture. The participating firms obtain an opportunity to share risks. Working with other firms reduces the investment costs of entering potentially risky new areas. Even though investment requirements are less than solely internal operations, the joint venture may still enjoy the benefits of economies of scale, critical mass, and the learning curve. Also, joint ventures allow firms the opportunity to gain knowledge. Firms may share technology in the interest of helping the joint venture. There is also a potential for sharing managerial skills in organization, planning, and control. This is the motivation of the February 2001 joint venture between Coca-Cola and Procter & Gamble, who have agreed to form a $4 billion sales joint venture of Coke's Minute Maid juice and distribution strength with P & G's chip and juice brands. In January 2001, Coke announced a similar joint venture with Nestle to codevelop tea drinks. This is all occurring as Pepsi wades through the required governmental approval process of its $14 billion December 2000 acquistion of Quaker Oats.

Joint ventures have proved to be particularly advantageous in the international setting. In some situations, local governments may not allow an acquisition. A joint venture presents an opportunity to combine some assets without violating such a regulation. International joint ventures usually reduce risks of firms operating in foreign countries. In addition, joint ventures have been used as a means of circumventing certain international trade barriers.

When high uncertainty is involved in the divestiture of a segment acquired by another firm, joint ventures can be an interim step. Or the parties might not be able to agree on a price. A common pattern is for the acquirer to pay cash for 40 to 45 percent of a segment being divested. A joint venture is used as a device for the selling firm to convey knowledge of manufacturing or distribution. The motivations and the incentives are all in the right directions. The better the selling firm does in teaching the acquirer the potentials of the segment, the more the segment will be worth. As a consequence, after a year or two the joint venture may be terminated by completing the purchase. Typically, the price received for the second segment is proportionally higher than that for the first segment because the acquirer better understands the potentials of the business. Value is created by minimizing employee turnover and avoiding the impairment of supplier and distribution networks.

Requirements for successful joint ventures can be summarized as follows.

1. Each has something to offer.
2. Careful preplanning is done.
3. Key executives are assigned to implement.
4. They may be used for information for an acquisition.
5. There is preplan termination, and often provisions are made for a buyout by one of the parties.

Although ventures can be an excellent tool to promote the interests of all parties, without the key ingredients noted above, joint ventures are destined for less than successful results.

ALLIANCES AND PARTNERSHIPS

The change forces in the world economy have become so powerful that they have accelerated the pace of change. Product life cycles are shorter. Potentials for accelerating product developments and new products are greater. Industry boundaries are blurred so that companies have opportunities in a wider range of industries and are impacted by competitors from more distant product-market activities.

In rapidly evolving industries (those related to the Internet and its backbone or infrastructure, data transmission, telecommunications, etc.), firms need to continuously broaden and sharpen their capabilities to be competitive. In these new industrial dynamics, alliances and partnerships have increasingly been used.

Alliances are less formal than joint ventures. A new entity need not be created. A formal contract may not be written. The relative sizes of participants may be highly unequal. Partner firms pool resources, expertise, and ideas so that the partners will have a continuing need for one another. Evolving relationships require adaptability and change over time. The alliance may involve multiple partners. Since the relationship is less legalistic, mutual trust is required. The speed of change in a relationship may be rapid. Firms may modify and move to other alliances as attractive possibilities emerge. Some creative people do not wish to be in the environment of large firms. But large firms may increase their access to creative people through alliances with small firms.

Alliances may have some advantages over mergers or joint ventures. They are more informal and offer flexibility. They may provide a firm with access to new markets and technologies with relatively small investments. Alliances provide the ability to create and disband projects with minimum paperwork. Working with partners possessing multiple skills can create major synergies.

Alliances have their own distinctive characteristics. Greater ambiguity and uncertainty is involved. The partner relationship evolves in ways that are difficult to predict. Today's ally may be tomorrow's rival—or may be a current rival in some other market. Managing the alliance relationship over time may be more important than crafting the initial partnership. Thus, initial understandings may have less to do with future success than adaptability to change.

The advantages and limitations on a comparative basis of acquisitions versus joint ventures versus strategic alliances are summarized in Table 6.1. Acquisitions involve greater risks and greater potential gains or losses. Joint ventures involve smaller investments. They may be of temporary duration, moving toward broader long-term goals. Strategic alliances can create complex relationships between multiple firms. The initial resource commitment may be quite small. The exchange of ideas may be valuable for the multiple-partner firms.

Some successful firms have used all the above forms of acquisitions, joint ventures, and alliances to increase their growth opportunities. AOL is at the center of an intricate web of alliances in many sectors. It is reported that companies such as Oracle have more than 10,000 business alliances. Announcements of new

TABLE 6.1

Acquisitions versus Joint Ventures versus Strategic Alliances

Acquisition	Joint Venture	Strategic Alliance
Allows 100% control	Firms intersect over narrow, well-defined segments	Useful for creation of complex systems between multiple firms
No need for interfirm consensus	Exploits distinctive or narrow opportunities	Blurs corporate boundaries
Less flexible	Generally only two firms involved	Partner is usually larger than in joint ventures (10 : 1 vs. 5 : 1)
Larger commitment of resources	Limited risk	Allows firms to focus on fewer core competencies
Risky	Joint production of single products	Less clear contributions and benefits
Often acquires more than is needed	Combines known resources	Difficult to anticipate consequences
May cause upheaval in corporate culture	Requires high-level management interaction	Gives firms access to people who would not work directly for them
May require accommodating different management systems	Rarely used in new markets or technologies	Often small resource commitment
Requires combining, harmonizing different information systems	Can be used to reduce risk in a merger transaction	Limited time duration
Requires combining different corporate cultures	Often across borders	Must be managed actively by senior executives
Requires rapid, effective integration	Tensions: Your firm wants to learn as much as possible, but not convey too much	The relationship likely to evolve in directions not initially planned
Remedy for strategic miscalculations		Managing over time requires adaptability to change and new knowledge
Most cost-cutting possible		Especially useful across borders
Can have partial investments as an interim step		Replacement for government-prohibited cross-border mergers
Can be across borders		

127

alliances occur almost daily in the press—this is of course true for mergers, takeovers, and joint ventures as well.

INVESTMENTS

Investments may be made for multiple reasons. One is to receive high returns from firms with attractive growth opportunities. A second motive may be to learn more about a potentially attractive new product-market opportunity for a firm. A third possibility is that the investment may facilitate the progress of the recipient firm. While the profitability outlook may be highly uncertain, the payoffs have high potentials.

EXCLUSIVE AGREEMENTS

Exclusive agreements usually involve rights for manufacturing or marketing. For example, in April 1997 Warner-Lambert entered into an exclusive agreement with Pfizer to comarket a cardiovascular drug, initially called turbostatin, later named Lipitor. This was in recognition of the size and aggressiveness of the Pfizer sales organization. Pfizer, unable to produce a statin of its own, was able to strengthen its offerings of cardiovascular drugs. Another example is the November 1999 exclusive agreement signed by USA Networks' Ticketmaster unit to provide ticketing services for all events at the Rio Suite Hotel & Casino in Las Vegas (a unit of Harrah's Entertainment). In January 2000, Healtheon/Web MD Corp. announced a wide-ranging 5-year agreement with CVS Corp.

The above examples illustrate how exclusive agreements help both parties. Each benefits from the strength and specialized assets of the other. As a result, some business activities can be performed at lower costs. Since a contractual arrangement is used, a more formal alliance is established.

LICENSING

Licensing is the granting of the know-how and sometimes the physical equipment required to produce specified products in return for a royalty fee arrangement. An example is an agreement between Abbott Laboratories and Antisoma PLC. Pharmaceutical company Abbott Laboratories and biotechnology company Antisoma PLC signed a global licensing agreement to develop and market Theragyn, Antisoma's main cancer therapy candidate. The deal may produce $100 million, excluding royalties, for Antisoma, based in the United Kingdom, including $13 million in Abbott funding for an issue of Antisoma shares. Theragyn is in late stages of development as a treatment for ovarian cancer. Abbott and Antisoma stated that data from a midstage safety and efficacy study suggest Theragyn can increase a patient's probability of living 10 years by about 75 percent, compared with 30 percent for control-group patients who received standard ovarian-cancer therapy (*The Wall Street Journal*, November 1, 1999).

The advantage of licensing to the licensor is that the royalties represent a high return on a relatively incremental investment. It speeds the entry into newer markets and helps build broader market recognition and acceptance.

The advantage to the licensee is that it adds new product lines that may fit well into its existing production and marketing organization. It thereby adds to its revenue sources. The knowledge gained may enable the licensee to produce related products on its own. Some of these products may take market shares from the product licensed and establish the licensee as a competitor.

FRANCHISING

Franchise agreements are contracts between the franchisor (parent) and the franchisee that grant the rights to use the parent's name, brand, reputation, and business model at a specified location within a designated market area. An illustration is the franchising operations of Mail Boxes Etc. (MBE), which has franchised 4000 centers worldwide. The outlets originally provided services that included 24-hour mailbox access, packaging, stamp sales, and parcel shipping. Established as an alternative to the post office, MBE has expanded its array of services to include copying, printing, faxing, and selling money orders, office supplies, passport photos, and duplicate keys.

The history of MBE shows the interaction between mergers and alliances. Anthony DeSio opened his first outlet in 1980. He was unable to obtain financing for expansion because potential sponsors or lenders could not visualize an attractive business potential. So MBE began to expand through franchising. By 1986 it was able to go public with about 275 locations. In 1990, UPS invested in 15 percent of MBE stock. In 1997, MBE formed a joint venture with USA Technologies to comarket MBE Express, which added self-service access to PCs (with Internet and e-mail capabilities), printers, copiers, and fax machines. U.S. Office Products acquired MBE in 1997 for $267 million. In 1999, MBE formed an alliance with iShip.com, which provides Internet shipping services. This history of MBE illustrates the interaction of the eight methods of expansion covered in this chapter.

The MBE story also illustrates the kind of benefits provided by a franchisor. These include established brand name with wide consumer recognition, a four-week training program, preopening support, ongoing support, a quarterly business evaluation program, marketing support, advantageous buying arrangements with MBE vendors, and national advertising campaigns including year-round TV advertising.

McDonald's is another success story with 28,000 restaurants worldwide. About 80 percent of the outlets are franchised. McDonald's owns most of the real estate on which the free-standing stores are located; as a result McDonald's is the world largest owner of commercial real estate.

In addition to restaurants, franchising is widely used in activities such as motels and hotels, automobile dealerships, tax services, travel agents, pest control services, and weight control. The listing provided by the International Franchise Association runs to some 80 categories of activities. The examples illustrate the basic characteristics of franchising activities. The operations are widely dispersed physically. The business activities are labor-intensive. The economic role of franchising is to minimize monitoring costs by having independent operators whose returns are tied to their own efforts and performance. The operations of outlets with independent owners can be compared to the performance of outlets owned by the franchisor. A key deci-

sion area is the negotiation of the original investment requirements and the size of the franchising fees. Risks to the franchisor include failures of owner-operators to conform to the
standards set by franchisors. Franchisees may also prefer to use
vendors different from the franchisor or related vendors.

SUMMARY

Growth opportunities in a firm may be achieved through both
internal and external means. (1) Internal growth has several
advantages. It usually offers the highest returns. There are no
cultural or implementation difficulties that may result from
external growth. However, internal growth may be time-con-
suming, and in some cases it may require skills that are outside
the abilities of a given firm.

There are several forms of external growth. (2) M&As may
allow firms to rapidly enter new markets, or may bring the firm
new and needed resources. (3) Joint ventures are separate business entities that are formed with other organizations. Joint
ventures allow firms to share unique skills and spread risk
among participating firms. Problems may arise owing to dis-
agreements between participating firms. (4) Like joint ventures,
alliances are agreements between different organizations, but
they tend to be less formalized. They usually involve less
investment, but also have greater difficulty with ambiguity of
the relationships between participating firms.

(5) Investments in other firms may allow firms to aid
another organization with potentially attractive prospects and
to learn about potentially new areas of growth opportunities.
(6) Exclusive agreements usually involve rights for manufacturing or marketing, allowing firms to utilize outside skills that
may be lacking within the organization. (7) Licensing can rapidly expand the market and achieve a high return on investment. The risk is that it may be creating new competitors. (8)
Franchising offers opportunities in many areas characterized
by dispersed operations, high labor intensity, and high monitoring requirements. Examples of outstanding successes
abound, but challenging organizational and management problems must be solved.

In summary, we have described eight methods by which growth opportunities may be enlarged. They are not mutually exclusive and may be self-reinforcing.

QUESTIONS AND PROBLEMS

6.1 What are the advantages and limitations of internal growth?

6.2 What are the advantages and limitations of growth by mergers?

6.3 Why have alliances increased in importance?

SOLUTIONS TO QUESTIONS AND PROBLEMS

6.1 Extensions of existing operations are usually related to some degree. The problems of combining different organizations and cultures are avoided. But new product programs developed internally may overstate revenues that can be achieved and understate costs. In addition, it may take too long to get to market.

6.2 A wide range of capabilities may be added rapidly. But synergy estimates may be overoptimistic, and premiums paid may be excessive. Implementation of combining different organizations and cultures may not be successfully achieved. High-quality management, experienced with acquisitions activity, increases the probability of success.

6.3 The pace of technological and market changes has been so rapid that firms must continuously survey for new opportunities and threats. Alliances require smaller investment outlays, but require special managerial skills for developing ambiguous relationships with other business entities.

CHAPTER SEVEN

Valuation

Valuation is a critical part of the merger process. A deal that may be sound from a business standpoint may be unsound from a financial standpoint if the bidder firm pays too much. The purpose of a valuation analysis is to provide a disciplined procedure for arriving at a price. If the buyer offers too little, the target may resist and, since it is in play, seek to interest other bidders. If the price is too high, the premium may never be recovered from postmerger synergies. These general principles are illustrated by the following simple model.

ANALYSIS

Mergers increase value when the value of the combined firm is greater than the sum of the premerger values of the independent entities.

$$NVI = V_{BT} - (V_B + V_T)$$

where NVI = net value increase
V_B = value of bidder alone
V_T = value of target alone
V_{BT} = value of firms combined

A simple example will illustrate. Company B (the bidder) has a current market value of $40 (it is understood that all the numbers are in millions). Company T (the target) has a current market value of $40. The sum of the values as independent firms is therefore $80. Assume that as a combined company (CC) synergies will increase the value to $100. The amount of value created is $20.

How will the increase in value be divided? Targets always (usually) receive a premium. What about the bidders? If the bidder pays a premium of less than $20, it will share in the value increase. If B pays a premium larger than $20, the value of the bidder will decline. If the bidder pays $50 for the target, a premium of 25 percent has been paid to T. The value increases are shared equally.

If B pays $60 for T, all gains go to the target. Company B achieves no value increase. If B pays $70 for T, the value of B will decline to $30.

In the mid-to-late 1980s Hershey Foods consummated three acquisitions that derived synergistic benefits from various and different sources. The acquisition of Luden's confectionery business was driven by a product line and facility rationalization that focused on four products: Fifth Avenue bar, Luden's cough drops, Mellow Mints, and Queen Anne chocolate-covered cherries. In addition, the distribution of these products could be expanded when placed with Hershey's sales force and logistic personnel. The second aquisition was consummated in Canada when Hershey Canada acquired the assets of Nabisco Brands-Confectionery division. Overnight, Hershey Canada's sales volume tripled, making it a major player in the Canadian confectionery market and through additional plant rationalization made use of underutilized chocolate production capacity. The final of these three acquisitions was the acquisition of Peter Paul/Cadbury in the United States. The synergy for this acquisition was the result of margin improvement and economies of scale.

All three cases involved sealed bids and in all cases the sellers tended to realize more than a fair share of the value of the synergies. In order for Hershey to realize shareholder value, the company must surpass the performance assumptions (growth, margins, capital utilization, etc.) embedded in the base scenario valuation.

THE USE OF STOCK IN ACQUISITIONS

A high percentage of the large transactions beginning in 1992 has been stock-for-stock transactions. Some hold the view that this does not represent real money. But this is not valid.

Suppose B exchanges 1.0 of its shares for 1.0 share of T. Since the combined firm is valued at $100, T will receive .5 × $100, which equals $50. The premium paid is 25 percent. Based on their previous $40 values, B and T each owned 50 percent of the premerger combined values. Postmerger, the percentages of ownership will remain 50–50.

If B exchanges 1.5 of its own shares per share of T, this is equivalent to paying $60 in value for the target. Company T shareholders will own 60 percent of the combined company. None of the synergy gains will be received by the bidder shareholders. Also note that the target shareholders will have 1.5 shares in the new company for every 1.0 share held by the bidder shareholders.

The situation is even worse if B pays more than $60 for the target. Assume B pays $70 for the target (1.75 to 1 shares). Since the combined company has a value of $100, the value of the bidder shares must decline to $36.36. The consequences are terrible. The shares of the bidder will decline in value by $3.64, or 9.1 percent. Furthermore, the B shareholders will own only 36.36 percent of the combined company; for every 1.0 share that they own, the target shareholders will own 1.75 shares.

The leading methods used in the valuation of a firm for merger analysis are the comparable companies or comparable transactions approach, the spreadsheet approach, and the formula approach. In this chapter we explain and illustrate the logic or theory behind each of these approaches.

COMPARABLE COMPANIES OR COMPARABLE TRANSACTIONS APPROACH

In the comparable companies or comparable transactions approach, key relationships are calculated for a group of similar companies or similar transactions as a basis for the valuation of companies involved in a merger or takeover. This approach is widely used, especially by investment bankers and in legal cases. The theory is not complicated. Marketplace transactions are used. It is a commonsense approach that says that similar companies should sell for similar prices. This straightforward approach appeals to businesspersons, to their financial advisers, and to the judges in courts of law called upon to render decisions on the relative values of companies in litigation.

First, a basic idea is illustrated in a simple setting, followed by applications to actual companies in an M&A setting. In Table 7.1, the comparable companies approach is illustrated. We are seeking to place a value on company W. We find three companies that are comparable. To test for comparability we consider size, similarity of products, age of company, growth rates, and recent trends, among other variables.

Assume that target companies TA, TB, and TC meet most of our comparability requirements. We then calculate the ratio of the enterprise market value to revenues, the ratio of the enterprise market value to EBITDA (earnings before interest, taxes,

TABLE 7.1

Panel A: Comparable Companies Ratios (Company W Is Compared with Companies TA, TB, and TC)

Ratio	Company TA	Company TB	Company TC	Average
Enterprise market value/ revenues	1.4	1.2	1.0	1.2
Enterprise market value/ EBITDA	15.0	14.0	22.0	17.0
Enterprise market value/ free cash flows	25.0	20.0	27.0	24.0

Panel B: Application of Valuation Ratios to Company W

Actual Recent Data for Company W		Average Ratio	Indicated Enterprise Market Value
Revenues	= $100	1.2	$120
EBITDA	= $7	17	119
Free cash flows	= $5	24	120
			Average = $120

depreciation, and amortization), and the ratio of the enterprise market value to free cash flows for the individual companies. The resulting ratios are given in panel A of Table 7.1. These ratios are then averaged, and the average ratios are applied to the absolute data for company W. For the averages to be meaningful, it is important that the ratios we calculate for each company be relatively close in value. If they are greatly different, which implies that the dispersion around the average is substantial, the average (a measure of central tendency) will not be very meaningful. In the example given, the ratios for the three comparable companies do not vary widely. Hence, it makes some sense to apply the averages.

We postulate that for a relevant recent time period, company W had revenues of $100 million, EBITDA of $7 million, and free cash flows of $5 million, as shown in panel B. We next apply the average market ratios from panel A to obtain the indicated enterprise value for company W. We have three estimates of the indicated enterprise value of W based on the ratio of enterprise market value to revenues, to EBITDA, and to free cash flows. The results are close enough to be meaningful. When we average them, we obtain approximately $120 million for the indicated enterprise market value for company W.

One of the advantages of the comparable companies approach is that it can be used to establish valuation relationships for a company that is not publicly traded. This is a method of predicting what its publicly traded price is likely to be. The methodology is applicable in testing for the soundness of valuations in mergers also. Both the buyer and the seller in a merger seek confirmation that the price is fair compared to the values placed on the other companies. For public companies, the courts will require such a demonstration if a suit is filed by an aggrieved shareholder.

The data in Table 7.1 can be reinterpreted to illustrate the comparable transactions approach. The data would then represent companies involved in the same kind of merger transactions as company W. In connection with merger transactions, a clarification should be made. When the term *enterprise market value* is used, it does not refer to the prevailing market price of the companies' common stock plus debt before the merger announcement.

In this context, *market* refers to the transaction price in deals recently completed. Typically, merger transactions involve a premium as high as 30 percent to 40 percent over the prevailing market price (before news of the merger transaction has leaked out). The relevant valuation for a subsequent merger transaction would be the transaction enterprise prices for comparable deals.

The result would be a higher indicated price. We will use 30 percent as the premium factor. The indicated enterprise market value of company W would be $156 million. The practical implication of this is that if company W were going to be purchased and no comparable transactions had taken place, we would take the comparable companies approach as illustrated in Table 7.1. But this would be only a starting point. There would then be some merger negotiations and probably some premium paid over prevailing market prices for the comparable companies.

In Table 7.1 we have illustrated the comparable companies and comparable transactions approaches using the ratios of enterprise market value to revenues, EBITDA, and free cash flows. In some situations, other ratios might be employed in the comparable companies or comparable transactions approach. Additional ratios could include sales or revenue per employee, net income per employee, or assets needed to produce $1 of sales or revenue. Note that market values are not included in the ratios just listed. The additional information could be used for interpreting or adjusting the average multiples obtained by using the comparable companies or comparable transactions approaches. Our experience has been that in actual merger or takeover transactions, investment bankers employ both the comparable companies approach and the comparable transactions approach and develop additional comparative performance measures as well.

For example in the Exxon/Mobil merger, J.P. Morgan Securities Inc. (the Exxon financial adviser) discussed five valuation checkpoints.

1. J.P. Morgan compared the return on capital employed by Exxon and Mobil for the years 1993 to 1998. J.P. Morgan observed that Exxon's ROC has been 2 to 3 percent above that of Mobil.

2. J.P. Morgan compared the price-to-earnings (P/E) multiple of the two. It observed that in recent years, Mobil had traded at an 8 percent to 15 percent discount to Exxon.

3. J.P. Morgan estimated future synergies to be $2.8 billion annually resulting in a potential value creation in the short-term of $22 to $25 billion, and in the long term of an additional $11 billion.

4. J.P. Morgan performed a contribution analysis based on historical data. It calculated the ratio of Exxon to the combined firms with respect to total revenues; earnings before interest, taxes, depreciation, and amortization, (EBITDA), after-tax operating cash flows, capital employed, oil and gas reserves, and refinery capacity. These ratios were mostly 70 percent to 73 percent compared with the 70 percent ownership share that Exxon shareholders would have in the combined company following the merger.

5. J.P. Morgan reviewed 38 "recently announced or closed large capitalization stock-for-stock transactions," finding a premium range of 15 percent to 25 percent. Based on closing share prices on November 24, 1998, two trading days before the merger announcement date, the implied premium to Mobil shareholders was about 20 percent.

Goldman Sachs as financial adviser to Mobil performed a similar analysis confirming the fairness conclusion with respect to the valuations implied by the terms of the merger.

Although the comparable companies and comparable transactions methods are widely used in practice, they have limitations. For example, J.P. Morgan referred to 38 "comparable" large-capitalization transactions. But there have not been 38 large oil industry transactions close to the late November announcement date. Also the application of the resulting range of 15 percent to 25 percent would give substantial differences in valuation. So clearly, the investment advisers must exercise some judgment in arriving at their fairness opinion. Since judgments are involved in the comparable analysis, it is supplemented by the discounted cash flow methodology.

DISCOUNTED CASH FLOW ANALYSIS

The discounted cash flow (DCF) analysis requires projections of the future free cash flows of a project or firm which are discounted back to the present by an applicable cost of capital. Since the patterns of future free cash flows can vary widely, we will perform a step-by-step explanation of the procedures. Also we will postpone discussion of how the cost of capital is calculated until we have completed the discussion of the DCF procedures.

The methodology of the discounted cash flow valuation is explained with reference to Table 7.2. In panel A we explain the abbreviations used in panel B. Panel B contains the basic input data. The first eight lines of panel B represent a condensed projected income statement. These data are projections or forecasts that have been developed by the bidder in analyzing the historical financial data of the target and the bidder's projections for the target based on its future prospects.

Line 1 in panel B is projected revenues. Line 2 deducts all operating costs except depreciation to obtain EBITDA. Line 3 deducts depreciation to obtain EBIT (earnings before interest expense and taxes). If other income and other expenses (except interest) are zero or net out to zero, EBIT is equal to NOI (net operating income). Line 5 deducts interest expense to obtain EBT (earnings before taxes). Line 7 deducts taxes to obtain net income (line 8).

The basic principle of the DCF valuation model is to value future expected cash flows. So we next describe how to go from net income to cash flows. In line 9, we add interest expense net of its tax shelter benefit to net income. So we add interest expense less its tax deduction, which is equivalent to interest expense multiplied by $1 - T$, as shown in line 9. The result in line 10 is NOPAT (net operating profit after tax). Using the data in the column for 2001, net income is $720, interest expense is $300, and the tax rate is 40 percent. So we have

$$\$720 + 300(1 - 0.40) = \$900 = \text{NOPAT}$$

It is useful to recognize that NOPAT can also be obtained by simply multiplying EBIT by $1 - T$ as follows:

$$\$1500(1 - T) = 1500(1 - 0.40) = \$900 = \text{NOPAT}$$

To NOPAT we add depreciation because it is a noncash expense. This gives us gross cash flows of $1400. Next we have to account for cash flows required by the capital expenditures of $900 and the changes in (net) working capital of $400 to obtain

T A B L E 7.2

DCF Spreadsheet Valuation (Zero Terminal Growth)

Panel A: Explanation of Abbreviations

EBITDA = earnings before interest expense, taxes, depreciation, and amortization
EBIT = earnings before interest expense and taxes
EBT = earnings before taxes
NOI = net operating income
NOPAT = net operating profits after tax

Panel B: Initial Growth Period

	Years	1 2001	2 2002	3 2003	4 2004	5 2005	$n+1$ 2006
1. Revenues		$10,000	$11,550	$13,340	$15,408	$17,796	$17,796
2. EBITDA		2,000	2,310	2,668	3,082	3,559	3,559
3. Depreciation		500	577	667	770	890	890
4. EBIT = NOI		1,500	1,732	2,001	2,311	2,669	2,669
5. Less: Interest expense		300	346	400	462	534	534
6. EBT = (4) − (5)		1,200	1,386	1,601	1,849	2,136	2,136
7. Less: Tax @ 40%		480	554	640	740	854	854
8. Net income = (6) − (7)		720	832	960	1,109	1,281	1,281
9. Add: Interest expense* $(1-T) = (5)*(1-T)$		180	208	240	277	320	320
10. NOPAT = $(4)*(1-T)=(8)+(9)$		900	1,039	1,201	1,387	1,602	1,602
10a. Add: depreciation		500	577	667	770	890	890
10b. Less: capital expenditures		900	1,039	1,201	1,387	1,602	890
10c. Less: changes in working capital		400	462	534	616	712	0
11. Free cash flow = (10) + (10a) − (10b) − (10c)		100	115	133	154	178	1,602
12. Discount factor @ 10.0%		0.909	0.826	0.751	0.683	0.621	
13. Present values of free cash flow		$ 91	$ 95	$ 100	$ 105	$ 111	
14. Sum of initial period present values		$ 502					

Panel C: Terminal Period

1. EBITDA of 2006	$ 3,559
2. Free cash flow, 2006	$ 1,602
3. Terminal period discount rate	12.0%
4. Terminal value in 2006	13,347
5. Present value factor: $1 / (1 + 0.10)^n$	0.6209
6. Present value of terminal period	$ 8,288

Panel D: Calculation of Equity Value

1. Sum of initial period present values	$ 502
2. Present value of terminal period	8,288
3. DCF enterprise value	$ 8,790
4. Add: excess cash	0
5. Less: debt	3,000
6. Equity value	$ 5,790
7. Number of shares outstanding	100
8. Value per share	$ 57.90

the net cash flows of $100 for 2001. The net cash flows are generally referred to as *free cash flow*, as labeled in line 11. In summary, free cash flow is calculated by adding tax shelter and depreciation to net income and deducting investment requirements. This is the cash flow part of DCF valuation. We next turn to the discounting procedure.

Discounting requires that each year's cash flow be divided by 1 plus the applicable discount rate or cost of capital. It should be clear at this point that DCF valuation simply applies the concepts of project capital investments analysis to the level of the firm. So line 12 represents the numerical values of $[1/(1 + k)^n]$ where k is the applicable cost of capital (10 percent) and n refers to the sequence of 5 years, as shown in panel B of Table 7.2. Line 13 presents the discounted or present values of each year's free cash flow. Line 14 is the sum of the initial 5-year period present values, which for this example is $502.

The $502 is the amount by which the value of the firm has been increased by the total investment projects of the firm for the first 5-year period of their lives. But the firm is always making a series of new investments so long as their earnings on the investment outlays exceed the cost of capital. The next step is to calculate what happens after the fifth year, or year 2005 in this example. The first 5 years are assumed to be a period of supernormal growth. It is a period during which the firm has competitive advantage or competitive superiority over its rivals. But as time passes, rivals may reduce costs, improve products, or by imitation and learning erode or eliminate the competitive advantage reflected in the data for the first 5 years in Table 7.2.

Many alternative possibilities could be considered. For simplicity of explanation we first assume that the competitive advantage has been completely lost and that the firm is unable to find any positive net present value investments. Its revenues in the sixth year and beyond will remain at $17,796. If so, its capital expenditures would be exactly offset by depreciation from year 6 on. Working capital will no longer grow because working capital needs are related to revenues which are no longer growing. The free cash flow for year 6 would be NOPAT and would be unchanged from the NOPAT of year 5, as shown in line 10 of panel B and in line 2 of panel C in the amount of $1602. Since depreciation and capital expenditures (both $890) offset each other, $1602 is also the free cash flow and under the model continues unchanged forever. The valuation of a constant amount that continues to infinity (forever) is shown by Eq. (7.1).

$$\text{Present value} = \frac{\text{cash flows}}{\text{discount rate}} = \frac{\text{cash flows}}{k} \qquad (7.1)$$

We use the discount rate of 10 percent for the initial period of competitive advantage. For the terminal period, the discount rate could be different. It could be lower on the argument that during the period of competitive advantage, competitors are seeking to erode the superiority. The counterargument is that when competitors have eliminated a firm's competitive advantage, the risk is even greater that revenues would decline rather than remain unchanged, so the terminal period discount rate would be higher. The actual choice depends upon the economic characteristics of the industry under analysis. Valuation is not mechanical. Valuation expresses the competitive outlook for a firm in quantitative terms.

In Table 7.2 for the terminal period, we illustrate a somewhat higher discount rate of 12 percent. When this is divided into the constant cash flow of $1602, we obtain $13,347, as shown in line 4 of panel C. But this is its value 5 years hence. We obtain the present value factor from a hand calculator or computer for period 5 at 10 percent which is 0.6209, resulting in a present value of the terminal period of $8288.

In panel D, we show the relationship between enterprise value and equity value. The DCF enterprise value is the sum of the initial and terminal period present values, or $8790 in our example. Since we have valued operating cash flows, we add excess cash which will generally be the marketable securities account, assumed to be zero in this example. We deduct total interest-bearing debt, assumed to be $3000, to obtain an equity value of $5790. If the firm has 100 shares outstanding, its market price per share would be $57.90.

Table 7.2 provides a vehicle for illustrating a simple example of the application of the spreadsheet discounted cash flow methodology. All the calculations could be made with a handheld calculator. The use of a computer speeds the process. More insights can be gained by considering some extensions to this model.

DCF with Spreadsheet Patterns

The data in the spreadsheet presented in Table 7.2 could come from internal company documents developed in its strategic and financial planning. We also observe spreadsheets of this

TABLE 7.3

DCF with Spreadsheet Patterns

Panel A
Inputs:

Time Relationships:

Base-year revenues	$8,658	
Revenue growth rate, initial period	15.5%	
Discount rate, initial period	10.0%	
Discount rate, terminal period	12.0%	
Terminal period growth rate	0.0%	
Terminal period depreciation	5.0%	
Terminal period capital expenditures	5.0%	
Terminal period changes in working capital	0.0%	
Tax rate	40%	

Base year	2000
Initial year of projection	2001
Last year of projection	2005

Panel B: Initial Growth Period

	Revenue Relation	1 2001	2 2002	3 2003	4 2004	5 2005	n + 1 2006
				Years			
1. Revenues		$10,000	$11,550	$13,340	$15,408	$17,796	$17,796
2. EBITDA	20.0%	2,000	2,310	2,668	3,082	3,559	3,559
3. Depreciation	5.0%	500	577	667	770	890	890
4. EBIT = NOI	15.0%	1,500	1,732	2,001	2,311	2,669	2,669
5. Less: Interest expense	3.0%	300	346	400	462	534	534
6. EBT = (4) − (5)		1,200	1,386	1,601	1,849	2,136	2,136
7. Less: Tax @ 40%		480	554	640	740	854	854
8. Net income = (6) − (7)		720	832	960	1,109	1,281	1,281
9. Add: Interest expense* (1 − T) = (5)*(1 − T)		180	208	240	277	320	320
10. NOPAT = (4)*(1 − T) = (8) + (9)		900	1,039	1,201	1,387	1,602	1,602
10a. Add: depreciation	5.0%	500	577	667	770	890	890
10b. Less: capital expenditures	9.0%	900	1,039	1,201	1,387	1,602	890
10c. Less: changes in working capital	4.0%	400	462	534	616	712	0
11. Free cash flow = (10) + (10a) − (10b) − (10c)		100	115	133	154	178	1,602
12. Discount factor @ 10.0%		0.909	0.826	0.751	0.683	0.621	
13. Present values of free cash flow		$ 91	$ 95	$ 100	$ 105	$ 111	

14. Sum of initial period present values	$ 502

Panel C: Terminal Period

1. EBITDA of 2006	$ 3,559
2. Free cash flow, 2006	$ 1,602
3. Terminal period discount rate	12.0%
4. Terminal value in 2006	13,347
5. Present value factor: 1 / (1 + 0.10)^n	0.6209
6. Present value of terminal period	$ 8,288

Panel D: Calculation of Equity Value

1. Sum of initial period present values	$ 502
2. Present value of terminal period	8,288
3. DCF enterprise value	$ 8,790
4. Add: excess cash	0
5. Less: debt	3,000
6. Equity value	$ 5,790
7. Number of shares outstanding	100
8. Value per share	$ 57.90

kind in many of the detailed studies of individual companies published by financial analysts employed by investment banking firms. Usually one can observe patterns in the data as shown in Table 7.3. Panel A summarizes the key input data that were already used in Table 7.2. Panel B in Table 7.3 has the same data as in Table 7.2 but inserts a new column which shows some key relationships to revenues. Line 1 presents the revenues data as before. Line 2 shows that EBITDA is 20 percent of revenues which implies that all costs except depreciation are 80 percent of revenues. Depreciation is shown as 5 percent of revenues.

Of course depreciation is more directly related to gross property, plant, and equipment but can also be expressed in relationship to revenues as shown in Table 7.4. Gross property, plant, and equipment is $5000 with an average 10-year life and therefore a depreciation rate of 10 percent per year. Since the revenues in 2001 are $10,000, we can also express depreciation as 5 percent of sales, as shown in Table 7.3. Similarly, interest-bearing debt is shown to be $3000 in Table 7.4 with an interest rate of 10 percent so that interest expense will be 3 percent of revenues. The net operating income margin is based on the cost relationships implied in lines 2 and 3. The relationships shown in lines 10b and 10c reflect internal

TABLE 7.4

Depreciation and Interest Expense Relationships

The initial condensed balance sheet is:				
Current assets (excluding marketable securities)		$2,000	Non-interest-bearing short-term debt	$1,000
Gross property, plant, and equipment	5,000		Interest-bearing debt	3,000
Less: accumulated depreciation	1,000			
Net property, plant, and equipment		4,000	Shareholders' equity	2,000
			Total liabilities and	
Total assets		$6,000	shareholders' equity	$6,000

A. Gross property, plant, and equipment (GPPE) has a 10-year life so depreciation is 10% of GPPE. Initial year revenues are $10,000 so depreciation is 5% of revenues.

B. Interest-bearing debt is $3000 with an interest rate of 10%, so interest expense is 3% of revenues.

company studies whose results are presented as key input data in panel A.

In Table 7.3, the input data in panel A and the revenue relationships in panel B are the value drivers of a company's stock price in the marketplace. The calculations proceed as in Table 7.2 to obtain the same valuation per share of $57.90. This must be so because the data are identical. The systematic relationships provide a sharper perspective and are valuable for financial planning. For example, if EBITDA could be improved by 1 percentage point, Table 7.5 shows that the indicated market price per share rises from $57.90 to $66.44, an increase of 14.7 percent. Recognition of the impact of the critical value drivers identified in Table 7.3 can provide powerful motivations for managers to control cost and to improve profit margins. Small changes in the value drivers can produce significant improvements in market prices. Clearly it is worthwhile to estimate these systematic relationships. Even if they are approximations, they provide a useful framework for company planning and performance improvements.

Formula Methods in Valuation

When the systematic relationships have been identified, the valuation procedures can also be expressed in compact formulas. Table 7.6 illustrates the formula approach. It is a calculation procedure equivalent to the steps shown in Tables 7.2 and 7.3. Panel A summarizes the value drivers. Panel B presents the formulas. Panel C shows the numerical calculations. Panel D is identical as in the previous two valuation tables. The indicated market value using the formula method produces results identical to the DCF spreadsheet valuations. All result in an intrinsic market value of $57.90 per share.

The formula in Table 7.6 panel B, Eq. (7.2), expresses in symbols the procedures illustrated in the spreadsheet methodology. In performing the calculations we use Eq. (7.2a) in which the summation term is simplified. We expressed $(1+g)/(1+k)$ as $1+h$ which enabled us to use the future sum of an annuity (App. A.3) formula. As before, we have two time segments —a period of competitive advantage with supernormal growth followed by

T A B L E　7.5

DCF with Spreadsheet Patterns

Panel A

Inputs

Base year revenues	$8,658
Revenue growth rate, initial period	15.5%
Discount rate, initial period	10.0%
Discount rate, terminal period	12.0%
Terminal period growth rate	0.0%
Terminal period depreciation	5.0%
Terminal period capital expenditures	5.0%
Terminal period changes in working capital	0.0%
Tax rate	40%

Time Relationships

Base year	2000
Initial year of projection	2001
Last year of projection	2005

Panel B: Initial Growth Period

	Revenue Relation	1 2001	2 2002	3 2003	4 2004	5 2005	n + 1 2006
1. Revenues		$10,000	$11,550	$13,340	$15,408	$17,796	$17,796
2. EBITDA	21.0%	2,100	2,425	2,801	3,236	3,737	3,737
3. Depreciation	5.0%	500	577	667	770	890	890
4. EBIT = NOI	16.0%	1,600	1,848	2,134	2,465	2,847	2,847
5. Less: Interest expense	3.0%	300	346	400	462	534	534
6. EBT = (4) − (5)		1,300	1,501	1,734	2,003	2,314	2,314
7. Less: Tax @ 40%		520	601	694	801	925	925
8. Net income = (6) − (7)		780	901	1,041	1,202	1,388	1,388
9. Add: Interest expense*(1 − T) = (5)*(1 − T)		180	208	240	277	320	320
10. NOPAT = (4)*(1 − T) = (8) + (9)		960	1,109	1,281	1,479	1,708	1,708
10a. Add: depreciation	5.0%	500	577	667	770	890	890
10b. Less: capital expenditures	9.0%	900	1,039	1,201	1,387	1,602	890
10c. Less: changes in working capital	4.0%	400	462	534	616	712	0
11. Free cash flow = (10) + (10a) − (10b) − (10c)		160	185	213	247	285	1,708
12. Discount factor @ 10.0%		0.909	0.826	0.751	0.683	0.621	
13. Present values of free cash flow		$ 145	$ 153	$ 160	$ 168	$ 177	
14. Sum of initial period present values		$ 804					

Panel C: Terminal Period

1. EBITDA of 2006	$ 3,737
2. Free cash flow, 2006	$ 1,708
3. Terminal period discount rate	12.0%
4. Terminal value in 2006	14,237
5. Present value factor: $1 / (1 + 0.10)^n$	0.6209
6. Present value of terminal period	$ 8,840

Panel D: Calculation of Equity Value

1. Sum of initial period present values	$ 804
2. Present value of terminal period	8,840
3. DCF enterprise value	$ 9,644
4. Add: excess cash	0
5. Less: debt	3,000
6. Equity value	$ 6,644
7. Number of shares outstanding	100
8. Value per share	$ 66.44

a second period extending to infinity. For the first term we start with revenues multiplied by the value drivers for NOPAT plus depreciation less investment requirements. The summation expression indicates that the free cash flows grow each year and are discounted year by year, as was illustrated in the Table 7.2

TABLE 7.6

Revenue Growth Formula

Panel A: Value Drivers

R_0	= initial-year revenues	$8,658
n	= number of supernormal growth years	5
m	= net operating income margin	15.0%
T	= tax rate	40.0%
g_S	= supernormal growth period growth rate	15.5%
d_S	= supernormal growth period depreciation	5.0%
I_{fgs}	= supernormal growth period capital expenditures (gross)	9.0%
I_{ws}	= supernormal growth period working capital expenditures	4.0%
k_S	= supernormal growth period cost of capital	10.0%
g_C	= terminal period growth rate	0.0%
d_C	= terminal period depreciation	5.0%
I_{fgc}	= terminal period capital expenditures	5.0%
I_{wc}	= terminal period working capital expenditures	0.0%
k_C	= terminal period cost of capital	12.0%
$1 + h$	= calculation relationship = $(1 + g_S) / (1 + k_S)$	1.0500

Panel B: Formula

$$V_0 = R_0[m(1 - T) + d_S - I_{fgs} - I_{ws}] \sum_{t=1}^{n} \frac{(1 + g_S)^t}{(1 + k_S)^t} +$$

$$\frac{R_0(1 + g_S)^n(m(1 - T) + d_C - I_{fgc}]}{k_C(1 + k_S)^n} \qquad (7.2)$$

$$V_0 = \frac{R_1[m(1 - T) + d_S - I_{fgs} - I_{ws}]}{1 + k_S} \left[\frac{(1 + h)^n - 1}{h} \right] +$$

$$\frac{R_0(1 + g_S)^n[m(1 - T) + d_C - I_{fgc}]}{k_C(1 + k_S)^n} \qquad (7.2a)$$

Panel C: Numerical Calculation

V_0 = 10,000 [0.15(1 − 0.4) + 0.05 − 0.09 − 0.04] [1 / (1 + 0.1)] [((1.05)^5 − 1) /
0.05] + 8658 [(1 + 0.155)^5] [0.15(1 − 0.4) + 0.05 − 0.05] / [(0.12) (1 + 0.1)^5]

= 10,000 (0.01) (0.9091) (5.5256)   present value of supernormal cash flows
  + 8658 (2.0555) (0.09) [(8.3333) (0.6209)]   present value of terminal value

= 502.3 + 8287.5

= $8,790

Panel D: Calculating Firm Value

Present value of supernormal cash flows	$ 502
Present value of terminal value	$ 8,288
Total present value of future cash flows	$ 8,790
Add: Marketable securities	0
Total value of the firm	$ 8,790
Less: Total interest-bearing debt	3,000
Equity value	$ 5,790
Number of shares	100
Value per share	$ 57.90

spreadsheet DCF valuation. The second expression, which is for the terminal period, starts with the revenues as of the end of the nth year of competitive advantage. These revenues are multiplied by the expression for NOPAT plus depreciation less investment requirements. The full second term is discounted at the terminal period cost of capital rate. The result is the value of the free cash flows as of the beginning of the terminal period. This is discounted back to the present. As before, enterprise value is the sum of the value of the cash flows during the period of competitive advantage and the value of the cash flows during the terminal period.

Thus far we have illustrated the situation of a firm that has a competitive advantage resulting in supernormal growth and profitability for a specified number of years, after which its revenues remain at a constant level. Patterns of future cash flows can take many different shapes. We will illustrate some widely used types.

The constant growth valuation model is frequently encountered. The formula is Eq. (7.3), shown in Table 7.7. The numerator is next year's cash flows. The denominator is the discount rate less the growth rate. The constant growth formula postulates that revenues of the firm grow at a specified constant rate for perpetuity. It is obvious that a firm cannot grow faster than the economy as a whole in perpetuity; otherwise the firm will become larger than the economy. Caution should be exercised in the use of this formula.

In Table 7.7, the growth rate of 5 percent and the other value drivers are based on analysis of the company and its industry. We insert the numbers in Eq. (7.3a) to obtain a valuation of \$20,088.

One of the useful applications of the constant growth model is in combination with a period of competitive advantage. This is illustrated in Table 7.8. Equation (7.4) repeats the first term in Eq. (7.2) and applies Eq. (7.3) to the terminal period. The procedures and calculations result in a market value per share of \$104.31. It is predictable that the value in Table 7.8 based on constant growth in the terminal period would be higher than in Table 7.3 and in Table 7.6 in which there was no growth in the terminal period.

TABLE 7.7

Constant Growth Valuation Model

Value Drivers

R_0 = \$8,696
m = 15.0%
T = 40.0%
g = 5.0%
d = 5.0%
I_{fg} = 2.0%
I_w = 1.0%
k = 10.0%

Formula and Valuation

$$V_0 = \frac{R_0[m(1-T)+d-I_{fg}-I_w](1+g)}{k-g} \qquad (7.3)$$

$$= \frac{R_1[m(1-T)+d-I_{fg}-I_w]}{k-g} \qquad (7.3a)$$

$$= 9130.8[0.15(1-0.4)+0.05-0.02-0.01]/(0.1-0.05)$$

$$= 9130.8(0.11)/0.05$$

$$= \boxed{\$20,088}$$

where R_0 = initial-year revenues
m = net operating income margin
T = tax rate
g = growth rate in revenues
d = depreciation
I_{fg} = capital expenditures (gross)
I_w = working capital expenditures
k = cost of capital

COST OF CAPITAL

To calculate the cost of capital of a firm, we first calculate the costs of its major individual components of financing: equity, debt, and preferred stocks. We begin with calculating the cost of equity.

TABLE 7.8

Revenue Growth Formula (Constant Growth in Terminal Period)

Panel A: Value Drivers

R_0	= initial year revenues	$8,658
n	= number of supernormal growth years	5
m	= net operating income margin	15.0%
T	= tax rate	40.0%
g_s	= supernormal growth period growth rate	15.5%
d_s	= supernormal growth period depreciation	5.0%
I_{fgs}	= supernormal growth period capital expenditures (gross)	9.0%
I_{ws}	= supernormal growth period working capital expenditures	4.0%
k_s	= supernormal growth period cost of capital	10.0%
g_c	= terminal period growth rate	4.0%
d_c	= terminal period depreciation	3.0%
I_{fgc}	= terminal period capital expenditures	2.0%
I_{wc}	= terminal period working capital expenditures	1.0%
k_c	= terminal period cost of capital	12.0%
$1 + h$	= calculation relationship = $(1 + g_s) / (1 + k_s)$	1.0500

Panel B: Formula

$$V_0 = R_0[m(1 - T) + d_s - I_{fgs} - I_{ws}] \sum_{t=1}^{n} \frac{(1 + g_s)^t}{1 + k_s)^t} +$$

$$\frac{R_0(1 + g_s)^n(1 + g_c)[m(1 - T) + d_c - I_{fgc} - I_{wc}]}{(k_c - g_c)(1 + k_s)^n} \quad (7.4)$$

$$V_0 = \frac{R_1[m(1 - T) + d_s - I_{fgs} - I_{ws}]}{1 + k_s} \left[\frac{(1 + h)^n - 1}{h} \right] +$$

$$\frac{R_0(1 + g_s)^n(1 + g_c)[m(1 - T) + d_c - I_{fgc} - I_{wc}]}{(k_c - g_c)(1 + k_s)^n} \quad (7.4a)$$

Panel C: Numerical Calculation

V_0 = 10,000 [0.15(1 − 0.4) + 0.05 − 0.09 − 0.04] [1/(1 + 0.1)] [((1.05)^5 − 1)/0.05] + 8658 [(1 + 0.155)^5] [1 + 0.04] [0.15(1 − 0.4) + 0.03 − 0.02 − 0.01] / [(0.12 − 0.04) (1 + 0.1)^5]

= 10,000 (0.01) (0.9091) (5.5256)   present value of supernormal cash flows
+ 8658 (2.0555) (1.04) (0.09) [(12.5) (0.6209)]   present value of terminal value

= 502.3 + 12,928.6

= $13,431

Panel D: Calculating Firm Value

Present value of supernormal cash flows	$ 502
Present value of terminal value	$ 12,929
Total present value of future cash flows	$ 13,431
Add: Marketable securities	0
Total value of the firm	$ 13,431
Less: Total interest-bearing debt	3,000
Equity value	$ 10,431
Number of shares	100
Value per share	$ 104.31

COST OF EQUITY

There are a number of techniques used to estimate the cost of equity. Each is reviewed below.

Capital Asset Pricing Model

The most widely employed method used in calculating the cost of equity is the capital asset pricing model (CAPM). In CAPM, the required return on equity is a risk-free return plus a risk component. For the economy as a whole, the risk-free rate would be related to the returns on U.S. government bonds. Because the discount factor used in valuation involves relatively long periods, the rates on relatively long-term bonds would be employed. Theory and practice generally begin with interest rate levels in the current economic environment since the long-term future is difficult to forecast. For the United States in early 2001, the yields on 10-year Treasuries were about 5.2 percent.

In the CAPM, the risk adjustment begins with the market-determined differential between equity yields and government bonds. The widely used historical data developed by Ibbotson Associates for the period January 1, 1926 to December 31, 2000, shows a geometric mean of 11 percent for large company stocks and 5.3 percent for long-term government bonds. This gives a spread of 5.7 percent as the market-determined differential, also called the market price of risk. Using the arithmetic mean, the spread is 13.0 percent minus 5.7 percent, which gives a 7.3 percent difference. The argument for the use of the geometric mean is that returns from investments should use compounded interest rates. The argument for the use of the arithmetic mean is that we are calculating an expected return which is calculated by some weighted arithmetic average of future returns. This view argues that when historical data are used as a guide, the arithmetic means should be used. Each view has some logic behind it.

For many years, based on patterns of the long-term relationships between returns on long- and short-term government bonds, on long- and short-term corporate bonds, and on equity groups such as large caps, small caps, high techs, etc., the market equity premium appeared to be in the range of 6.5 percent to 7.5 percent. But by the mid-1990s, a paradigm for a new economy began to emerge. Analysts moved toward using 4 percent to 5 percent as the market price of risk.

A number of arguments have been offered to justify a lower market risk premium in the "new economy." The U.S. economy had experienced a period of sustained economic growth for almost two decades. Price inflation was reduced to the 1 percent to 2.5 perccent levels. Unemployment was low, yet wage costs were relatively flat into mid-1999. High rates of productivity from the new technologies also helped keep costs low. The restructurings of the 1980s made U.S. firms more cost-efficient. These are the kinds of factors used to support the argument that the economy as a whole had become one of relatively stable, attractive growth, with lower risks of severe reverses.

With the decline in stock prices from their peak levels in March 2000 and forecasts of a recession in the U.S. economy beginning to be reflected in declining revenue and profit reports during the first quarter of 2001, the above arguments for lowering the expected market price of risk become weakened.

To illustrate the CAPM, we use 7 percent for the market price of risk. The 7 percent is multiplied by the firm's beta to obtain an estimate of the risk adjustment for an individual firm. The beta of a firm is a measure of how the return on its common stock varies with returns on the market as a whole. Returns on the market as a whole have been conveniently measured by use of the S&P 500, all stocks on the New York Stock Exchange, or other broad groupings. Thus, if the return on the market increased by 10 percent, a firm with a beta of 1.2 would experience a rise in its returns of 12 percent (and conversely if the market fell by 10 percent). Thus, high beta stocks exhibit higher volatility than low-beta stocks in response to changes in market returns.

The beta for the market as a whole must necessarily be 1, by definition. With a risk-free rate of 5.2 percent, and a market price of risk of 7 percent, we can write an equation for the expected return on the market:

Expected return on the market = 5.2% + 7% (1) = 12.2%

From this relationship, we can generalize to individual firms.

Required return on equity of a firm = 5.2% + 7%(beta)

If the beta of the firm is 1.2, its required return will be 13.6 percent. If the beta of the firm is 0.8, its required return will be 10.8 percent, according to CAPM. In our example, we will use a 1.2 beta level firm. Thus, the cost of equity for a firm with a beta of 1.2 would be 13.6 percent compared with a required return of 10.8 percent for a 0.8 beta firm. Betas have been calculated for individual firms by most of the brokerage houses and data sources such as Value Line. Betas for companies are illustrated below.

Exxon Mobil	0.80
May Department Stores	1.00
General Motors	1.10
Yahoo	1.60

Oil companies have low betas because their returns are most sensitive to the price of oil and less sensitive to movements in the general economy. Sales of mostly nondurable goods are tied more directly to the economy. Thus a department store, which sells mostly nondurable consumer goods, such as May Department Stores, would have returns that fluctuate as the return of the market as a whole. The betas of companies like General Motors are likely to be greater than 1 because the sales of durable goods fluctuate more than the economy as a whole. When buyers become pessimistic about the economic outlook, they can make automobiles or machinery last longer and post-pone purchases. We would expect the beta of an Internet company to be high because Internet companies depend heavily on advertising as a source of revenues. Advertising outlays are especially sensitive to economic prospects.

We have illustrated how to calculate the cost of equity using the CAPM. We next discuss other methods. To make comparisons with alternative calculations of the cost of equity, we call our firm the Brown Company, assign it a beta of 1.2, and use 13.6 percent as its CAPM measure of the cost of equity.

The Dividend Growth Model

The dividend growth model states that the value of equity is equal to the expected dividend divided by the difference between the cost of equity and the growth rate of dividends in perpetuity. Solving this expression for the cost of equity for a firm gives

Cost of equity = Expected dividend yield + expected growth rate

Cost of equity of Brown Company = 2.7% + 11% = 13.7%

The expected dividend yield of 2.7 percent is taken from a projection of the Brown Company dividend yield for 2002 to 2004. The 11 percent expected long-term growth rate in dividends is based on medium-term growth projections. The resulting 13.7 percent is consistent with the CAPM result.

Bond Yield Plus Equity Risk Adjustment

A third approach provides a check on the previous two. The yield on a firm's equity should be greater than the yield on its bonds, since equity claims are junior to the prior claims of creditors. Here, the firm's equity risk adjustment is in relation to the yield on its bonds. Brown Company's long-term bonds were generally rated Baa in January 2001, and the yield on Baa bonds was in the 8.0 percent range. Historical data on the equity returns to Brown Company shareholders suggest a spread over its bond yields of about 5 percent. We add 5 percent to the 8 percent bond yield to obtain 13 percent.

We have three estimates of the cost of equity capital. They average about 13.4 percent. This is the figure we shall employ as our component cost of equity. We next consider the cost of other methods of financing.

COST OF DEBT

The cost of debt should be on an after-tax basis because interest payments are tax-deductible. Therefore, the cost of debt capital is calculated as follows:

$$k_b(1 - T) = \text{after-tax cost of debt}$$

Here T is the corporate tax rate used previously. Thus, if the before-tax cost of debt were 8 percent and the firm's effective corporate tax rate were 40 percent, the after-tax cost of debt would be 4.8 percent.

We start with the firm's before-tax cost of debt and multiply it by the factor $(1 - T)$ to obtain the relevant after-tax cost. How do we obtain the before-tax cost of debt in practice for an actual firm? Two main procedures may be used: (1) We can look in any investment manual to determine the rating of the firm's outstanding publicly held bonds. Various government agencies and investment banking firms periodically publish promised yields to maturity of debt issues by rating categories. (2) We can take a weighted average of the yield to maturity for all the firm's publicly traded bonds.

We use an estimate of 8 percent for the before-tax cost of debt for Brown Company based on the Baa rating of its long-term debt. Its after-tax cost of debt, using a tax rate of 40 percent, would be 4.8 percent.

Preferred stock is a third source of financing. Most preferred stocks have no maturity and pay a fixed dividend. The cost of preferred stock is, therefore, the promised dividend divided by its current market price. Preferred stocks have somewhat greater risk than debt because of its junior position. So this will make for a higher required yield. But preferred stock dividends received by another corporation are not fully subject to the corporate tax. This makes for a lower required yield. The two influences tend to balance out so the yield on preferred stock is about the same as the yields on long-term debt. We would therefore expect Brown Company's yield on preferred stock to be around 8 percent with no tax deduction for payments. Most companies use little or no preferred stock in part due to this lack of tax deductibility of dividends paid. So we shall not use preferred stock in our example.

Weighted Average Cost of Capital

To calculate the marginal weighted cost of capital, we first calculate financing proportions at book values and at market values for Brown Company.

Financial Proportions at Book Value (Millions)

Interest-Bearing Debt	$ 2,500	47%
Shareholders' Equity	2,800	53%
Total	$ 5,300	

Financial Proportions at Market Value (Millions)

Interest-Bearing Debt*	$ 2,500	16%
Shareholders' Equity* ($25×510.3)	12,758	84%
Total	$15,258	

Taking these financial proportions as a guide, we use a financial structure consisting of 30 percent debt and 70 percent equity to calculate the weighted average cost of capital for Brown Company:

$$0.134(0.70) + 0.048(0.30) = 0.0938 + 0.0144 = 0.1082$$

Accordingly, the appropriate discount rate to use in calculating a valuation of the Brown Company is the 10.82 percent cost of capital.

CAPITAL STRUCTURE AND THE COST OF CAPITAL

A decision with respect to capital structure was required to obtain the proportions of debt and equity used in calculating the weighted average cost of capital (WACC, or k). We present some materials to provide a basis for making such a decision.

First we consider the reasons why firms sell equity. The finance literature argues that firms sell equity when management judges the stock to be overvalued. We believe this to be an overgeneralization. Book equity increases with retained earnings. Earnings are retained to finance growth. Retained earnings represent the cheapest form of financing. If a firm paid out all of its earnings as dividends and then raised outside equity to finance

---

*The market value of shareholders' equity is calculated as the number of shares outstanding times the market price of the common stock. The market value of debt is assumed to be the same as its book value.

growth, it would have subjected shareholders to their personal tax on dividends and would have to pay investment bankers to sell the additional equity. Depending upon the investment requirements to support growth, it is possible that the use of retained earnings would result in a debt ratio on the low side. Under such circumstances, the firm could use share repurchases and/or sell debt to rebalance its financial structure.

A strong inducement to sell debt is that the interest on debt is deductible as an expense for tax purposes. Even without the tax consideration, a firm might seek to use debt, which carries a fixed interest payment, to magnify the gains on equity. This is called *trading on the equity*. We have seen many examples of this during the boom environment of the 1990s. A case in point is the telecommunication equipment industry. The great prospects for the use of fiber optics led to heavy investments in companies to produce fiber optics and telecommunication companies which used them in their operations. Both existing and new companies made heavy use of debt, seeking high returns and high stock values. However, as the use of debt results in high debt-to-equity ratios, at some point the risk of financial distress affects both the cost of debt and the required return on equity.

One consequence of rising debt ratios is a deterioration in bond ratings and rising cost of debt. This is illustrated by Table 7.9. The patterns in Table 7.9 reflect financial conditions as of mid-January 2001. Heavy debt ratios have already imposed severe penalties on required returns to bonds below the investment grade of BBB. Ten-year Treasuries were yielding about 5.2 percent. AAA corporate bonds have yields to maturity of 7.2 percent, representing a differential of 2 percentage points or 200 basis points. Leverage ratios measured by debt-to-equity for top-grade corporates would be 25 percent or less. The associated EBIT-to-fixed-charges ratio would be 7 times or better.

Table 7.9 shows that as the leverage ratios increase, associated with lower fixed charge coverage ratios, bond ratings decline and debt costs increase. BBB bonds carry leverage ratios in the 67 to 90 percent range and require yields about 80 basis points higher than AAAs. The table shows a required yield on junk bonds of 640 basis points above the AAAs—more than 800 basis points higher than 10-year U.S. Treasuries. The market for junk

T A B L E   7.9

Leverage, Ratings, and Debt Costs

Debt/Equity Ratio (Percent)	EBIT/Fixed Charges	Bond Rating*	Debt Costs (Percent)
25 or less	> 7×	AAA	7.2
25 to 43	4× to 8 ×	AA	7.3
43 to 67	3× to 5×	A	7.6
67 to 90	1.75× to 2.5×	BBB	8.0
90 to 233	1× to 2×	BB	13.6
233 and above	0.75× to 1.25×	B	16.0

* Bond ratings are related to leverage ratios and pretax fixed charge coverage. Other factors include firm size, prospective growth rates in sales and profitability, industry, and competitive factors.

bonds is subject to extreme fluctuations in market attitudes. In periods of optimism, the spread in relation to Treasuries can drop as low as 300 basis points. The spreads as high as 840 basis points against the junk bonds result in their realized yields (measured from the mid-1980s when they first came to wide use) being 1 to 2 percentage points higher than U.S. Treasuries.

The message of Table 7.9 is that high debt ratios associated with low fixed charges coverage ratios can lead to high debt costs and higher cost of capital to business firms. Another method of measuring the risk of high leverage ratios is the impact on a firm's beta. The relationship between a leveraged equity beta and an unleveraged beta is shown by the following equation:

$$\beta_e = \beta_u \left[1 + \frac{B(1 - T)}{S} \right] \qquad (7.5)$$

where β_e = leveraged equity beta
β_u = unleveraged equity beta
B = market value of debt
S = market value of equity
T = tax rate

We illustrate how this equation works. Suppose a firm's unleveraged beta is 0.8. Assume a tax rate of 40 percent and a leverage ratio B/S of ⅔. Using Eq. (7.5), the leveraged equity beta is 0.8[1 + ⅔(0.6)], or 1.12. If the leverage ratio were 0.5, the leveraged beta would be 1.04.

It can be seen that the unleveraged equity beta reflects the business risk of the firm. The difference between the leveraged beta and the unleveraged beta reflects the financial risk resulting from the use of leverage. So the equation can be used to calculate a target leverage ratio based on the firm's target equity beta. Suppose the firm had a target equity beta of 1.12. From our previous analysis we can use the equation to solve for the target B/S which would be ⅔.

We can generalize the above by the use of Fig. 7.1 which shows the relationship between leverage measured by B/S and the costs of debt, equity, and the resulting WACC or k. With no debt, the unleveraged firm's cost of equity and WACC would be k_u. As shown in Table 7.9, for a debt ratio of up to 25 percent equity, the debt rating remains at AAA. As the leverage ratio begins to rise beyond that point, its cost increases moderately until it reaches the below investment-grade status when it rises sharply. The cost of equity curve is similar. But equity is junior to debt, so as the cost of debt rises, the cost of equity rises even faster. The level of the WACC curve first falls because the proportion of lower-cost debt increases. At some point the WACC curve rises because the increased costs of debt and equity offset the higher debt proportion. Since the WACC curve falls and then rises, it must have some low point. This optimum capital structure range is shown in Fig. 7.1. The range is more like a flat saucer than a steep cup.

VALUATION IN MERGERS

We now show the application of our valuation framework in analyzing mergers. We do this by an actual example, the Tribune's acquisition of the Times Mirror.

Deal Terms

The deal was announced on March 13, 2000. Tribune agreed to pay about $6.4 billion in a combination of cash and stock. It planned to purchase up to 28 million Times Mirror shares for cash

FIGURE 7.1

Effects of bankruptcy costs and taxes on the cost of capital

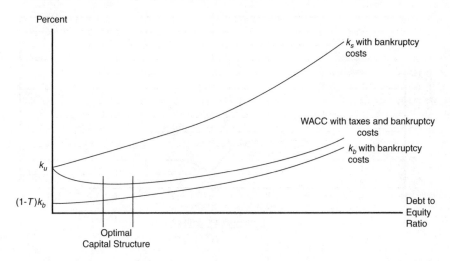

at $95 per share. Following that exchange, the remaining shares were to be exchanged for 2.5 shares of Tribune stock. The $95 offer was about twice the preannouncement price per share of Times Mirror. The stock market reaction to the merger is shown in Fig. 7.2. The announcement of the merger caused Times Mirror stock to increase from $47.94 to $85.63 (+79 percent). Meanwhile, Tribune fell from $37.19 to $30.81 (-17 percent), although it recovered the next day. The $95 offer to Times Mirror shareholders was a 98 percent premium over the closing price of the day before. Although the premium was well over the market price, analysts noted that it was only about a 10.5 multiple on Times Mirror's expected 2000 EBITDA. Most newspaper deals had been in the 11 to 14 times EBITDA multiple range.

VALUATION ANALYSIS

Cost of Capital

We begin our valuation analysis with the calculation of the cost of capital. We use CAPM to determine the cost of equity. We use a risk-free rate of 5.2 percent and a market risk premium of 7

F I G U R E 7.2

Stock prices for Tribune and Times Mirror

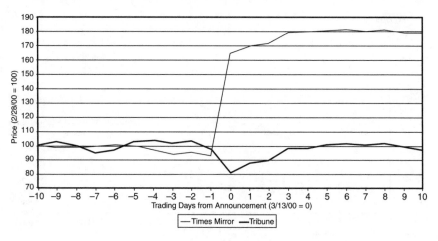

percent. We use Value Line beta estimates of 0.8 for Times Mirror, and 1.05 for Tribune. Beta estimates are subject to error. However, we believe it plausible that Times Mirrror would have a beta tied more closely to the special characteristics of the newspaper industry which might make it less responsive to the broader economic forces reflected in overall market movements. Tribune had already been moving into broader areas outside the newspaper business which could plausibly bring its beta closer to 1. The resulting cost of equity calculations are:

Times Mirror: $0.052 + 0.8(0.07) = 10.8\%$

Tribune: $0.052 + 1.05(0.07) = 12.55\%$

We next proceed to calculate the weighted average cost of capital (WACC). We estimate the capital structure of Tribune to be 25 percent debt and that of Times Mirror to be 30 percent debt. Because Tribune was getting into high-risk, high-growth areas, a lower debt structure was plausible. Since Times Mirror had increased efficiency, divested unprofitable lines, and was focusing on the tried and dependable in its own industry, it was plausible that it could carry a higher ratio of debt. We are reflecting their policy, not ours. Sticking to traditional business areas can be more risky in the face of industry changes. The estimated tax rate for Tribune is 40 percent and that for Times Mirror is 41 percent. Because both firms are relatively healthy financially, we estimate an 8 percent cost of debt. These assumptions yield the following WACC calculation:

Times Mirror: $(0.7)(.108) + 0.3(1 - 0.41)0.08 = 8.976\%$

Tribune: $(0.75)(0.1255) + 0.25 (1 - 0.40)0.08 = 10.6125\%$

Individual Companies

To determine if the merger will create value, it is first necessary to determine the value of the individual companies before the merger. Tables 7.10 and 7.11 illustrate premerger values of Tribune and Times Mirror. These are made using historical value driver patterns, the WACC calculated above, and certain judgments about the future based on the characteristics of the industry. Tribune had a higher operating margin, and we judged it to have greater prospects for growth, thanks to its television possibilities. (Eq. 7.4a from Table 7.8) We judged Times Mirror (Table 7.11) to have relatively high margins, but few prospects for future growth, based on the nature of the newspaper industry. (Eq. 7.2a from Table 7.6) The prices per share that resulted from our assumptions in Tables 7.10 and 7.11 were somewhat under the prices of the two firms before the merger was announced.

Why Tribune Was Interested in Times Mirror

The Tribune Company was looking to build its base of print and broadcast media outlets. Tribune's strategic vision was to become a leading media company in the major markets of the nation. It had a broad collection of assets in Chicago (*Chicago Tribune*, WGN television, Chicago Cubs) and was looking to build similar portfolios elsewhere. Tribune already owned television station KTLA in Los Angeles and saw advantages to adding the *Los Angeles Times*. Tribune's vision is to build portfolios of media assets in major markets and then to cross-sell advertising on its

TABLE 7.10

Valuation of Tribune

Panel A: Value Drivers

R_0	= initial year revenues	$3,222
n	= number of supernormal growth years	10
m	= net operating income margin	29.0%
T	= tax rate	40.0%
g_S	= supernormal growth period growth rate	8.0%
d_S	= supernormal growth period depreciation	0.7%
I_{fgs}	= supernormal growth period capital expenditures (gross)	0.6%
I_{ws}	= supernormal growth period working capital expenditures	0.9%
k_S	= supernormal growth period cost of capital	10.6125%
g_C	= terminal period growth rate	3.0%
d_C	= terminal period depreciation	0.7%
I_{fgc}	= terminal period capital expenditures	0.6%
I_{wc}	= terminal period working capital expenditures	0.9%
k_C	= terminal period cost of capital	10.6125%
$1 + h$	= calculation relationship = $(1 + g_S) / (1 + k_S)$	0.9764

Panel B: Numerical Calculation

$$V_0 = 3479.8 \, [0.29(1-0.4)+0.007-0.006-0.009] \, [1/(1 + 0.106125)] \, [((0.9764)^{10} - 1)/ \\ (-0.0236)] + 3222 \, [(1 + 0.08)^{10}] \, [1+0.03] \, [0.29(1-0.4)+0.007- 0.006-0.009] \, / \\ [(0.106125-0.03) \, (1+0.106125)^{10}]$$

$= 3479.8(0.166) (0.9041) (9.0014)$ present value of supernormal cash flows
    $+ 3222 (2.1589) (1.03) (0.166) [(13.1363) (0.3647)]$ present value of terminal value

$= 4700.7 + 5698.2$

$= \$10,399$

Panel C: Calculating Firm Value

Present value of supernormal cash flows	$ 4,701
Present value of terminal value	$ 5,698
Total present value of future cash flows	$ 10,399
Add: Marketable securities	0
Total value of the firm	$ 10,399
Less: Total interest-bearing debt	2,400
Equity value	$ 7,999
Number of shares	237
Value per share	$ 33.75

T A B L E 7.11

Valuation of Times Mirror

Panel A: Value Drivers

R_0	= initial year revenues	$3,190
n	= number of supernormal growth years	4
m	= net operating income margin	19.0%
T	= tax rate	41.0%
g_s	= supernormal growth period growth rate	5.0%
d_s	= supernormal growth period depreciation	0.4%
I_{fgs}	= supernormal growth period capital expenditures (gross)	0.4%
I_{ws}	= supernormal growth period working capital expenditures	0.6%
k_s	= supernormal growth period cost of capital	8.976%
g_c	= terminal period growth rate	0.0%
d_c	= terminal period depreciation	1.0%
I_{fgc}	= terminal period capital expenditures	1.0%
I_{wc}	= terminal period working capital expenditures	0.0%
k_c	= terminal period cost of capital	8.976%
$1 + h$	= calculation relationship = $(1 + g_s) / (1 + k_s)$	0.9635

Panel B: Numerical Calculation

$$V_0 = 3349.5\ [0.19(1-0.41)+0.004-0.004-0.006]\ [1/(1+0.08976)]\ [((0.9635)^4 - 1)/$$
$$(-0.0365)] + 3190\ [(1 + 0.05)^4]\ [0.19(1-0.41) + 0.01-0.01]\ /\ [(0.08976)\ (1 + 0.08976)^4]$$

$$= 3349.5\ (0.1061)\ (0.9176)\ (3.7864) \quad \text{present value of supernormal cash flows}$$
$$+ 3190\ (1.2155)\ (0.1121)\ [(11.1408)\ (0.709)] \quad \text{present value of terminal value}$$

$$= 1234.8 + 3433.6$$

$$= \$4668$$

Panel C: Calculating Firm Value

Present value of supernormal cash flows	$	1,235
Present value of terminal value	$	3,434
Total present value of future cash flows	$	4,668
Add: Marketable securities		0
Total value of the firm	$	4,668
Less: Total interest-bearing debt		1,300
Equity value	$	3,368
Number of shares		72
Value per share	$	46.78

various properties. This strategy is seen as a means of increasing the margins on advertising revenue, since advertisers would be willing to pay more for the increased exposure.

The strategy of building a portfolio of media properties presents the possibility for cooperation between the different media branches. Perhaps the television stations could rely on some of the news-gathering resources of the newspapers, and vice versa. In the Los Angeles market alone, there is already talk that Tribune could attempt to bolster its KTLA news broadcasts by building direct ties between the *Los Angeles Times* and the television broadcast.

Tribune also believed that the merger would help it build its overall national footprint. The deal gave the combined company a media presence in 18 of the top 30 markets in the country. In addition, its Internet sites would have a combined 3.4 million unique monthly visitors and projected 2000 revenues of $55 million. This national reach is another critical motivation for the merger. Tribune envisions being able to increase advertising revenue by being a means for advertisers to reach markets across the United States.

Some of the latent strategies of Times Mirror might be implemented more effectively by Tribune because it was further along the way in developing positions in alternative media, particularly the Internet and its future developments. Thus, Tribune could view an improvement in growth and operating margins at Times Mirror from its advanced position in implementing new strategies.

Why Did the Chandlers Agree to Sell to Tribune?

Clearly they gained from the recapitalization of September 3, 1999, and the substantial premium in the purchase price. Perhaps without being acquired Times Mirror could have achieved the same results—but over a longer time and with much greater uncertainty.

The Value of the Combined Companies

Table 7.12 (using Eq. 7.4a) presents our pessimistic judgments for the combined company. Following Tribune's logic, we determined

T A B L E   7.12

Valuation of Combined Tribune/Times Mirror (Pessimistic)

Panel A: Value Drivers

R_0	= initial year revenues	$6,266
n	= number of supernormal growth years	8
m	= net operating income margin	27.0%
T	= tax rate	40.0%
g_S	= supernormal growth period growth rate	8.0%
d_S	= supernormal growth period depreciation	0.6%
I_{fgs}	= supernormal growth period capital expenditures (gross)	0.6%
I_{ws}	= supernormal growth period working capital expenditures	0.9%
k_S	= supernormal growth period cost of capital	9.00%
g_C	= terminal period growth rate	1.0%
d_C	= terminal period depreciation	1.0%
I_{fgc}	= terminal period capital expenditures	1.0%
I_{wc}	= terminal period working capital expenditures	0.0%
k_C	= terminal period cost of capital	9.00%
$1 + h$	= calculation relationship = $(1 + g_S) / (1 + k_S)$	0.9908

Panel B: Numerical Calculation

$$V_0 = 6767.3 \, [0.27(1-0.4)+0.006-0.006-0.009] \, [1/(1+0.09)][((0.9908)^8-1)/(-0.0092)]$$
$$+ \, 6266 \, [(1+0.08)^8] \, [1+0.01] \, [0.27(1-0.4)+0.01-0.01-0] \, / \, [(0.09-0.01)(1+0.09)^8]$$

= 6767.3 (0.153) (0.9174) (7.7478)   present value of supernormal cash flows
+ 6266 (1.8509) (1.01) (0.162) [(12.5) (0.5019)]   present value of terminal value

= 7359.6+11,904.6

= $19,264

Panel C: Calculating Firm Value

Present value of supernormal cash flows	$ 7,360
Present value of terminal value	$ 11,905
Total present value of future cash flows	$ 19,264
Add: Marketable securities	0
Total value of the firm	$ 19,264
Less: Total interest-bearing debt	3,700
Equity value	$ 15,564
Number of shares	347
Value per share	$ 44.85

that there should be some new opportunities in owning television and newspaper media sources in the same markets. Because of this factor, we judged that the combined company would retain value drivers that are similar to Tribune. However, there are risks to such a judgment. If Tribune's multimedia strategy does not work outside of Chicago, or if the FCC does not grant Tribune certain broadcast licenses, the share price will suffer. With these estimations of the value drivers, Tribune's share price increases only slightly.

In the more optimistic valuation projections (Table 7.13 based on Eq. 7.4a), the earlier completion of the strategic goals of Times Mirror results in a sales growth rate of 9 percent and strengthens the period of competitive advantage for Tribune to 10 years.

The results from Tables 7.12 and 7.13 have been used in Tables 7.14 and 7.15. Tribune was to pay about $2.6 billion cash, and stock with a premerger value of $4.1 billion. After a relatively brief initial decline, Tribune returned to its previous levels. In June, Tribune began a decline in price that took it to $34.62 on August 14, 2000. Its 52-week range was $28 to $61. The Value Line of May 26, 2000, while expressing criticism of the acquisition and the subsequent price decline of Tribune, commented that Tribune was "now suitable for patient investors with horizons out to the 2003–2005 time frame."

Division of Gains to the Shareholders of Tribune and Times Mirror

In Table 7.14, a pessimistic scenario of the Tribune acquisition of Times Mirror results in a negative value of the total transaction, but substantial gains go to Times Mirror stockholders. As shown, the premerger market values of the Tribune ($9.7 billion) and Times Mirror ($3.7 billion) total $13.4 billion. The Tribune paid $2.7 billion in cash and $4.1 billion in equity or a total price of $6.8 billion. If we assume a negative response by the market and say a postmerger value (for the combined firm) of only $15.6 billion, the value of the Tribune dropped by $0.9 billion, which represents the postmerger value less the "payment" to Times Mirror stockholders and the Tribune's premerger value. Of course the old Times Mirror stockholders now own

T A B L E 7.13

Valuation of Combined Tribune/Times Mirror (Optimistic)

Panel A: Value Drivers

R_0	= initial year revenues	$6,266
n	= number of supernormal growth years	10
m	= net operating income margin	27.0%
T	= tax rate	40.0%
g_S	= supernormal growth period growth rate	9.0%
d_S	= supernormal growth period depreciation	0.6%
I_{fgs}	= supernormal growth period capital expenditures (gross)	0.6%
I_{ws}	= supernormal growth period working capital expenditures	0.9%
k_S	= supernormal growth period cost of capital	9.00%
g_C	= terminal period growth rate	1.0%
d_C	= terminal period depreciation	1.0%
I_{fgc}	= terminal period capital expenditures	1.0%
I_{wc}	= terminal period working capital expenditures	0.0%
k_C	= terminal period cost of capital	9.00%
$1 + h$	= calculation relationship = $(1 + g_S) / (1 + k_S)$	1.000

Panel B: Numerical Calculation

V_0 = 6829.9 [0.27(1−0.4)+0.006−0.006−0.009] [1/(1+0.09)] [10]+6266 [(1+0.09)^{10}]
[1+0.01] [0.27(1−0.4)+0.01−0.01−0] / [(0.09-0.01) (1+0.09)^{10}]

= 6829.9 (0.153) (0.9174) (10) present value of supernormal cash flows
+ 6266 (2.3674) (1.01) (0.162) [(12.5) (0.4224)] present value of terminal value

= 9587.0+12,815.5

= $22,403

Panel C: Calculating Firm Value

Present value of supernormal cash flows	$ 9,587
Present value of terminal value	$ 12,816
Total present value of future cash flows	$ 22,403
Add: Marketable securities	0
Total value of the firm	$ 22,403
Less: Total interest-bearing debt	3,700
Equity value	$ 18,703
Number of shares	347
Value per share	$ 53.90

T A B L E 7.14

Tests of Merger Performance—Pessimistic Scenario ($ Billion)

	Market Caps	Proportions
Premerger		
Tribune	$ 9.7	72.4%
Times Mirror	3.7	27.6%
Total	$13.4	100.0%
Postmerger		
Combined value	$15.6	
Cash paid to Times Mirror shareholders	2.7	
Stock paid to Times Mirror shareholders	4.1	
Remainder	$8.8	
Tribune premerger	9.7	
Gain from merger		−$0.9
Portion to Tribune (237/347 shares outstanding)		− $0.6	68.3%
Portion to Times Mirror (110/347 shares outstanding)		− $0.3	31.7%
Distribution of Gains		
Gains to Tribune	−$0.6	−29.5%
Gains to Times Mirror	$2.8	129.5%

a portion ($31.7 percent) of the combined Tribune company, and consequently share in that decrease in market value ($0.3 billion). Consequently, the Tribune stockholders absorb a $0.6 billion decrease in value. The Times Mirror stockholders experience a total gain of $2.8 billion, which is the value of the cash ($2.7 billion) and Tribune stock ($4.1 billion) offset by their proportion of the postmerger loss of value (−$0.3 billion) and the premerger value ($3.7 billion).

Table 7.15 shows a case where the market reacts optimistically to the acquisition as the postmerger market values rises to $18.7 billion. As above, the Tribune paid $6.8 billion in cash and stocks for Times Mirror resulting in a net postmerger value of $11.9 billion or a $2.2 billion gain when compared to the Tribune's

T A B L E 7.15

Tests of Merger Performance—Optimistic Scenario ($ Billion)

	Market Caps	Proportions
Premerger		
Tribune	$ 9.7	72.4%
Times Mirror	3.7	27.6%
Total	$13.4	100.0%
Postmerger		
Combined value	$18.7	
Cash paid to Times Mirror shareholders	2.7	
Stock paid to Times Mirror shareholders	4.1	
Remainder	$11.9	
Tribune premerger	9.7	
Gain from merger		$2.2
Portion to Tribune (237/347 shares outstanding)		$1.5	68.3%
Portion to Times Mirror (110/347 shares outstanding)		$0.7	31.7%
Distribution of Gains		
Gains to Tribune	$1.5	28.4%
Gains to Times Mirror	$3.8	71.6%

premerger market capitalization of $9.7 billion. The Times Mirror stockholders share in this gain via the Tribune shares they now hold (or 31.7%) to the extent of $0.7 billion, which leaves $1.5 billion gain in value for the Tribune stockholders.

Comments

We have used the DCF valuation models to illustrate a methodology for analyzing mergers. The particulars of this case are less important than the approach utilized. The important generalization is that the mergers must make sense in terms of the economics of the industry. The firm should also be sound from a social standpoint—it should intensify competition rather than dampen it.

The use of historical data in valuation is only a starting point. The most valuable part of a valuation exercise is the business economics analysis of the industry dynamics and the firm's position in it. This provides a basis for the judgments on value driver levels. It also establishes a framework for strategic and competitive policy planning. The appropriate model for a synergistic merger requires analysis of its impact on the combined firm instead of the acquired firm alone. We demonstrate that for a plausible valuation model only modest improvements in the value drivers are sufficient to recover the premium paid. The results would depend on the underlying business economics of the transaction.

NEGOTIATIONS

Much has been written about negotiations. Frequently real estate examples are used. Merger analysis provides a more fruitful area to discuss the nature of negotiation. The reason is that considerable data can be developed on the history and future prospects of the companies involved. Critical is an understanding of how the data should be interpreted in relation to the competitive position of the firm in its industry.

Usually some market price data are available on transactions that are comparable at least to some degree. Even for targets that are privately owned, some guidance can be obtained from publicly traded companies. Comparisons can be made with respect to growth rates, profit measures such as EBITDA, ROCE (return on capital employed), ROIC (return on invested capital), the q ratio (market capitalization of debt and equity divided by the relevant amount of capital invested), MVA (market value added—subtracting the denominator of the q ratio from its numerator), EG (economic gain) or EP (economic profit) or EVA (economic value added)—all three are one-period measures of MVA, and RTS (returns to shareholders measured by the sum of capital gains and dividends with reference to a base market value).

Analysis can be made of revenue growth, cost structures, investment rates, employment growth, and quality of top management and employees. This represents a form of due diligence on the managerial, cultural, and financial dimensions of the combining companies. The sample items listed in this and the above paragraph are all reflected in the spreadsheet financial projections we described earlier in the chapter. We have described the value drivers as growth in revenues, operating profit margin, tax rates, investment requirements, free cash flow patterns, and the applicable cost of capital. We have shown how the value drivers establish current enterprise value estimates. These procedures provide useful inputs for negotiation discussions. They facilitate an informed basis for sensitivity analysis. Different judgments about future revenue growth rates, cost structures, investment requirements, competitive pressures, and cost of capital can be instantly calculated. This kind of exercise can provide some boundaries for value estimates. Also a planning framework is created for the future operations of the combined firms. In addition, a basis is established for a continuous postmerger review or audit performance in relation to projections. These reviews can contribute to the strategic planning efforts for continued performance improvements and value enhancements.

The area of M&As (mergers and acquisitions, alliances, and joint ventures) offers attractive opportunities for principled negotiation. By this we mean using standards of fairness in seeking to meet the interests of both parties. Since firms are being combined, it is important to produce agreements that build good future relationships.

The literature on negotiation offers guides for negotiation strategy and techniques. A basic requirement is to start with good preparation. We need a strategic vision. The firm needs to assess its strengths and weaknesses. The firm identifies the resources and capabilities required and what it brings to the deal.

A key consideration in buying a company is realistic identification of gains, synergies, and their sources, whether in revenue enhancement and/or cost reductions and/or possibilities for new and strengthened strategies. This is the basis for developing a solid quantification of the firm's BATNA (best alternative to a negotiated agreement). In merger valuation, quantification of BATNA is facilitated. Value relationships can be analyzed with references to comparable companies and comparable transactions. The active markets for buying and selling business entities and segments provide quantitative information. All the parties can benefit. For the buyer, it is imperative that the premiums paid have a sound foundation in estimates of synergy and savings.

SUMMARY

Valuation is central to the merger process. Fundamentally, firms should merge only if the value to shareholders will be enhanced. Target firms usually justify resisting hostile mergers by claiming that a proposed merger undervalues the potential of the firm. Meanwhile, bidding firms must determine a value of the target that is sufficiently high for the target to accept, but not so high as to eliminate the anticipated gains from the merger. This analysis becomes even more complex in stock-for-stock transactions, where bidders must analyze how much of the combined company will be owned by bidder and target shareholders.

The comparable companies and comparable transactions approaches seek to determine value based on the historical values and ratios of similar companies and acquisitions. These methods are especially useful for valuing companies that are not publicly traded. The comparables methodology can also provide a useful checkpoint for other valuation methods. However, judgment is required.

The most widely accepted valuation method is the discounted cash flow method. The DCF methodology values the firm as the sum of the free cash flow of the firm discounted at the appropriate weighted average cost of capital. This method can use spreadsheet projections. In addition, analysis can yield systematic relationships between revenues, cost structures, and investment requirements. These can produce estimates of the key drivers of value: revenue growth, operating income, effective tax rate, financing costs, working capital, fixed investment requirements, the applicable cost of capital, and the length of time over which the firm can achieve a competitive advantage. The use of these key value drivers facilitates the use of computers in achieving effective sensitivity analysis.

Valuation is inherently a judgment. It combines science and art. The art of doing valuation is to make an initial estimate based on rational, best judgment estimates of the determinants (value drivers) of value. Then based on alternative scenarios, a sensitivity analysis of the relationship between valuations to the input value drivers is made. The process itself can improve understanding of the firm's competitive position and lead to value enhancements.

The valuation techniques introduced in this chapter are equally applicable to divestitures (Chapter 8) and share repurchases (Chapter 9). These techniques are effective tools that allow a seller to value a division, subsidiary, or line of business. Additionally, a company can perform a "self-valuation" to determine its own self-assessed, intrinsic value compared with the current market price. If the intrinsic value exceeds the current market price, a share repurchase opportunity exists.

QUESTIONS AND PROBLEMS

7.1 Fill in the blanks below, and discuss your results.

Panel A

Comparable Companies Ratios
(Company W Is Compared with Companies TA, TB, and TC)

Ratio	Company TA	Company TB	Company TC	Average
Enterprise market value/ revenues	2.0	2.5	1.0	_____
Enterprise market value/ EBITDA	20	10	5	_____
Enterprise market value/ free cash flows	30	20	25	_____

Panel B

Application of Valuation Ratios to Company W

Actual Recent Data for Company W		Average Ratio	Indicated Enterprise Market Value
Revenues	= $200	_____	_____
EBITDA	= $10	_____	_____
Free cash flows	= $5	_____	_____
		Average =	_____

7.2 *a.* The risk-free rate is 5.5 percent, and the market price of risk is 7 percent. The firm's beta is 1.2. What is the firm's cost of equity using CAPM?

b. The firm has an A bond rating and a cost of debt of 8 percent. Its tax rate is 40 percent. Its capital structure is 40 percent debt and 60 percent equity. What is the firm's weighted average cost of capital (WACC)?

7.3 A firm has free cash flows of $1000 which are expected to grow at a 4 percent rate to perpetuity. Its cost of capital is 9 percent. What is an estimate of its present value?

SOLUTIONS TO QUESTIONS AND PROBLEMS

7.1

Panel A

Comparable Companies Ratios
(Company W Is Compared with Companies TA, TB, and TC)

Ratio	Company TA	Company TB	Company TC	Average
Enterprise market value/ revenues	2.0	2.5	1.0	1.8
Enterprise market value/ EBITDA	20	10	5	11.7
Enterprise market value/ free cash flows	30	20	25	25.0

Panel B

Application of Valuation Ratios to Company W

Actual Recent Data for Company W		Average Ratio	Indicated Enterprise Market Value
Revenues	= $200	1.8	$360
EBITDA	= $10	11.7	117
Free cash flows	= $5	25.0	125
			Average = $201

The average ratios are based on multiples that differ

widely for the different companies. The average ratios are therefore not dependable guides to comparable values. Additional methods would have to be employed to improve the estimated enterprise value of company W.

7.2

   a. Cost of equity = 5.5% + 7%(1.2) = 13.9%

   b. WACC = 13.9%(0.60) + 8%(1 − 0.40)(0.40) = 10.26%

7.3 Use the constant growth formula. The numerator will be $1000(1 + 0.04). The denominator will be 0.09 − 0.04. Its value would be $1040 divided by 0.05, which is $20,800.

CHAPTER EIGHT

Restructuring and Financial Engineering

In previous chapters, we have described alternative paths to growth. In this chapter, we discuss methods of reorganizing the assets, operations, and ownership structures of the firm to enhance organizational values.

RESTRUCTURING

The main forms of restructuring are (1) divestitures, (2) equity carve-outs, (3) spin-offs, and (4) tracking stocks. We discuss each in turn.

Divestitures

Divestitures represent the sale of a segment of a company to another entity. The divestiture by a seller generally represents focusing on a narrower core of activities. The buying firm seeks to strengthen its strategic programs. In April 1998, Cooper Industries sold its auto parts business, Cooper Automotive, to Federal Mogul. This transaction reflected competitive forces in the auto business. Cost-cutting pressure from auto manufacturers pushed the auto parts makers to deliver complete systems of parts, rather than individual items. Cooper's strategy was to focus on its strengths in tools and hardware, along with electrical products. Federal Mogul had a 5-year strategic acquisition program that would enable it to manufacture complete engine systems. In addition, the crown jewel of the deal was Cooper's brake and friction product business, which would help Federal Mogul become a major supplier of brake systems.

The key reason for divestitures is that they are worth more as a part of the buyer's organization than as a part of the seller's. Often the seller seeks to shed unrelated activities or activities it feels that it is not managing effectively. The buyer is seeking to further strengthen an existing business. In a soundly conceived divestiture, the stock prices of both companies increase.

In January 1979, Hershey Foods completed the acquisition of Friendly Ice Cream Corporation (FIC) for approximately $165 million. FIC was a chain of moderately priced restaurants, primarily located in the northeastern part of the United States. Unfortunately, for years there was very limited synergy creation and virtually no cross-training of key executives from Hershey's other lines of business. In the mid-to-late 1980s, Friendly's growth started to sputter and no one knew how to correct it. Fortunately, a restauranteur came along and offered to buy FIC. Working with Friendly's latest strategic plan, the management at Hershey Foods valued (using the techniques from Chapter 7) the Friendly Ice Cream business. The offer put on the table by the restauranteur exceeded Hershey's view of the economic potential of continuing to run the business. A deal was quickly struck.

Equity Carve-outs and Spin-offs

In an equity carve-out, a company sells up to 20 percent of the stock of a segment. Notable recent deals include the equity carve-outs of General Motors (GM) and of Du Pont. In 1998, Delphi was created by a decision of the GM board of directors, and it was incorporated in September in Delaware. On January 1, 1999, GM supplied Delphi with the assets and liabilities that had been the Delphi Automotive Systems segment of GM. In February, an equity carve-out of 17.7 percent of the Delphi stock was made, with GM holding the remaining 82.3 percent. In the following April, all the remaining shares of Delphi were distributed in a spin-off as a dividend of 0.7 share of Delphi per share of GM common stock. Upon completion of the spin-off, executives of GM on Delphi's board resigned. Delphi became a fully independent, publicly traded company.

The Du Pont spin-off of Conoco involved a share exchange. In its initial equity carve-out, Du Pont sold 150 million A shares at $23, raising $3.45 billion. The spin-off of the remainder of Conoco was made through a share exchange at the option of the Du Pont shareholders, who would receive 2.95 shares of class B stock of Conoco. Each share of the class B stock carried five votes; class A shares had only one vote per share.

The two examples illustrate the general characteristics of equity carve-outs. The Conoco carve-out and spin-off created a separate petroleum company and focused Du Pont more on the chemical business. Du Pont raised a substantial sum in the process. In addition to the $3.45 billion from the initial public offering (IPO), Conoco repaid debt of $9.22 billion to Du Pont, and in the share exchange, Du Pont received $11.95 billion share value for a total of $24.62 billion on an after-tax basis.

So in the equity carve-out, substantial funds can be raised. The parent can focus more directly on its core business. Each segment can improve efficiency by focus. In the segment spun off, performance of managers can be measured directly. Compensation can be tied to performance. The literature argues that motivation and incentives can be strengthened.

Tracking Stocks

Tracking stocks are separate classes of the common stock of the parent corporation. They were first issued in 1984 when GM used a tracking stock to buy EDS, creating a class of common identified as E stock (called a letter stock at the time). Similarly, in 1985, when GM acquired Hughes Aircraft, a new class called H was used. In May 1991, U.S. Steel Company became USX for the steel business and created a USX-Marathon stock for the oil business (called a target stock at the time). In September 1992, USX created a third tracking stock when it sold shares of the USX-Delhi group stock in an IPO.

Each tracking stock is regarded as common stock of the parent for voting purposes.

The tracking stock company is usually assigned its own name. DLJ calls its tracking stock DLJdirect. Georgia Pacific created Timber Co. Ziff-Davis formed ZDNet. The special characteristics of Internet companies have stimulated the use of tracking stocks. Internet companies trade at high valuations, which makes it difficult for "old economy" companies to compete with or to acquire such rivals. This has led a number of them to establish or acquire interests in separately traded entities for their e-commerce businesses. Examples are Disney/Infoseek and AT&T/Excite@home.

Tracking stock is similar to a spin-off in that financial results of the parent and the tracking stock companies are reported separately. But in the tracking stock relationship, the board of the parent continues to control the activities of the tracking segment; the spin-off becomes an independent company. Tracking stock companies trade separately so dividends paid to shareholders of each company can be based on their individual cash flows. The performance and compensation of managers can be measured at the tracking stock company level. Managerial compensation can be based on performance of the tracking stock company and its stock price behavior. One of the criticisms of tracking stocks is that the subsidiary is still subject to control of the parent.

THE CHOICE OF RESTRUCTURING METHODS

Spin-offs are best when the main business of the parent is not likely to make substantial contributions to the segment. Clearly, GM's automotive business did not inherently contribute to the computer processing and data analysis business of EDS, which subsequently was spun off. In some cases, a conflict of interest may be involved. This was the reason that Lucent was one of the spin-offs in the 1995–1996 split-up of AT&T. A major part of Lucent was the old Western Electric, which manufactured central station telephone exchange equipment as well as other products sold to the operating companies, which after 1984 had become competitors to their former parent. Also, a segment with high margins and high growth can command higher stock price multiples when its performance might be made less certain by less favorable prospects for the parent. The converse could be true as well.

Tracking stocks can also isolate subsidiaries with high profit and growth opportunities. Tracking stock subsidiaries can benefit from the strong financial position of the parent. Tracking stocks may be useful for companies with segments that share significant synergies. If a parent of a tracking stock company has losses, overall corporate taxes can be reduced. Since the parent continues to control the tracking stock subsidiary, potential conflicts of interest raise some concerns.

CHANGING OWNERSHIP STRUCTURES

The most complete form of ownership change is represented by taking a public company private through a leveraged buyout (LBO). When the former managers are the prime movers in the transaction, it is called a management buyout (MBO). The basic idea is to raise the necessary funds to purchase control from the existing public shareholders, using financing with a large percentage debt component, providing management with a high percentage of the remaining small equity base. A turnaround was usually involved in the sense that fundamental operating changes were made to increase profitability and value.

Highly leveraged transactions have been used prior to the 1980s, when LBOs became substantial in dollar volume. The high degree of diversification activity that took place during the conglomerate merger movement of the 1960s resulted in many firms having segments that did not receive informed guidance by top management. During the 1980s, LBOs were one of the methods for unwinding the diversification of the 1960s.

Table 8.1 presents data on the value of LBO transactions in relation to total merger activity between 1982 and 1999. In the 1986–1989 period, LBOs represented more than 20 percent of the total dollar value of completed mergers. While the $62 billion value of LBOs in 1999 was almost back to the $65.7 billion peak in 1989, the LBO percentage of total mergers was still only 4.4 percent. As Table 8.1 suggests, LBOs went through three distinct periods.

TABLE 8.1

Value of LBO Transactions ($ Billion)

Year	Value of Total Completed Mergers	Leveraged Buyouts	% of Total Mergers
1982	$ 60.7	$ 3.5	5.8
1983	52.7	4.5	8.5
1984	126.1	18.7	14.8
1985	145.5	19.7	13.5
1986	204.9	45.2	22.1
1987	178.3	36.2	20.3
1988	238.5	47.0	19.7
1989	323.9	65.7	20.3
1990	207.5	15.2	7.3
1991	141.2	7.0	5.0
1992	124.9	9.6	7.7
1993	178.2	11.0	6.2
1994	276.9	13.0	4.7
1995	384.8	20.9	5.4
1996	560.2	29.0	5.2
1997	768.9	28.7	3.7
1998	1323.3	41.0	3.1
1999	1393.9	62.0	4.4
Yearly Averages			
1982–1985	$96.3	$11.6	12.1
1986–1989	236.4	48.5	20.5
1990–1992	157.9	10.6	6.7
1993–1995	280.0	15.0	5.3
1996–1999	1011.6	40.2	4.0

Source: *Mergers & Acquisitions,* almanac issues.

The 1982–1989 Period

The first period was from 1982 to 1989, when strong growth occurred. Many segments were being shed by companies with valuations in the range of 3 to 5 times EBITDA. With new management or previous management energized and motivated by its substantial equity positions, efficiency and profitability were improved. These LBOs were mainly in consumer nondurable goods industries with stable cash flows, such as food and retailing. The Safeway LBO in 1987 is an example. Within 3 to 4 years, debt was reduced from as high as 90 percent of total capitalization from the stable cash flows.

With profitability restored and attractive growth opportunities, a company could be sold in a secondary initial public offering (SIPO). The data show that a substantial portion of the proceeds received were used to further reduce the debt to almost normal industry standards. The value of shares held by management had greatly increased. While debt was substantial in the initial LBO financing and provided valuable tax shields to the company, the main motivation was to provide management with the incentives from owning a substantial portion of the relatively small equity base. Management ownership of equity typically moved from 1 to 2 percent to as high as 15 to 20 percent.

Debt also played a significant role in the initial stage of taking the company private. Often a commercial bank or insurance company provided the senior debt financing often secured, making it a relatively low-risk investment. The other sources between common equity and the senior debt were called *mezzanine financing*, consisting of senior unsecured debt, subordinated debt, and preferred stock. Sometimes the mezzanine financing required some options to buy equity as compensation for their junior position.

LBO activity was highly successful during this initial period from 1982 to 1989. The numerous empirical studies agreed in finding annual returns above 25 percent, with many even higher. The reasons for the success in the early stages of the LBO movement can be enumerated. One, segments were available at relatively low valuation multiples. Two, the firms and segments taken over in LBOs and MBOs were not performing up to their potentials. Three, managers were given substantial equity stakes in entities whose performance could be measured and evaluated as independent entities. Four, investors and managers benefited from harvesting the gains in secondary public offerings or sales to other companies.

The 1991–1992 Period

The successes during this initial period attracted a substantial flow of capital into the activity. The large pool of funds from both operating firms as strategic buyers as well as financial buyers reached several hundred billion. Well-known financial buyers with capital to invest greater than $1 billion included Kohlberg, Kravis & Roberts; Morgan Stanley Capital Partners; E.M. Warburg, Pincus & Company; Clayton, Dubilier & Rice; Thomas H. Lee Company; GS Capital Venture Partners; The Blackstone Group; Forstmann Little & Company; and Hicks, Muse, Tate & Furst. But there were many others as well, so that the total funds available for LBOs far exceeded the opportunities for profitable investments. This competition pushed valuation multiples from the 3 to 5 times EBITDA to 10 and higher; often the difference between the winning bid and others was exceedingly high. In addition, the unwinding of the diversification activities of the 1960s sharply reduced the opportunities. The demise of the leading investment banking firm, Drexel Burnham Lambert, was disruptive. Legislation required that investments in below-investment-grade debt securities (junk bonds) by financial institutions such as the savings and loan companies had to be marked down to market. This aggravated the already adverse developments in the junk bond market. As shown in Table 8.1, leveraged buyout activity in 1991 and 1992 dropped below $10 billion per year.

The Post-1992 Period

The third period of LBO activity began after 1992. The economy experienced sustained economic growth, stock prices moved continuously higher, interest rate levels and financing availability were favorable. This more favorable economic environment helped stimulate the resurgence of LBOs. Innovative approaches were developed by LBO sponsor companies and financial buyers. LBOs were applied increasingly beyond industries with stable earnings to high growth technology-driven industries.

The financial structure of LBO transactions after 1992 moderated the excesses of the late 1980s. With respect to the prices paid, the price-to-EBITDA ratios moved down from 8 to 10 and above level toward the 5 to 7 range. Compared with equity ratios as low as 5 to 10 percent, equity in the initial capital structures moved up to 20 to 30 percent. The ratio of cash flows to interest and other financial requirements moved up to 2 or better. This contrasts with the deals in the late 1980s, when asset sales in the first year of the LBO were necessary to meet financial obligations and interest payments were in the form of more subordinated debt, an arrangement called *PIK* (payment in kind).

The financial press provides numerous cases of innovative approaches by LBO sponsors. For example, Clayton, Dubilier & Rice Inc. (CD&R) has emphasized a partnership relationship with members who have considerable previous managerial experience. It structures the transaction, owns the majority of the equity, controls the company it acquires, provides experienced executives, and establishes management incentives by linking compensation to performance. CD&R has emphasized buying undermanaged segments of larger companies to achieve a turnaround. Financial buyers may also develop joint deals with corporate strategic buyers to purchase companies on a leveraged basis.

The increased participation by commercial banks is described in detail in a comprehensive survey by Allen (1996). He describes the increased use of syndication of high leveraged transactions to other banks and the development of a highly liquid secondary loan trading market. He emphasizes a continued close client-focused relationship by the commercial bank. This embraces not only LBO and M&A activity but also the broad gamut of financial services the client company may require. He also describes a range of capital structure strategies tailored to the characteristics of the transaction. Similar innovative approaches have been developed by investment banking firms and other financial intermediaries.

Financial buyers (LBO sponsors, investment banks, commercial banks) have faced increased competition from corporate buyers. All have adopted new strategies. One is the leveraged buildup. The leveraged buildup identifies a fragmented industry characterized by relatively small firms. Buyout firms based on partners with industry expertise purchase a firm as a platform for further leveraged acquisitions in the same industry (Allen, 1996, p. 27). They seek to build firms with strong management, developing revenue growth while reducing costs, with the objectives of improved margins, increased cash flow, and increased valuations.

Requirements for a Successful LBO

In both the early 1980s and after 1992, LBOs have earned superior returns to investors in all stages. (1) The most important reason is the improvement in operations, reducing cost and increasing cash flows. This is achieved by bringing in management with experience and competence in the operations of the company. (2) The percentage of equity ownership by management strengthened management incentives. (3) Valuations in the LBO purchase transaction must be 5 to 7 times of EBITDA. (4) Higher percentage of equity in financial structures provides greater flexibility in making the additional investments that may be required. (5) Financial buyers may assist in formulating strategies and providing managerial expertise.

LBOs guided by these principles can achieve returns to investors higher than returns from broad stock indexes such as the S&P 500.

Leveraged Recapitalizations

Substantial ownership changes also take place in leveraged recapitalizations. Leveraged recapitalizations substitute for the acquisition of a company that would create substantial goodwill whose write-off would burden reported future earnings. A typical pattern is to issue a large amount of debt whose proceeds are used to pay a large cash dividend to existing stockholders. The cash dividend may be in excess of the preactivity market price of the stock. Essentially, a substantial stock buyback has taken place for the shareholders. The result is a highly leveraged company with a debt-to-equity ratio as high as 5 to 1, whose equity shares sell at a small fraction of their preactivity level. These shares are referred to as *stubs*. Existing management may take additional shares of common stock in lieu of the cash dividend payments, substantially increasing their ownership fraction. Thus, the ownership control has been substantially changed without creating the requirement of future goodwill write-offs.

Another variation is for a financial buyer to become the majority owner. As before, the target company issues a large amount of debt, whose proceeds are used to pay a cash dividend to existing shareholders or used in a stock buyback program. The financial buyer acquires sufficient shares to own 80 percent with 20 percent owned by the original shareholders. The deal can be structured so that from an accounting standpoint, the transaction is a recapitalization of the target, with no goodwill at the target level. If the financial buyer uses a new shell company as an acquisition vehicle, it may record the goodwill.

In both of the examples described above, the transaction can avoid the creation of goodwill that will reduce the reported earnings of the subject company. So the leveraged recapitalization is an alternative to an outright acquisition or merger as a method of changing ownership control.

Dual-Class Recapitalizations

In dual-class recapitalizations (DCRs), firms create a second class of common stock with inferior voting rights and higher dividend payments. An illustrative DCR creates class A shares with one vote per share, but with a higher dividend rate. The class B shares have a lower dividend rate, but can cast multiple votes, as high as 10 per share. As a result of a DCR, the control group will own about 60 percent of the common stock voting rights, but have a claim of only about 25 percent of the dividends paid. Often the control group represents founding families or their descendants with two or more of the top executives related by either blood or marriage. Examples of well-known firms that have employed dual-class recapitalizations in the past include American Fructose, Chris Craft, Church & Dwight, Helena Curtis, Hershey Foods, J.M. Smucker, and Wrigley.

The main reason for DCRs is for top management to maintain control so that long-term programs can be pursued. The pressure to show improving results quarter by quarter is reduced. If the operations of the firm were relatively complicated, it would be especially difficult to evaluate managerial performance. Another reason is that managers develop firm-specific capabilities. The managers would be subject to the risk that outside shareholders would support an acquisition offer before the longer-term plans have come to fruition. Shareholder approval is required for a DCR. Apparently, the higher dividend and the prospect of higher future stock values result in shareholder approval.

Another Hershey Foods example is illustrative of dual-stock recapitalization motives. As mentioned in Chapter 3, in the mid-1980s Hershey Foods wanted to expand their business via acquisition. Numerous companies were identified as potential target companies. Each of these target companies carried an estimated price tag of over $1 billion. Hershey Foods has a unique ownership structure in that its founder, Milton S. Hershey, left a trust for the benefit of the Milton S. Hershey School. The provisions of the trust stated that Hershey Foods must remain under the control of the trust. In the mid-1980s, the trust's ownership slipped to slightly over 50 percent. In addition, the trust did not have excess cash available to participate in an equity offering to maintain their 50 percent interest, and Hershey Foods had only $300–$400 million of unused debt capacity.

Without the ability to issue additional equity or finance the deal with debt, the board and management team decided that a dual-class recapitalization would alleviate one barrier of expansion. Each common stockholder was offered an even exchange of one share of publicly traded common stock for a super voting (10 votes per share) Class B share of stock. The common stock would continue to carry only one vote, but pay a 10 percent higher dividend. The Milton S. Hershey Trust converted a number of its common shares to the super voting class B shares, while most common stockholders held their common shares and received a 10 percent increase in dividends. The Trust secured over 70 percent of the total corporate votes while holding just over 50 percent of the shares. As a result, Hershey could have issued almost $2 billion of added common stock before encroaching on the 50 percent majority ownership interest of the Hershey Trust. It also provided an excellent takeover defense (see Chapter 10) since through this dual-class recapitalization, the board and a management-friendly Milton Hershey Trust controlled an even larger portion of Hershey Foods.

Empirical studies support the value-increasing motives of DCRs. Compared with LBO firms, DCRs achieve higher growth rates in sales and number of employees. The DCRs have higher ratios of R&D expenditures to sales. They also use a higher percentage of their cash flows for capital expenditures than the LBO firms. Dual-class firms have lower leverage ratios and do not change them as a consequence of the recapitalization. A large proportion of the dual-class firms sell more equity following the recapitalization. On balance, it appears that the superior voting shares are used by the control group to improve firm performance.

THE USE OF ESOPs

ESOPs are employee stock ownership plans that invest in the securities of the sponsoring employer firm. ESOPs are defined contribution employee benefit pension plans that invest at least 50 percent of the assets in the common shares of the sponsoring corporation. ESOPs are stock bonus plans or combined stock bonus plans and money purchase plans which invest primarily in the employer securities. The plans may receive stock or cash, which is used to buy stock.

The ESOP Association (*www.esopassociation.org*), headquartered in Washington, D.C., estimates that for the year 2000 there were about 11,500 ESOPs covering some 8.5 million employees. During most of the 1990s, there were about 10,000 ESOPs. Most ESOPs are leveraged, using borrowed funds to purchase employer securities held by the ESOP trustee. The ESOP Association estimates that 1500 companies are 100 percent owned by the ESOP. About 4 percent of ESOP companies are unionized. In 1999, ESOPs owned approximately $500 billion in sponsored stock.

ESOPs have been used in three major ways. (1) Owners of privately held firms can achieve tax-free liquidity, maintaining control of the firm. (2) ESOPs offer the opportunity for tax-advantaged financing. (3) ESOPs have been used as a takeover defense.

Tax-Free Liquidity

An example will best convey how an owner of a private company can sell a substantial portion of the firm's equity tax-free. Let's assume that John Smith is the 100 percent owner of Acme

Company, which represents his entire estate in case of death. At his death, his estate would be forced to sell the company to pay the estate taxes. Smith has received an offer to buy his company by a strategic buyer in a similar line of business. Because Smith is only 55 years old, he wants to continue to operate his company. But he recognizes the need for additional liquidity.

An ESOP can come to his rescue. Acme Company has received a professional appraisal of $6 million; Acme has 300,000 shares of stock outstanding. An ESOP is created with all the employees of Acme as beneficiaries. The ESOP borrows $2 million from a financial intermediary. The ESOP uses the funds to buy 100,000 shares of Acme stock from Smith. The loan to the ESOP is guaranteed by Acme Company, secured by the 100,000 shares held in trust. Acme Company will make ESOP contributions on an amortized basis to cover both interest and principal by the end of 10 years.

Smith has received $2 million in cash. If these funds are invested in the securities of other U.S. corporations within 12 months, the proceeds are not taxable to Smith. This tax-free rollover is allowable under a 1984 tax law if the ESOP owns at least 30 percent of the firm's stock. As the loan is repaid, the Acme shares belonging to the ESOP trust are allocated to the account of each individual employee participating in the plan. The advantage to Smith is that he has achieved a nontaxable $2 million which he can invest in a diversified portfolio.

Tax Advantages

Acme Company can deduct dividends paid on the ESOP shares held by the trust if they are used to repay ESOP debt. Another tax advantage relates to excess pension asset reversions. In 1986, an excise tax was placed on reversions of excess assets from the defined benefit plan. If the excess pension assets are placed in an ESOP, the excise tax is lower.

ESOPs as a Takeover Defense

The use of ESOPs as a takeover defense is illustrated by a leading case example. In 1988, Shamrock Holdings, the investment vehicle for part of the Disney family, made an offer for the Polaroid Corporation chartered in Delaware. A Delaware anti-takeover law provided that if the management of a company resisted an offer, the hostile bidder would be required to obtain 85 percent of the shares outstanding. Shortly after the Shamrock bid, Polaroid established an ESOP, placing 15 percent of its shares in an ESOP trust. Since management controls the trust and its voting of shares, Shamrock was unable to obtain the 85 percent acceptance of the offer. Shamrock contested the Polaroid action, but lost all its legal appeals. Many other companies announced ESOPs shortly after the Polaroid-Shamrock decision.

Evaluation of ESOPs

When Congress adopted ESOP legislation in 1974, it was persuaded by arguments that stock ownership by employees would reduce their conflicts with management. U.S. workers would become owners of common stock and have a second income from cash dividends. At a minimum, it was argued that worker productivity would increase and company performance would improve.

In 1987, the General Accounting Office (GAO) reviewed prior studies of ESOPs and corporate performance. None of the studies reviewed found significant gains in either profitability or productivity. Only one of the studies reported a significant improvement in sales growth. Later studies of ESOP performance found mixed results. United Airlines adopted an ESOP in July 1994, but flight attendants were unwilling to participate because they felt that the pay cuts required were too large. The ESOP at United has not been successful in avoiding continuing conflicts over wages. Avis set up a 100 percent ESOP in 1987, but employees were not granted board seats or voting rights. A 100 percent ESOP plan was adopted at Weirton Steel Corporation in 1984. At Northwestern Steel & Wire Co., employees accepted pay cuts to obtain 59 percent ownership and one-half of the board seats in a 1987 ESOP. Worker conflicts were not avoided in the two steel companies.

One problem is that management has been unwilling to grant employees full shareholder rights. Management has maintained control of the trusts that administer the plans.

Charges have been made that ESOPs have been used by management as instruments for increasing their control.

The academic studies of ESOPs have produced mixed results. ESOPs have the potential for improving worker productivity, and individual examples can be cited as evidence of spectacular successes. But the general evidence is inconclusive.

SUMMARY

Restructuring can increase value. The main forms of restructuring are divestitures, equity carve-outs, spin-offs, and tracking stocks. Divestitures move resources to the higher-value users. Equity carve-outs raise funds for the parent firm and prepare the way for the spin-offs to shareholders of the remaining shares. Tracking stocks result in separate reporting, but the parent continues to control the tracking segment.

Changed ownership structures include LBOs, leveraged recapitalizations, and dual-class recapitalizations. LBOs take a company private, make initial heavy use of debt financing, usually involve an improvement in operations, and increase the ownership position of management to strengthen motivation. Leveraged recapitalizations use substantial debt increases to make large cash dividends or share repurchases; management ownership positions are increased. A financial buyer is often involved in LBOs and leveraged recapitalizations. Dual-class recapitalizations provide top management with magnified voting rights and the other shareholders with larger claims to dividends to support programs with longer-term payoffs.

The argument for employee stock ownership is that as part owners employees have a greater stake in the firm's profitability. But ESOPs do not provide direct stock ownership. Dividends and voting rights are passed through only with respect to shares actually allocated to the accounts of participants. Participants typically do not receive any distribution of securities from the plan until they separate from service.

ESOPs can help the owners of privately held companies cash out some of their holdings. The funds received are not taxable if ESOPs hold at least 30 percent of the shares and the funds are invested in U.S. corporations within 12 months.

REFERENCES

Allen, Jay R., "LBOs—The Evolution of Financial Structures and Strategies," *Journal of Applied Corporate Finance*, 8, Winter 1996, pp. 18–29.

U.S. General Accounting Office, *Employee Stock Ownership Plans: Little Evidence of Effects on Corporate Performance*, Washington, D.C., October 1987.

QUESTIONS AND PROBLEMS

8.1 Why would divestitures have a positive effect on stock prices of both the seller and the buyer?

8.2 How can companies gain by giving away a segment to their existing shareholders?

8.3 What do leverage recapitalizations accomplish for an investor group?

8.4 What does an LBO accomplish?

8.5 From the standpoint of shareholders, why are tracking stocks less valuable than stocks in a spin-off?

SOLUTIONS TO QUESTIONS AND PROBLEMS

8.1 The economic basis for divestitures is to move assets to companies for which the segments have greater value. The selling company benefits because the buyer values the segment at a higher level than the seller. The value increase can be shared between buyer and seller. Since the buyer has a relatively unique fit with the segment purchased, the value increase is less likely to result in a general bidding which pushes all the gains to the seller.

8.2 The spin-off is a tax-free dividend to shareholders. The dividend is of value to shareholders. A new entity has been created with its own management. The spin-off is usually publicly traded. Its new management may have the required expertise for improved performance. In a separate company, the improved performance can be measured and can result in rewards to its managers. Thus the incentives to management are strengthened. The company which has made the spin-off is more focused and thereby can improve its own performance as well.

8.3 The investor group can obtain control of a company without the necessity of a goodwill write-off of the premium paid.

8.4 When it is a segment of a company, it is a spin-off for cash to the parent. Management of the new firm has expertise. Its performance can be measured. Its stock ownership benefits from the increased value of the new company. Other forms of executive compensation can also be granted. When the segment goes public again, the value of shares held by management would reflect the performance improvements.

8.5 The parent continues to control the tracking stock subsidiary, but not the new spin-off entity. In creating a spin-off, the terms chosen by the parent may be more favorable to the parent than to the new entity. But potential conflicts of interest with a tracking stock subsidiary are also present in the creation, but continuing as well.

CHAPTER NINE

Cash Flows, Dividends, and Share Repurchases

Dividend policy deals with the issues of how much cash flow should be paid out to stockholders, what form to use, and how much is reinvested in the firm. In simplified models of pure theory, dividend policy is irrelevant. In the complexities of the real world, dividend policy can increase the value of a firm. The purpose of this chapter is to describe how the sound use of the firm's cash flows can enhance value for shareholders.

THE FACTUAL BACKGROUND ON DIVIDENDS AND SHARE REPURCHASES

Table 9.1 presents data on dividend payout patterns in the U.S. economy as a whole since 1960. The percent changes in after-tax profits, positive and negative, are much higher than for dividends. The patterns are summarized in Table 9.2. Clearly the volatility of profits is much greater than that for dividends. The mean percent profit changes in the positive direction are 44.6 percent greater than for dividends. The evidence shows that dividend payments increase only after some lag as profits increase.

Table 9.3 presents information of share repurchases in relation to the data on dividends. The percent share repurchase to dividends has risen from virtually nothing in 1980 to almost 75 percent in 1999. Between 1984 (when share repurchases

T A B L E 9.1

Dividend Payout Patterns, 1960–1999 ($ Billion)

Year	After-Tax Profits	Percent Change (After-Tax Profits)	Dividends	Percent Change (Dividends)	Dividend Payout (Percent)
1960	29.6		13.4		45
1961	30.6	3.38	13.9	3.73	45
1962	37.5	22.55	15.0	7.91	40
1963	41.4	10.40	16.2	8.00	39
1964	46.8	13.04	18.2	12.35	39
1965	55.0	17.52	20.2	10.99	37
1966	58.2	5.82	20.7	2.48	36
1967	56.8	−2.41	21.5	3.86	38
1968	57.0	0.35	23.5	9.30	41
1969	53.8	− 5.61	24.2	2.98	45
1970	46.9	−12.83	24.3	0.41	52
1971	57.0	21.54	25.0	2.88	44
1972	67.5	18.42	26.8	7.20	40
1973	74.3	10.07	29.9	11.57	40
1974	62.2	−16.29	33.2	11.04	53
1975	81.6	31.19	33.0	−0.60	40
1976	95.9	17.52	39.0	18.18	41
1977	117.5	22.52	44.8	14.87	38
1978	133.3	13.45	50.8	13.39	38
1979	133.9	0.45	57.5	13.19	43
1980	112.9	−15.68	64.1	11.48	57
1981	136.8	21.17	73.8	15.13	54
1982	137.1	0.22	76.2	3.25	56
1983	175.8	28.23	83.6	9.71	48
1984	214.6	22.07	91.0	8.85	42
1985	224.8	4.75	97.7	7.36	43
1986	193.0	−14.15	106.3	8.80	55
1987	218.2	13.06	112.2	5.55	51
1988	266.4	22.09	129.6	15.51	49
1989	252.8	−5.11	155.0	19.60	61
1990	260.9	3.20	165.5	6.77	63
1991	282.6	8.32	178.4	7.79	63
1992	308.4	9.13	185.5	3.98	60
1993	345.0	11.87	203.1	9.49	59
1994	386.7	12.09	234.9	15.66	61
1995	457.5	18.31	254.2	8.22	56
1996	502.7	9.88	297.7	17.11	59
1997	557.6	10.92	333.7	12.09	60
1998	541.7	−2.85	348.6	4.47	64
1999	589.1	8.75	364.7	4.62	62

TABLE 9.2

Relative Volatility, Profits, and Dividends

	Mean Percent Changes	
	Positives	**Negatives**
After-tax profits	13.30	−9.36
Dividends	9.20	−0.60

TABLE 9.3

Share Repurchase versus Cash Dividends, 1980–1999

Year	Dividends ($ billion)	Share Repurchase ($ billion)	% Share Repurchase to Dividends
1980	64.1	0.3	0.5
1981	73.8	0.6	0.8
1982	76.2	0.7	0.9
1983	83.6	6.8	8.1
1984	91.0	27.3	30.0
1985	97.7	20.3	20.8
1986	106.3	28.2	26.5
1987	112.2	55.0	49.0
1988	129.6	37.4	28.9
1989	155.0	63.7	41.1
1990	165.5	36.1	21.8
1991	178.4	20.4	11.4
1992	185.5	35.6	19.2
1993	203.1	38.3	18.9
1994	234.9	73.8	31.4
1995	254.2	99.5	39.1
1996	297.7	176.3	59.2
1997	333.7	181.8	54.5
1998	348.6	236.2	67.8
1999	364.7	245.4*	67.3

Growth Rates

1984–1998	10.10%	16.70%	
1992–1998	11.90%	40.30%	

Source: Department of Commerce, Bureau of Economic Analysis; Securities Data Company.
*Estimate.

began to be large) and 1999, the growth rate in share repurchases has been 16.7 percent per annum compared to 10 percent per annum for dividends. The growth rate of share repurchases has been even higher since 1992. For firms in the Standard and Poor's 500 index, the dollar amount of share repurchases exceeded dividends by 1998 (Liang and Sharpe, 1999).

It is useful to put these growth rates into perspective. Table 9.4 shows the compound annual growth rates in after-tax profits and dividends in relation to the economy as a whole. For most time segments, profits and dividends have grown faster than gross domestic product. This is particularly true since 1982. The growth in the consumer price index has been relatively low except for the decade between 1972 and 1982. But clearly both profits and dividends are propelled by the growth in the overall economy.

Despite the increasing importance of share repurchases, dividend payouts have increased over time, as shown in Table 9.5. In the 1960s and 1970s dividend payouts were in the 40 percent range. Between 1983 and 1990 payouts averaged 52 percent. For 1991 to 1999 payouts rose to 60 percent. Other evidence suggests that the number of firms paying dividends has sharply decreased (Fama and French, 2000). This results from the increase in the number of new firms whose need for funds to finance rapid growth precludes dividend payouts. In the older economy, mature firms have higher payouts as their internal needs for funds decline.

In Table 9.6, dividends plus share repurchases are related to after-tax profits. A strong upward trend is shown. In 1984, cash

TABLE 9.4

Compound Annual Growth Rates in Selected Series, 1960–1999

	1960–1966	1966–1972	1972–1982	1982–1990	1991–1999
GNP	6.97%	7.82%	10.07%	7.06%	8.87%
After-tax profits	11.93	2.50	7.34	8.38	9.62
Dividends	7.52	4.40	11.02	10.18	9.35
CPI	1.52	4.34	8.73	3.86	2.23

T A B L E 9.5

Dividend Payout Patterns ($ Billion)

Year	After-Tax Profits	Dividends	Dividend Payout (Percent)
1960–1966	299.1	117.6	39
1967–1972	339.0	145.3	43
1973–1982	1085.5	502.3	46
1983–1990	1806.5	940.9	52
1991–1999	3971.3	2400.8	60

return to shareholders in the form of dividends plus share repurchases was 55 percent. By 1998, the percentage grew to 108 percent. This is a surprising result. How can firms as a whole pay out more than they earned? The answer is that cash flows are more relevant than after-tax profits. As the growth rates of firms in the mature segment of the economy slow, cash flows from working capital and depreciation increase. As firms grow rapidly, they have to invest in receivables, inventories, and equipment; with slower growth these investments are liquidated to some degree.

We have summarized the broad patterns in dividends and share repurchases. We next consider the factors that influenced cash payouts and the choice between dividends and share repurchases.

FACTORS INFLUENCING PAYOUTS

Many factors influence payouts. Some are legal requirements; others, institutional; still others, economic.

Investment Growth Opportunities

The single most important factor is an economic one. If the firm can earn more with the funds than its investors, it is better for the firm and its investors to keep the funds in the business. The concepts are illustrated in Table 9.7 and Fig. 9.1. The downward sloping line illustrates investment return opportunities.

T A B L E 9.6

Dividend plus Share Repurchases to After-Tax Profits, 1984–1999 ($ Billion)

Year	After-Tax Profits	Dividends	Share Repurchase	Total	Percent of After-Tax Profits
1984	214.6	91.0	27.3	118.3	55.13
1985	224.8	97.7	20.3	118.0	52.49
1986	193.0	106.3	28.2	134.5	69.69
1987	218.2	112.2	55.0	167.2	76.63
1988	266.4	129.6	37.4	167.0	62.69
1989	252.8	155.0	63.7	218.7	86.51
1990	260.9	165.5	36.1	201.6	77.27
1991	282.6	178.4	20.4	198.8	70.35
1992	308.4	185.5	35.6	221.1	71.69
1993	345.0	203.1	38.3	241.4	69.97
1994	386.7	234.9	73.8	308.7	79.83
1995	457.5	254.2	99.5	353.7	77.31
1996	502.7	297.7	176.3	474.0	94.29
1997	557.6	333.7	181.8	515.5	92.45
1998	541.7	348.6	236.2	584.8	107.96

T A B L E 9.7

Investment Returns

k	10%	10%	10%	10%	10%	10%	10%	10%	10%	10%	10%	10%	10%	12%	16%	24%
r	120%	110%	100%	90%	80%	70%	60%	50%	40%	30%	20%	10%	0%	−10%	−20%	−30%
Investment	0	10	20	30	40	50	60	70	80	90	100	110	120	130	140	150
MVA (incremental)		10.5	9.5	8.5	7.5	6.5	5.5	4.5	3.5	2.5	1.5	0.5	−0.5	−1.7	−3.1	−4.9
MVA (cumulative)		10.5	20.0	28.5	36.0	42.5	48.0	52.5	56.0	58.5	60.0	60.5	60.0	58.3	55.2	50.3
MVA + Investment		20.5	40.0	58.5	76.0	92.5	108.0	122.5	136.0	148.5	160.0	170.5	180.0	188.3	195.2	200.3

It represents a schedule developed by firms in their capital budgeting processes.

In Fig. 9.1 consider the line that represents projects ranked by their prospected returns. The cost of capital line is horizontal up to a point and then begins to rise, as discussed in Chap. 7 on valuation. In principle, the firm should invest $110 million where the return from the project just equals its applicable cost

FIGURE 9.1

Investment Returns

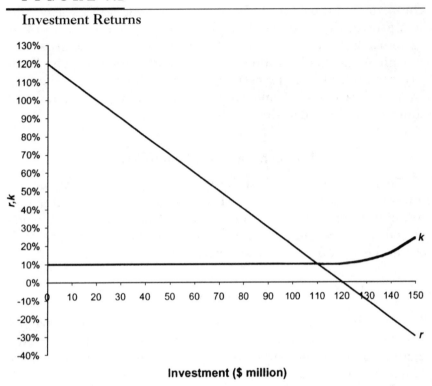

Investment ($ million)

of capital. Since the better projects earn more than the applicable cost of capital, for the projects as a group the average returns are greater than the cost of capital. The total dollar amount of net present value (NPV) added to the market worth of the firm is maximized for a total outlay for new projects of $110 million. For our example, the investment of $110 million will add $60.5 million to the value of the firm for that period.

If the cash available from operations of the firm were $120 million, as a first approximation the firm would invest $110 million and have $10 million available to return to investors for that time period. If the cash from operations were $80 million, the firm would need an additional $30 million of financing. If in subsequent periods new investment return schedules (capital budgets), with segments above the applicable cost of capital, economic value would be added to the firm in each time period. The firm would be said to have growth opportunities. It would be a growth firm and would be likely to pay out a low percentage of cash flows, or none at all, because of the value growth it is achieving. This is standard capital budgeting analysis. Cash payouts are linked to investment opportunities. This is the fundamental economic framework for formulating dividend and share repurchase decisions.

Uncertainty and Instability

If a firm is subject to instability and high uncertainty in its investment opportunities, it may modify the above pattern by retaining more earnings than an investment schedule for one period would call for. It would build up cushions for some periods and draw off them for other periods.

Tax Influences

Tax laws have impacts in a number of ways. Corporations pay taxes on their income. Cash returned to shareholders is taxed again. For example, suppose a corporation has income before taxes of $100 million. If its tax rate is 35 percent, it has $65 million left after taxes. If it paid out all this in dividends and its investors were subject to a 39 percent personal income tax, it would pay $25.35 million. Thus the total taxes paid on the $100 million would be $60.35 million or 60.35 percent. If the corporation paid the $65 million in the form of a share repurchase, its stockholders might be subject to only a 20 percent capital gains rate or $13 million, saving $12.35 million.

Shareholders obviously prefer to pay a capital gains tax rate to a higher ordinary personal income tax. So taxes influence the choice of cash dividends versus share repurchases. Alternatively if the firm can invest money to obtain a return greater than its cost of capital, its shareholders can achieve the capital gains rate in another way. Retained earnings or internal funds invested at a rate in excess of the firm's cost of capital will increase the firm's stock price over time. If the shareholders want the cash, they can sell an amount of stock equivalent to what the cash dividends would have been and pay a capital gains tax rather than ordinary personal income tax rates.

Costs of External Financing

So internal financing has tax savings. Clearly it makes no sense for a firm to pay dividends and then go out and sell additional stock to finance growth opportunities. In addition to tax aspects, external financing involves other expenses. One, the flotation costs to paid investment bankers could be in the range of 2 to 5 percent. Two, external equity financing may involve an information asymmetry cost. Investors may feel that management is selling additional equity shares because it judges them to be overvalued. This may cause the price of the stock to decline.

Informational Content or Signaling

Dividend increases may be regarded by investors as management's judgment or expectation that the underlying earnings growth is strong enough to maintain the higher dividend even if temporary unfavorable fluctuations occur. Thus an increase in dividends may be taken as a signal of continued earnings growth. A cut in dividends would convey the opposite kind of information. Hence, dividend increases follow cash flow increases with a lag. The company seeks a cushion against a dividend cut. The negative information conveyed by dividend reductions would cause its stock price to decline.

Investor Clientele Effects

Orphans and widows may require a dependable flow of dividends to meet their living expenses. They would prefer a high dividend payout. In general, shareholders in low tax brackets would not suffer the tax disadvantage of dividends to the same degree as investors in high tax brackets. The latter would be interested in a low dividend payout that resulted in share price increases so that income could be taken in the form of gains taxed at lower capital gains rates. Because of the divergence of investor clienteles, it is recommended that a firm can improve its share price by announcing a clear and relatively fixed dividend policy. The firm can then attract the clientele whose needs are best met by the dividend policy the firm has established.

THE GROWTH OF SHARE REPURCHASES

The preceding section described the reasons why dividend policy can influence shareholder value. We now analyze the nature of the growth of share repurchases. We first briefly describe four major types of share repurchases:

1. Fixed-price tender offers (FPTs)
2. Dutch auctions (DAs)
3. Transferable put rights (TPRs)
4. Open-market repurchases (OMRs)

Fixed-Price Tender Offers

A firm offers to buy a specified fraction of shares within a given time period. The tender price offered is usually higher than the prevailing market price of the stock at the time of the offer. Most fixed-price tender offers are at least fully subscribed. If the offer is oversubscribed—more shares are offered than are sought—the firm can buy the shares back on a pro rata basis. Alternatively, the firm may elect to buy back all shares (more than the original target number or fraction) at the tender offer price. If the tender offer is undersubscribed, the firm may extend the offer, hoping to have more shares tendered over time; or the firm may cancel the offer if it includes a minimum acceptance clause; or the firm may simply buy back whatever number or percentage of shares was actually tendered. In a fixed-price tender offer, the firm usually pays any transfer taxes involved, and the shareholder pays no brokerage fees.

Dutch Auctions

In a Dutch auction, the firm announces the number of shares it would buy in a specified time period and the price range in which shareholders may offer to tender. For example, the current price of the stock may be $14. The company may offer to buy 4 million shares at a price range of $15 to $19 per share. Typically, the price offers will be at intervals such as 10¢ or 25¢. At the offer price that results in 4 million shares being offered, all shares offered at or below that price will be purchased at that price. Thus, even though some shareholders may have offered to sell at $16, if $16.70 is the price at which 4 million shares are offered, all shares offered at prices below $16.70 will still receive the $16.70 per share.

Oversubscription is possible in a Dutch auction if the reservation prices of the shareholders are lower than the lower range price terms. Oversubscription may also occur from the lumpiness of bidding schedules. For example, if at $16.70 less than 4 million shares were offered but at $16.80, 4,100,000 shares were offered, the company might accept only a fraction of shares (4.0/4.1) of the amount tendered by each shareholder, or it might take the full 4.1 million shares at $16.80.

Transferable Put Rights

A firm announces a purchase of 5 percent of its outstanding common shares. Each shareholder would receive one TPR for every 20 shares held. Thus, if a firm has 100 million shares outstanding and is seeking to repurchase 5 million shares or 5 percent, 5 million TPRs will be issued, and for every 100 shares a shareholder will receive five TPRs.

A secondary market develops in which TPRs are bought and sold. If the prevailing market price of the stock is $14 and the TPR gives the shareholder the right to put the stock to the company at $15.50, trading will take place in the TPRs. Shareholders who feel that the stock is worth less than $15.50 will be glad to have the opportunity to put the stock to the company at $15.50. These shareholders or other investors will be buyers of the TPRs. On the other hand, shareholders who feel that the stock is worth more than $15.50, for example $16 or even $18, will want to continue to hold their stock and sell their TPRs.

Open-Market Repurchases

A firm announces that it will repurchase some dollar amount (for example, $5 billion or $10 billion) of its common stock from time to time in the open market. This is the most frequent type of share repurchase, outnumbering the other three methods by a factor of more than 10 to 1. However, open-market repurchases generally involve a smaller percentage of total shares outstanding than the other methods. OMRs probably average about 5 percent of shares outstanding versus around 16 percent for fixed-price tender offers.

Open-market repurchases differ from the first three described with respect to the credibility of their signaling power. FPTs provide shareholders with a put option with a fixed exercise price for a specified trading period; they are usually "in the money" in the sense that the tender price represents a premium over the preexisting market price. Dutch auctions require that the shareholders specify an exercise price with the risk that if they ask for too high a premium, their shares may not be repurchased. Transferable put rights are tradable, and since the exercise price is above the preexisting price, they will have value. OMRs are simply an announcement that the board of directors has approved the use of a dollar amount of funds or the funds required to buy a specified number of shares in the future. The time period over which the open-market repurchases are to be made may not be specified. Indeed, sometimes the stock price of the firm may rise with the announcement of the OMR; having accomplished its objective, the firm may not actually repurchase any shares. The signaling credibility, therefore, is clearly weaker for the OMR than for the other forms of share repurchase.

REASONS FOR SHARE REPURCHASES

The main types of share repurchase programs have been described. While their characteristics vary to some degree, the factors associated with the growth in the use of stock buybacks apply to all of them. We next discuss these forces.

Greater Flexibility

We have shown that dividend cuts have adverse effects on stock prices. If a firm uses both cash dividend payouts and share repurchases, it achieves greater flexibility. With share repurchases, management can convey to shareholders that cash will be returned when funds are available in excess of needs to finance sound investment programs. Thus, if a company's growth prospects are improved, the initial expansion may be financed in part by a cut in dividends, but followed by a share repurchase. When the resulting increases in cash flows are larger than investment requirements at the time, share repurchase can be used without committing the company to a permanent higher dividend level.

Tax Savings

Through 2000, cash dividends to shareholders were subject to a maximum individual tax rate of 39.6 percent; the return of cash to shareholders in the form of share repurchases may qualify for the long-term capital gains rate of 20 percent. This represents a tax savings of potentially as much as 19.6 cents on each dollar received. Shareholders can choose whether or not to participate in a stock buyback program. They can defer their tax payments to make their own selection of when to sell.

Change Financial Structure

The debt-to-equity ratio is one measure of the firm's financial structure. The standard procedure for measuring debt is to first deduct excess cash and marketable securities holdings. So a share repurchase with excess cash not only reduces equity, but also increases debt. Thus, the leverage ratio can be quickly increased. A similar result occurs if a firm sells additional debt in order to make share repurchases. If the firm has been operating with less than the optimal debt leverage ratio, the share repurchase will move the firm toward that ratio. If so, it may lower the firm's cost of capital, with a resulting increase in share price and market value.

Offset Stock Options

Stock options have become increasingly used by firms in executive compensation programs and extended broadly to recruit or retain target employees. As stock options are exercised, the number of the firm's shares outstanding continuously increases.

Conceivably, this could create downward pressure on the firm's stock price. Share repurchases can be used to offset this potential dilutive effect.

Takeover Defense

Share repurchases may be used as a takeover defense for two reasons. One, the share repurchase plan may be viewed more favorably than the takeover. Two, when a firm tenders for a percentage of its shares, the shareholders who offer their shares for sale are those with the lowest reservation prices. Those who do not tender have the higher reservation prices. Hence, for a takeover bidder to succeed with the remaining higher reservation price shareholders, the premium offered will have to be higher. The required higher premium may deter some potential acquirers from making bids (Bagwell, 1992).

Information Content and/or Signaling

Probably the strongest reason for share repurchases is associated with their information content. The market has generally come to associate announcement of share repurchases with future improvements in cash flows of the company. Empirical studies find an association between the announcement of share repurchases and subsequent improvements in cash flows.

In response to an announcement of a share repurchase by a firm, its market price may rise with the expectation of future increases in cash flows. If, as time goes by, the firm's cash flows actually increase, this provides some confirmation and the probability of further cash flow increases may be strengthened. Empirical studies confirm that the positive market price response to the announcement of a share repurchase may continue over the second and third years (Ikenberry, Lakonishok, and Vermaelen, 1995). What we have described is the information content in a share repurchase announcement.

The announcement of a fixed-price tender offer may also be associated with signaling. In a fixed-price tender, the firm typically offers a premium over the prevailing market price. If officers and directors do not sell their shares, they have put themselves at risk. Since they are paying a premium, if the subsequent cash flows of the firm do not increase to support a higher market price, they will suffer capital losses. So if officers and directors put themselves at risk in announcing a premium fixed-price tender offer, this would be a strong signal of their belief in higher future cash flows.

In open market share repurchases, the firm may instruct the specialist who handles the stock to execute its purchase orders in weak markets. Hence, no premium might be involved. Obviously, firms with declining stock prices might be tempted to signal higher cash flows to bolster their stock. Financial analysts who follow companies are likely to distinguish between true and false signals. From time to time, financial publications list companies that have announced share repurchases which did not help their faltering stock prices.

So fixed-price tender offers at a premium, with officers and directors at risk, are likely to convey strong signals of improvement in future cash flows. Open market share repurchases are more likely to require confirming evidence. Note further that it is not share repurchase, as such, that causes the share price increase. Credible information of future cash flow changes causes the share price changes.

The financial literature also reports that share repurchases may be part of a more general restructuring program in which the firm is engaged (Nohel and Tarhan, 1998). If the firm has embarked on a general program to improve its efficiency and performance and a share repurchase program is a part of that restructuring, the influence on share prices is likely to be positive. But the restructuring may be the stronger causal force.

Accounting Treatment

The basic accounting entry when shares are repurchased is to reduce (debit) shares outstanding and to reduce (credit) cash by the outlay required. Accounting principles permit the charge (debit) to the shareholders' equity account to be at cost or market. The common practice is for firms to charge the shareholders' equity account with the actual amount paid for the shares (at market). The results can best be made concrete by a simplified accounting model of a stock buyback, shown in Table 9.8. Panel A of the table postulates a firm with a net income of $1000 million, shares outstanding of 500 million, a P/E multiple of 30 times, and a buyback of 50 million shares. Panel B presents the balance sheet before and after the buyback. The results in panel C are calculated in panel D. Before the buyback, earnings are $2 per share. The market price per share, applying the P/E multiple, is $60. The book value per share is $6000 divided by 500, which is $12 per share. Market capitalization is $60 times the 500 million shares outstanding, which gives $30,000 million. The return on book equity is the $1000 million net income divided by $6000 million, which is 16.67 percent. The debt-to-equity ratio is $4000 debt less $3000 excess cash, which equals $1000 divided by $6000, or 16.67 percent.

We can now illustrate the accounting effects of the stock buyback. We postulate that in an open market share repurchase program, 50 million shares are bought at $60, for a total of $3000. This is the debit to the book shareholders' equity, which is reduced to $3000 million. The net income is postulated to be reduced by the 3 percent after-tax earnings on the $3000 excess cash, or $90. The resulting $910 is divided by 450 to give $2.02 as the new EPS after the buyback. If the P/E ratio of 30 continues to hold, the resulting market price per share rises to $60.60. Market capitalization declines to $27,270 million— which makes sense because fewer shares are outstanding. The book shareholders' equity per share is $3000 million divided by the 450 million shares remaining, or $6.67. The return on book equity rises to 30.33 percent. The debt ratio rises to 133 percent.

The stock buyback, using generally accepted accounting principles (GAAP), would increase EPS, the market price per share, and the return on book equity. However, these represent accounting cosmetics. If the more fundamental reasons for share repurchases are not present, a sound economic basis for stock price increases has not been met. See, for example, "Stock Buybacks Gain Popularity, but Price Pops Aren't Guaranteed" (*The Wall Street Journal*, March 6, 2000, p. C17). A *Barron's* article (February 14, 2000, p. 20), entitled "No Elixir," listed 50 companies that bought back the biggest percentage of their shares in 1999. It noted that "big corporate stock repurchase programs

TABLE 9.8

Accounting for a Stock Buyback—Use Excess Cash

Panel A: Inputs

Net income	$1,000 million
Earnings rate on excess cash	5%
Shares outstanding	500 million
P/E ratio	30
Tax rate	40%
Shares for buyback	50 million
Share price buyback	$60.00
Buyback	50 million shares @ $60 = $3,000 million

Panel B: Balance Sheets ($ million)

	Before Buyback	After Buyback
Cash	$4,000	$1,000
Other assets	$6,000	$6,000
Total assets	$10,000	$7,000
Total debt	$4,000	$4,000
Book shareholders' equity	$6,000	$3,000
Total claims	$10,000	$7,000

Panel C: Financial Effects

Net income	$1,000	$910
EPS	$2.00	$2.02
Market price per share	$60.00	$60.60
Book value per share	$12.00	$6.67
Market capitalization (million)	$30,000	$27,270
Return on book equity	16.67%	30.33%
Debt-to-equity ratio	16.67%	133%

Panel D: Calculations after Buyback

Net income = net income less after-tax 5% $(1 - T)$ earnings on $3,000 excess cash
$$= \$1,000 - 90 = \$910$$
EPS = net income / new shares
$$= \$910 / (500 - 50) = \$910 / 450$$
$$= \$2.02$$
Market price per share = $2.02 × 30 = $60.60, 0.60/60.00 = 1.0% increase
Book value per share = $3,000 / 450 = $6.67
Market capitalization = $60.60 × 450 = $27,270
Return on book equity = $910 / $3,000 = 30.33%
Debt-to-equity ratio = $4,000 / $3,000 = 133.33%

failed to prevent most of these stocks from dropping last year." See also "Buybacks for All the Wrong Reasons" (*The New York Times*, December 17, 2000, section 3, p. 1). In "Buybacks Binge Now Creates Big Hangover" (*The Wall Street Journal*, December 18, 2000, pp. C1, 2), data are compiled for a sampling of S&P 500 companies covering the years 1998 through 2000. The article listed the amounts by which share prices of selected companies had declined below their repurchase prices. Illustrative examples and the dollar amounts of paper losses include Hewlett-Packard at $3.2 billion; Intel, $4.6 billion; and Microsoft, $2.7 billion. The losses of Gillette ($473 million) and McDonald's ($359 million) were modest by comparison. Perhaps from a long-term investor's standpoint, gains may be achieved in the longer term. Nevertheless, at a minimum, the timing of the repurchases was ill advised. But it may also be possible that financial engineering manipulations, described in the following section, were becoming unraveled.

STOCK BUYBACKS IN A FINANCIAL ENGINEERING FRAMEWORK

In one scenario, stock buybacks play a key role in financial engineering which produces excellent achievement in performance metrics. Mergers consummated with differentially higher price-earnings (P/E) ratios create high accounting growth rates in earning per share (EPS). In the process, firms in promising growth areas are added to the corporate portfolio. Managerial capabilities are retained by stock options. The grant of stock options is not recognized as a cost in U.S. GAAP accounting. The grant of stock options is carried in footnotes with the cost estimated using the Black-Scholes option pricing model. When the stock options are exercised, the difference between the value of the stock and the exercise price is treated as income taxed at the ordinary personal tax rate. The gain to the option recipient can be taken as a corporate tax deduction. This reduces the effective tax rate of the corporate issuer. The stock option income tax benefits listed in the cash flow statement of Microsoft's year 2000 annual report (p. 25) were $5.535 billion.

As the options are exercised, the number of common shares of the company increases. Stock buybacks can be used to offset the increase in the number of shares, increasing the rate of growth of EPS. The accounting method for recording share repurchases reduces book equity, thereby increasing the GAAP reported return on equity. If the firm does not have excess cash to accomplish the share repurchase, it can issue debt to use the proceeds for buybacks.

The continued rise in company stock prices creates opportunities for more financial engineering. The company can sell puts, which during an extended period of rising stock prices will expire worthless. Gains on the put transactions are not taxable to the issuer. Microsoft reported $472 million "put warrant proceeds" for 2000. Companies such as Microsoft and Intel were also investing in numerous small companies. This provided several advantages. It kept them current on new technologies. It gave them information on new potential investment areas. The informal advisory relationship enabled them to appraise the quality of management. Since these were in high-growth areas, the returns on the investing companies at IPOs were substantial, or the investments could become attractive acquisitions.

Stock Dividends and Stock Splits

A stock dividend is paid in additional shares of stock instead of cash and simply involves a bookkeeping transfer from retained earnings to the capital stock account. In a stock split there is no change in the capital accounts; instead, a larger number of shares of common stock is issued. In a two-for-one split, stockholders receive two shares for each one previously held. The book value per share is cut in half, and the par, or stated, value per share of stock is similarly changed.

From a practical standpoint there is little difference between a stock dividend and a stock split. The New York Stock Exchange considers any distribution of stock totaling less than 25 percent of outstanding stock to be a stock dividend and any distribution of 25 percent or more a stock split. Since the two are similar, the issues outlined below are discussed in connection with both stock splits and stock dividends.

Many hypotheses have been put forth to explain why corporations have stock splits. Logically, a paper transaction that doubles the number of shares outstanding without changing the firm in any other way should not create shareholder wealth out of thin air. The exact effect of stock splits on shareholder wealth has been studied extensively. The pioneering study by Fama et al. (1969) measured unexpected stock price changes around split ex dates. Monthly data for 940 splits between 1927 and 1959 revealed no significant changes in shareholder wealth in the split month. However, for a subsample of firms that split and increased their dividends, they found an increase in shareholders' wealth in the months following the split. For a dividend decrease subsample they found a decrease in shareholders' wealth. These results are consistent with the idea that splits are interpreted as messages about dividend increases, or about higher future cash flows.

A study by Grinblatt, Masulis, and Titman (1984) used daily data and looked at shareholder returns on the split announcement date as well as the split ex date. They examined a special subsample of splits where no other announcements were made in the 3-day period around the split announcement and where no cash dividends had been declared in the previous 3 years. For this sample of 125 "pure" stock splits they found a statistically significant announcement return of 3.44 percent. They interpret stock split announcements as favorable signals about the firm's future cash flows. Surprisingly, they also find statistically significant returns (for their entire sample of 1360 stock splits) on the split ex date. There is no good explanation for this result.

One often hears that stocks split because there is an "optimal" price range for common stocks. Moving the security price into this range is alleged to make the market for trading in the security "wider" or "deeper," hence there is more trading liquidity. Copeland (1979) reports that contrary to the above argument, market liquidity is actually lower following a stock split. Trading volume is proportionately lower than its presplit level, brokerage revenues (a major portion of transactions costs) are proportionately higher, and bid-ask spreads are higher as a percentage of the bid price. Taken together, these empirical results point to lower postsplit liquidity.

Brennan and Copeland (1988) present a signaling model of stock splits. Because transaction costs are a higher percentage of the value of a share traded for low-priced stocks than for high-priced stocks, stock splits are a costly signal. If two companies are alike in every way except that managers of the first company believe that their firm will experience higher cash flows in the future, then the first company can benefit from a stock split because the price increase from signaling higher future cash flows will exceed the cost of (temporarily) lower liquidity. This theory predicts that the target split price, and not the split factor, will be related to the announcement date return. In other words, the market will react more favorably to a $50 stock that splits 2-for-1 down to the $25 price range than to a $200 stock that splits 4-for-1 to the $50 price range. This is exactly the empirical result that Brennan and Copeland find. In addition, McNichols and David (1990) report that after the event there are unexpected positive increases in the earnings of companies that have stock splits. It seems, therefore, that stock splits are best explained as signals about better future prospects for the firm.

SUMMARY

The empirical evidence on dividends suggests that the following conclusions are warranted. Dividend changes are interpreted as signals about the future prospects of the firm. The market reacts strongly and immediately to announcements of positive dividend increases. There is evidence that shareholders self-select into clienteles, with high-tax-bracket shareholders migrating toward low-payout firms and low-tax-bracket shareholders selecting high-payout firms.

Firms with many profitable growth opportunities (high-growth firms) will use their internally generated funds without paying dividends. Older, more mature firms will pay dividends because not all internally generated funds will be exhausted by investment opportunities. When one firm is internally financing its profitable investments and the other is financing externally, incentives for a merger between them are produced. Internal equity financing is cheaper than external equity financing.

One reason for share repurchase is its association with expectations of higher future cash flows. Since share repurchases are not made on a regular basis as dividends are, they give a firm greater flexibility. When its investment needs were high, the omission of share repurchases would not adversely affect share prices, as would dividend reductions.

Share repurchases are a tax-efficient method of returning cash to shareholders. Stock buybacks are a method of quickly changing a firm's financial structure. Stock buybacks can offset the growth in shares outstanding that would otherwise take place as stock options are exercised. A share repurchase may also have the effect of a takeover defense. Stock buybacks are likely to improve accounting measures of performance.

Stock splits and stock dividends simply divide shareholders' equity into more units. Since they are signals of prospects for future cash flow improvements, they are associated with stock price increases.

REFERENCES

Bagwell, Laurie Simon, "Dutch Auction Repurchases: An Analysis of Shareholder Heterogeneity," *Journal of Finance*, 47, March 1992, pp. 71–105.

Brennan, Michael J., and Thomas E. Copeland, "Beta Changes around Stock Splits: A Note," *Journal of Finance*, 43, 1988, pp. 1009–1014.

Copeland, Thomas E., "Liquidity Changes Following Stock Splits," *Journal of Finance*, 34, 1979, pp. 115–141.

Fama, Eugene F., Lawrence Fisher, Michael C. Jensen, and Richard Roll, "The Adjustment of Stock Prices to New Information," *International Economic Review*, 10, 1969, pp. 1–21.

Fama, Eugene F., and Kenneth R French, "Disappearing Dividends: Changing Firm Characteristics or Lower Propensity to Pay?" *Journal of Financial Economics*, 60, 2001, pp. 3–43.

Grinblatt, Mark S., Ronald W. Masulis, and Sheridan Titman, "The Valuation Effects of Stock Splits and Stock Dividends," *Journal of Financial Economics*, 13, 1984, pp. 461–490.

Ikenberry, David, Josef Lakonishok, and Theo Vermaelen, "Market Underreaction to Open Market Share Repurchases," *Journal of Financial Economics*, 39, October-November 1995, pp. 181–208.

Liang, J. Nellie, and Steven A. Sharpe, "Share Repurchases and Employee Stock Options and Their Implications for S&P 500 Share Retirements and Expected Returns," Working Paper, Federal Reserve Board, Division of Research and Statistics, November 1999.

McNichols, Maureen, and Ajay David, "Stock Dividends, Stock Splits and Signaling," *Journal of Finance*, 45, 1990, pp. 857–880.

Nohel, Tom, and Vefa Tarhan, "Share Repurchases and Firm Performance: New Evidence on the Agency Costs of Free Cash Flow," *Journal of Financial Economics*, 49, 1998, pp. 187–222.

QUESTIONS AND PROBLEMS

9.1 Herman Company has $2 million of backlogged orders for its patented solar heating system. Management plans to expand production capacity by 30 percent with $6 million investment in plant machinery. The firm wants to maintain a 45 percent debt-to-total-asset ratio in its capital structure; it also wants to maintain its past dividend policy of distributing 20 percent of the after-tax earnings. In 2000, earnings were $2.6 million. How much external equity must the firm seek at the beginning of 2001?

9.2 As an investor, would you rather invest in a firm with a policy of maintaining a constant payout ratio, a constant dollar dividend per share, or a constant regular quarterly dividend plus a year-end extra when earnings are sufficiently high or corporate investment needs are sufficiently low? Explain your answer.

9.3 How would each of the following changes probably affect aggregate payout ratios? Explain your answer.
  a. An increase in the personal income tax rate
  b. A liberalization in depreciation policies for federal income tax purposes
  c. A rise in interest rates
  d. An increase in corporate profits
  e. A decline in investment opportunities

9.4 Gorlin Corporation's common stock is selling for $45.00 per share following a 2-for-1 stock split. This stock price represents a P/E ratio of 15. Prior to the stock split the P/E ratio was 10, and dividends per share were $1.00. The postsplit dividend is $0.75 per share.

a. What was the presplit stock price?

b. By what percentage has the stock price increased?

c. By what percentage has the dividend increased?

9.5 Swerdlin Company has $30 million of excess cash that is available for distribution to its shareholders.

a. Assuming dividend income is taxed at a 40 percent rate and capital gains income is taxed at a 20 percent rate, calculate the impact on shareholder wealth of a $30 million cash dividend distribution versus a $30 million share repurchase.

b. Under what circumstances, if any, would Swerdlin's shareholders be better off having Swerdlin retain and reinvest at least part of the cash in short-term financial instruments rather than pay it out to shareholders?

9.6 The market value of Atlas Company equity is $20 per share. The intrinsic or true value per share in the judgment of management is $30 per share. The cost of equity for Atlas is 10 percent. What would be the rate of return in a share repurchase if these data were correct?

SOLUTIONS TO QUESTIONS AND PROBLEMS

9.1
Earnings	$2,600,000
Percent of earnings retained	0.8
Retained earnings	$2,080,000
New assets	$6,000,000
Percent financed by equity	0.55
Equity financing needed	$3,300,000
Retained earnings	2,080,000
External equity needed	$1,220,000

9.2 The way this question is worded, each individual would have to make up his or her own mind. In our opinion, investors who intend to invest in companies that maintain a relatively high payout are probably seeking income and would much prefer to receive a stable dollar dividend per share. Investors who are not seeking current income would probably, over the long run, seek companies that retain a relatively large percentage of their earnings. These investors would probably not be particularly concerned about whether the company paid a stable dividend. They would, of course, be concerned with earnings and the trend in earnings.

9.3 *a.* From the stockholders' point of view, an increase in the personal income tax would make it more desirable for a firm to retain and reinvest earnings. Consequently, an increase in personal tax rates should lower the aggregate payout ratio or cause borrowing on personal account to increase to offset its personal taxes.

b. If the depreciation charges were raised, the rise would tend to reduce reported profits vis-à-vis cash flows, because most firms set up a reserve for deferred taxes, that is, "normalize" reported profits. With higher cash flows, payout ratios would tend to increase. On the other hand, the change in tax-allowed depreciation charges would increase rates of return on investment, other things being equal, and this might stimulate investment, reduce redundant cash flows, and consequently reduce payout ratios. On balance, it is likely that aggregate payout ratios would rise, however, and this has in fact been the case.

c. If interest rates were to increase, the increase would make retained earnings a relatively attractive way of financing new investment. Consequently, the payout ratio might be expected to decline.

d. An increase in corporate profits would probably lead to an increase in dividends, but not necessarily to an increase in the payout ratio. If the aggregate profit increase was a cyclical increase that could be expected to be followed by a decline, then the payout ratio might fall, because firms do not generally raise dividends in response to a short-run profit rise.

e. If investment opportunities for firms declined while cash flows remained relatively constant, an increase would be expected in the payout ratio. The shareholders can reinvest the funds in companies with better growth opportunities.

9.4 a. Postsplit: Price/EPS = 15 ⇒ $45/EPS = 15 ⇒ EPS = $3 per new share

Post-split EPS	$ 3.00
2-for-1 stock split	× 2
Presplit EPS	$ 6.00
Presplit P/E ratio	×10
Presplit stock price	$60.00

b.
Postsplit stock price	$45.00
2-for-1 stock split	× 2
Equivalent presplit stock price	$90.00

$$\frac{\$90 - \$60}{\$60} = 50\% \text{ increase in stock price}$$

c.
Postsplit dividend	$0.75
2-for-1 stock split	× 2
Equivalent presplit dividend	$1.50

$$\frac{\$1.50 - \$1.00}{\$1.00} = 0.50 = 50\% \text{ increase in dividend}$$

9.5 a.
Dividend of	$30 million
Tax @ 40 percent	12 million
After-tax income	$18 million

Share repurchase of	$30 million
Tax @ 20%	6 million
After-tax income	$24 million

After-tax income to shareholders is $6 million higher with a share repurchase.

b. Swerdlin's shareholders would be better off having Swerdlin retain and reinvest the cash in short-

term financial instruments if the company antici-
pates positive-NPV investment opportunities in
the near future. Although the short-term financial
securities are probably zero-NPV investments, the
cost to obtain additional financing in the near
future can be avoided by holding the funds temporarily in marketable securities.

9.6 The following can be used:

Rate of return in share repurchase

$$= \frac{\text{cost of equity}}{1 - \text{percent undervaluation}}$$

$$= \frac{\text{cost of equity}}{\text{ratio of market to intrinsic value}}$$

$$= \frac{10\%}{\$20/\$30}$$

$$= 15.0\%$$

CHAPTER TEN
Takeover Defenses

In Chap. 1, we discussed a number of the "change forces" that affect the world economy. These change forces were in general the result of (1) improvements in communications, information, and technology; (2) industry deregulation and opening of international borders; (3) efficiency of operations, including economy of scale and the combining of complementary activities; (4) restructuring activities of firms and industries—vertical versus horizontal integration; (5) supportive economic and financial environments; and (6) individual entrepreneurship. The catalysts have been strong and growing stronger.

A firm is a prime acquisition target when the value of its shares does not fully reflect the potential value of the business. In Chap. 8, we discussed methods for "unlocking" the value of the firm through restructuring ownership relationships, specifically divestitures of lines of business or entire divisions, spin-offs, equity carve-outs, and tracking stocks. Also, in Chap. 8, we examined financial restructuring through leveraged buyouts, leveraged recapitalizations, dual classes of stock, general recapitalizations, exchange offers, tracking stocks, and ESOPs. In Chap. 9, we reviewed share repurchases and dividend policy. In many ways, these chapters began the discussion about takeover defenses. All these techniques are designed to "unlock" the value of a company's stock so that its "intrinsic" economic value is reflected in its stock price.

After a general discussion, this chapter presents additional takeover defenses. The defensive strategies will not limit the impact of the "change forces" and prevent the takeover of the firm. They are designed to slow down a potential hostile acquirer while management has time to fully consider additional alternatives to enhance the value of the firm above and beyond the initial acquisition offer.

VULNERABLE TARGET COMPANIES

The general change forces discussed above affect every industry and every company to varying degrees. Economic pressures can make the value of a particular company more or less attractive in the hands of different owners. Industry consolidation leading to economies of scale provides additional synergies that may be available to only the acquiring firm. Shifts in the economic dynamics of an industry, such as Dell successfully concentrating on only personal computer sales while limiting its activities in many other segments of the value chain of the information industry, provide additional catalysts for stock price premiums. Any company will be hard pressed to ward off the general change forces. However, any company can still be better positioned so that its management can seek the best offer possible.

Companies that may not have followed the restructuring advice in Chaps. 8 and 9 may find themselves in a particularly vulnerable position. Characteristics of these types of firms include undervalued assets and/or strong cash positions.

Undervalued Assets

In the late 1970s and early 1980s, T. Boone Pickins, Mesa Petroleum's CEO, found it less expensive to buy petroleum companies with proven reserves than to explore for new oil. The stock price of those target companies did not fully reflect the market value of the petroleum reserves. Conservative accounting conventions did not allow the target companies to fully reflect the underlying market value of their major asset. In these cases, the assets were ripe for picking through acquisitions of the entire companies.

At one point, Hershey Foods targeted the acquisition of American and Italian Pasta Company (AIPC). AIPC primarily produced "store-brand" pasta. Additional expansion into store-brand pasta was not the catalyst for this acquisition. Instead, the primary motive of the acquisition was to acquire the sole production facility of AIPC. This plant was one of the most efficient pasta factories in the world. Its capabilities would cost Hershey a significant amount to reproduce. The acquisition route was deemed an immediate and lower-cost alternative until the federal government antitrust agencies challenged the acquisition. Hershey walked away from the acquisition and built its own world-class pasta manufacturing facility, which delayed Hershey's efficiency realization.

These two cases illustrate a situation in which the stock price is below the replacement value (or current market value) of the assets. This situation makes a firm particularly attractive to an acquirer without considering the ongoing value of the underlying business.

Another type of undervalued asset is a subsidiary, division, line of business, etc., that is undervalued by the stock market. In those cases, a business unit may have its performance underappreciated by the stock market or may be an actual "drain" to the value of the entire firm because of inferior performance that diverts management's attention. In these cases, an acquirer may be better positioned to unlock the intrinsic value of that asset.

Strong Cash Position and Unused Debt Capacity

Some companies hoard cash and marketable securities. These companies are particularly vulnerable to acquisitions since that cash will be captured by the acquiring company and used to pay for the acquisition. As we noted in Chap. 7 on valuation, the value of a company's equity is the value of the operations (discounted cash flow analysis of operating cash flow and residual value) less the value of the outstanding debt plus the value of the cash and marketable securities. In a perfect world, the acquiring company pays out the full value of the cash and marketable

securities to the target company's stockholders through the negotiated deal structure. However, this is a topic that tests both parties' negotiating skills.

Related to a strong cash position is unused debt capacity.
Certain industries typically have capital structures that include
a significant amount of debt. For example, in Table 10.1, the
food processing industry in 2000 had 50.8 percent of its capital
financed with debt on a historical book basis or 15.0 percent on
a market value basis. Regardless of how the leverage is measured, the financially conservative nature of Tootsie Roll and
Wrigley is very clear. Both of these companies use minimal to no
debt. All else being the same, a potential acquirer could buy
either of these companies and finance a large portion of the

TABLE 10.1

2000 Food Processing Industry Capital Structure (Percent)

	Capitalization Ratio*	
	Book	Market
Campbell Soup	96.9	10.0
ConAgra	46.4	19.7
Dean Foods	53.6	37.9
General Mills	85.9	14.7
Heinz	64.7	19.6
Hershey Foods	42.3	12.3
Interstate Bakeries	39.4	23.6
Kellogg	61.2	12.9
Nabisco	49.0	21.9
Quaker Oats	68.4	6.7
Tootsie Roll	1.6	0.4
Wrigley	0.0	0.0
Industry average	50.8	15.0

* The capitalization ratio is calculated as the book or market values of

$$\frac{\text{Long-term debt}}{\text{Long-term debt} + \text{equity}}$$

acquisition via debt. In particular, the unused debt capacity of the targeted company itself could enhance the amount of debt a potential acquirer has available to complete the transaction.

Aligned with a strong cash position is strong annual cash flow. First, strong annual operating cash flow, as we saw in Chap. 7, provides the basis on which to value the firm and may support an intrinsic value greater than the current stock price. Second, strong annual cash flows also provide the wherewithal to service additional levels of debt.

TAKEOVER DEFENSES

Any company is subject to a potential takeover. The first step, well before an acquisition attempt is made, is to have a plan of action in place. What will the board's response be to an unfriendly takeover? What is the difference between a friendly and an unfriendly acquirer? What is the fair value of the corporation? What steps are appropriate to take before an attempted acquisition, and what steps is the company willing to take after the unwanted overture is made?

By valuing the corporation's strategic plan, the company can routinely perform a self-acquisition valuation. The value of a company, as discussed in Chap. 7, is based upon projected performance. The corporation's strategic plan represents the best set of assumptions prepared by the most knowledgeable people. What does the company see as its value, and how does it compare to the offer at hand?

This section reviews numerous defensive tactics, many of which can be implemented beforehand. When an unfriendly offer comes, time is of the essence. Corporate response needs to be quick. In the early days, silence or no comment may be appropriate as the board weighs numerous alternative courses of action.

There are six different broad categories of defensive measures that a company can employ to ward off unwanted acquisition advances:

- Operating performance
- Financial techniques
- Restructuring and financial engineering

- Antitakeover charter amendments
- Other board or management methods
- Postacquisition bid techniques

The first two categories of defensive measures are centered on the ongoing performance of the firm, both the operations and the financial structure. The third category, restructuring and financial engineering, reflects a dynamic management self-review that aggressively seeks to maximize the value of the firm without any prodding by an unwanted acquirer. Antitakeover charter amendments are specific provisions included in the corporation's charter. In addition to charter amendments, the board and management have other defensive measures that can be put into place before an unwanted offer is presented. Finally, there are a series of measures that can be implemented after an offer is presented.

Each of these six categories is discussed in turn below.

OPERATING PERFORMANCE

In the valuation chapter, it was very clear that in order to enhance the value of a business, the corporation must focus on growth of the business (as measured by growth in sales), the efficiency of operations (or profit margin), and the appropriate injection of capital into the operations. These three areas not only are good defensive tactics, but also are sound business practices. Table 10.2 lists defensive operating performance tactics.

Additionally, operating performance must meet or exceed expectations to fully unlock the value of the firm. Of course, a company can help establish (or "manage") those expectations.

Growth in the operations of a business can be achieved through sustained organic business growth, joint ventures or other business arrangements, and an aggressive acquisition program. Throughout the life cycle of a firm, sustaining organic business growth becomes a more difficult task. Product revitalization and expansion is key to stimulating future organic growth. A dynamic management team will also seek out joint ventures or other business arrangements that can capitalize upon another firm's expertise. Finally, the last growth tactic is

T A B L E 10.2

Defensive Operating Performance

Growth in operations
- Sustain core business growth
- Joint ventures or other business arrangements
- Acquisition of other companies

Efficiency of operations
- Analyze operations to get "true" profit picture
- Enhance productivity
- Divest businesses that do not generate cash

Efficiency of capital management
- Limit working capital investment
- Invest cash flow in positive NPV projects
- Invest cash flow in positive NPV acquisitions

Meet or exceed expectations

---

for the company itself to acquire other companies. Key acquisitions can augment the core business growth, improve the efficiency of the operations, result in positive net present value for the firm, and utilize excess cash or the debt capacity of the firm.

The efficiency of the operations must first be analyzed to understand the "true" cost of doing business and the resulting profit picture. Relatively recent processes such as activity-based cost (ABC) accounting help to identify areas for improvement or areas to leverage and capitalize on. Once a profit and cost profile is developed, productivity enhancement can zero in on selected areas. Enhancement can be found through increased productivity, economies of scale (e.g., leveraging fixed costs of doing business), or even outsourcing of nonstrategic functions. Productivity enhancement can result from the implementation of technology or an enterprisewide information system such as an efficient resource planning (ERP) system by SAP, Baan, and Oracle. Oracle claims more than $1 billion in annual savings due to the implementation of its own ERP software. Many corporations are also finding that a productivity program originated by General Electric (Six Sigma) is increasing productivity and resulting in substantial savings and increased profits. Finally, the overall corporate efficiency of operations can be enhanced when inefficient operations, such as plants, products, and businesses, are divested.

Capital management techniques must ensure managers are not over- or underinvesting in the working and fixed capital needs of the business. Dell Computer Corporation's working capital management (specifically inventory management) is clear example of best-demonstrated practices. Through efficient processes and just-in-time inventory systems, Dell has been able to reduce its days outstanding in inventory to approximately 6 days from a level of 31 days just 5 years earlier. By reducing its inventory investment, Dell has reduced its capital needs by $1.4 billion.

A fixed capital investment program is also very important; it ensures that management invests in positive net present value projects. Underinvesting is also a concern. Old technology can lead to inefficient operations that will ultimately put a company at a disadvantage. The demise of Montgomery Ward, which filed for Chapter 11 bankruptcy protection in December 2000, demonstrates a company that is still feeling the effects of a 22-year decision not to open any additional stores.

DEFENSIVE FINANCIAL TECHNIQUES

The defensive financial techniques are not only good defensive tactics, but are sound business practices as well. As discussed above, a company is particularly vulnerable if it has a hoard of cash or vast amounts of the unused debt capacity. The unwanted acquirer uses both the excess cash and the unused debt capacity to secure or enhance financing for the target company. Defensive financial techniques are designed to alleviate these positions and result in the company simply issuing debt or dispersing its cash. But how best to accomplish this? See Table 10.3.

If the company can identify positive net present value investments to enhance its operation, the company can invest in itself by expanding its capacity, introducing new products, increasing its efficiency, or acquiring new businesses.

Another effective technique is for the company to "recapitalize" and repurchase its stock, increase its dividends, or pay a

T A B L E 10.3

Defensive Financial Techniques

Liquidate marketable securities.

Issue debt.

Structure debt so that if an acquisition occurs, the debt must be paid off.

Repurchase stock.

Increase dividends.

Pay a one-time, extraordinary dividend.

---

one-time extraordinary dividend. Recapitalization through stock repurchase has multiple effects. Yes, it uses excess cash or unused debt capacity, but it also reduces the number of available shares and concentrates the outstanding shares into the hands of fewer stockholders. A share repurchase program may also act as a price support while sending positive signals to the market.

An additional antitakeover defensive tactic can be incorporated into a debt agreement. That is, the debt can become due and payable if an acquisition occurs. So if a company is acquired, the acquirer must repay the target's debt. In that way, the acquirer must come up with additional financing rather than assume the target's outstanding debt, which may also have more favorable interest rates.

DEFENSIVE RESTRUCTURING AND FINANCIAL ENGINEERING

Chapter 8 developed numerous restructuring alternatives. These restructurings also may prove to be a viable defensive tactic. Table 10.4 presents the techniques noted in Chap. 8.

The ownership reorganization is designed to enhance the current market value of the company by separating the company into individual businesses. The first two items listed in Table 10.4 concern divesting either assets or complete businesses. This recognizes that the asset or business may be more valuable in some other hands.

For example, in 1979, Hershey Foods acquired a northeastern U.S. restaurant chain called Friendly's Ice Cream Corporation.

T A B L E 10.4

Defensive Restructuring and Financial Engineering

Ownership reorganization
- Sell off assets to unlock "true" value
- Divest businesses to realize true value
- Spin-offs and split-ups
- Equity carve-outs
- Tracking stock

Employee stock ownership plans (ESOPs)

Financial restructuring
- Leveraged buyouts and leveraged recapitalization
- Dual class of stock recapitalization—super voting stock
- Recapitalization
- Exchange offers
- Reorganization
- Liquidation

Reorganize in an antitakeover friendly state

Friendly's offered a menu of moderately priced sandwiches and dinner entrees along with ice cream. Hershey supplied capital to Friendly's and helped it expand through new restaurant additions and the acquisition of small restaurant chains. By 1988, growth was waffling, margins were stabilized or slipping, and capital needs were intensifying. In 1988, Friendly's strategic plan projected the revenue, income, and cash flow for the restaurant chain through 1995. By estimating a residual value and valuing the cash flows at the cost of capital (see Chap. 7), a "value" of the business was obtained. As Hershey's management was considering alternatives, a restauranteur by the name of Don Smith inquired about buying the chain for $375 million. He understood the restaurant business and knew how to improve its operations. To him the restaurant business was more valuable than to Hershey. Hershey consummated the deal within months of the initial offer and realized more value for its shareholders than by trying to manage the business.

Additional ownership reorganizations include spin-offs, split-ups, equity carve-outs, and tracking stock. These techniques are more fully discussed in Chap. 8.

An employee stock ownership plan (ESOP) concentrates shares of stock in the hands of employees. While the benefits of ESOPs are detailed in Chap. 8, in the case of a defensive technique, the benefits are quite clear. ESOP shares remain unavailable in any unfriendly takeover situation.

Financial restructuring such as the recapitalization discussed in the section above is an appropriate defensive tactic. As mentioned, cash amounts or unused debt capacity provides the funds so that the firm can repurchase its shares. The fewer shares outstanding, the more difficult it may be for an unfriendly acquirer to obtain shares.

Finally, a company can reorganize in an antitakeover friendly state to avail itself of an atmosphere more conducive to slowing or thwarting unwanted acquisition overtures.

ANTITAKEOVER CHARTER AMENDMENTS

Another category of defense mechanisms is referred to as *antitakeover amendments* to a firm's corporate charter. The charter consists of articles of incorporation, which are first filed by the corporation's founders, and a certificate of incorporation, which the state provides once the articles have been approved. The charter gives the corporation its legal life. The charter provides power to the corporation in line with that state's laws. A corporation's bylaws supplement the charter with rules that specifically govern the internal management of the firm. A number of antitakeover amendments can be attached to the corporation's charter. These are often referred to as *shark repellents*.

Table 10.5 describes six general amendments, each of which is described in greater detail below.

Board of Director Provisions

Board antitakeover amendments are initiated to enhance the position of the board while maintaining its power.

T A B L E   10.5

Antitakeover Charter Amendments

Board provisions
- Classified or staggered board
- For-cause provision
- Maximum number of members
- Elect standby directors

Fair price provisions

Supermajority votes
- For acquisitions
- To cancel supermajority
- To amend charter

Super voting stock (dual recapitalization)

Eliminate cumulative voting

Antigreenmail amendment

Limit shareholder action
- Curtail consent solicitation
- Advance notice of meeting
- Ability to call special meetings
- Scheduling shareholder meetings
- Setting and controlling meeting agendas

The first board-related shark repellent considered is a staggered or classified board of directors. In a staggered board, its members are not all elected at one time. Their appointments are staggered over time. After the initial period, for example, a nine-member board will have only three members of the board elected for a 3-year term, annually. In the first year, the first class of three board members would be elected, the second year the next class of three members, the third year the final class of three members, and in the fourth year the process would begin again with the board seats from the first class up for election. This provision ensures that new majority shareholders would have to wait two cycles (or 2 years) before gaining control of the board.

A second board provision strengthens the staggered board by allowing the removal of a board member only *for cause*. That is, a board member cannot be arbitrarily removed. This provision creates a limited number of reasons why a member of the board can be removed. Again, this amendment limits an acquirer's ability to quickly replace an unfriendly board and strengthens the staggered board amendment.

Another board provision limits the number of directors. In that way, an acquirer cannot "pack the board" with added members and more quickly assume control of the board.

A final board provision allows for the election of standby directors. A standby director is elected with a class of directors and assumes a board seat, if one of that class of board members dies. This provision eliminates the early replacement of a classified seat.

Taken together, the board provisions provide for a slowdown in the process of an unfriendly acquirer to gain control of the board. The added provisions anticipate and thwart a hostile acquirer's ability to remove, overwhelm, or take advantage of a board member's death.

Fair Price Amendment

A fair price amendment requires that an acquirer pay a fair price for all of the corporation's outstanding stock. A fair price may be determined as an historical multiple of the company's earnings or even a predetermined multiple of earnings or book value of the target company. Additionally, in the case of a two-tier tender offer, the fair price amendment forces the acquirer to pay all target shareholders the same amount. This maintains a level of equality for those target stockholders who tender their shares in a second tier with those target shareholders who tender their stock in a first tier. Consequently, the acquirer cannot offer more to the first group, thereby putting undue pressure on the target stockholders who do not want to hastily tender their shares. This removes one catalyst available to a potential acquirer.

Supermajority Votes

Supermajority voting amendments require shareholder approval by at least two-thirds vote and sometimes as much as 90 percent of the votes of the outstanding stock for transactions involving change in control. In most supermajority voting amendments, the board has discretion in imposing the supermajority rule. This way the board has flexibility to impose the supermajority provision in the case of an unfriendly takeover and to not enforce it in the case of a friendly acquirer. Thus, the supermajority rule may not apply in the case of a merger approved by the board. In other cases, a supermajority vote may be necessary to cancel the supermajority vote for an acquisition.

In addition, some supermajority voting amendments have been extended to include supermajority voting to amend the corporation's charter.

Super Voting Stock

Dual class capitalization, or super voting stock, was already discussed in general in Chap. 8 and is included in Table 10.4. As discussed, companies may have more than one class of stock for many reasons, say to separate the performance of individual operating divisions. Dual class capitalization is also a defensive tactic whereby a firm may issue shares with different numbers of votes per share. One class of shares has more votes per share than the other class of stock. For example, some super voting shares have 10 or more votes per share.

Although the creation of super voting stock is no longer permitted under today's policies of the Securities Exchange Commission, New York Stock Exchange, American Stock Exchange, and NASDAQ, it is a technique that was successfully used in the past.

Eliminate Cumulative Voting

In a situation in which three board members are being elected, cumulative voting allows a stockholder to cast all his or her votes for one board seat. For example, under cumulative voting, a stockholder of 1000 shares in an election for three board members can cast 3000 votes. That could be 1000 votes to each of three candidates or all 3000 votes to one candidate. By allowing cumulative voting, minority shareholders with enough shares may gain control of a board seat.

The nature of cumulative voting is illustrated by the following formula:

$$R = [DN / (T + 1)] + 1 \qquad (10.1)$$

where R = number of shares required to elect desired number
of directors
D = desired number of directors to elect
N = total number of shares (votes) outstanding
T = total number of directors to be elected

So, in our example, if a stockholder held 1000 shares of stock out of a total of 3900 shares, or 25.6 precent, that stockholder would need only 976 shares to secure 1 board seat out of 3 available positions:

$$R = [(1 \times 3900) / (3 + 1)] + 1 = 976 \qquad (10.1a)$$

Said differently, the stockholder with 1000 shares when electing 3 directors may cast all 3000 votes for 1 candidate. The remaining two candidates would receive a total of 8700 votes (or 2900 shares times 3 votes per share). Thus board candidate 2 could receive 3001 votes while board candidate 3 could receive 3001 votes. Board candidate 4 could only receive the remaining 2698 votes and consequently would not be elected. The cumulative voting process secures one seat for the minority stockholder.

By eliminating cumulative voting and forcing only 1 vote per share per candidate there is no sharing of power with a minority stockholder. For example, board member 1, the minority's (1000 shares) candidate receives a vote of 1000; the majority's (2900 shares) candidate receives a vote of 2900—the majority wins. Minority board candidates 2 and 3 each receive 1000 votes, but are not elected because the majority's candidates 2 and 3 each receive 2900 votes. In this way the majority stockholders do not let the minority shareholder obtain any intrusion onto the board.

Antigreenmail Amendment

During the 1980s, it was not uncommon for a company or investment firm to purchase a block of stock in a target company and then to begin to clamor about an acquisition. The target firm, viewing the situation as a hostile takeover, would offer to buy back the shares at a premium price over what the acquirer paid for it. In this way, the phrase *greenmail* was coined as a variation on *blackmail*.

Antigreenmail charter amendments prohibit or greatly discourage greenmail. The provision generally requires a shareholder vote with the approval of a majority or supermajority of the nonparticipating shareholders before a greenmail repurchase is consummated. The greenmail payment cannot be made if it is not approved by the shareholders.

Limit Shareholder Action

The board of directors controls the logistics around stockholders' meetings. These logistics are important and can be used to impede the desires of an unwanted acquirer. The stockholder meeting is very important to the unfriendly acquirer since this forum will provide the necessary venue for the shareholder vote.

A consent solicitation may add seats to the board, remove specific board members, or elect new board members without a special stockholders' meeting, if the necessary board provisions are not in place. This consent solicitation, which has been established in some states, speeds up the process to conduct a stockholder vote without setting up a special meeting. Once again, a company's charter or bylaws can be amended to limit this process.

An advance-notice provision is contained in some corporations' bylaws. These bylaws may require advance notice of 2 months before a special meeting can be held. Additionally, the board has the power to call special meetings, to schedule those meetings, and to set the meeting agenda.

The antitakeover charter amendments are designed to use the corporation's charter and its supporting bylaws to limit unfriendly acquisition attempts.

OTHER BOARD OR MANAGEMENT METHODS

In addition to antitakeover charter and bylaw amendments, the management team and board of directors have other techniques to deal with unfriendly acquisition attempts. Table 10.6 lists these methods.

T A B L E 10.6

Other Board or Management Methods

Poison pills
- Flip-over plan
- Flip-in plan
- Dead-hand provisions
- Back-end plans
- Poison puts

Authorization of preferred equity privately placed with favorable vote

Parachutes
- Golden parachute
- Silver parachute
- Tin parachute

Negotiate contracts for labor, rent, etc., that increase with management change

Poison Pills

A poison pill is a defensive strategy that involves a security with special rights exercisable by a triggering event. The triggering event could be the announcement of an acquisition attempt or the accumulation of a certain percentage of stock by another corporation. Poison pills come in two general varieties that may be used together. The two varieties are flip-over and flip-in plans. A flip-over plan provides for a bargain purchase price of the acquirer's shares; a flip-in program provides a bargain purchase price of the target company.

The poison pill, like the other takeover defenses, must be justified as protection to the corporation and its shareholders. While a poison pill does not prevent an unwanted takeover, it does strengthen the board's negotiating position. If a bidder comes in with a substantial offer, the board may redeem the poison pill. A *dead-hand provision* allows only the members of the board who initiated the poison pill to modify or redeem the provision. Once again, the dead-hand provision prevents an unfriendly acquirer from seizing control of the board and removing the pill.

A *back-end plan* is a different variety of a poison pill. A back-end plan provides the target shareholders with rights. At the option of the target's stockholder, a right and a share of the target's stock can be exchanged for cash or senior debt at a specific price set by the target's board. This effectively communicates the board's asking price for the company.

A poison put takes the form of a bond with a put option attached. The put option only becomes effective if an unfriendly acquisition takes place. The bonds are put (or sold back) to the acquiring company, thus putting an additional drain on the cash requirements of closing the deal.

While these forms of poison pills may not prevent an unfriendly takeover, once again they slow the process, initiate more intense negotiations, and open the door for more attractive offers.

Authorization of Preferred Equity

Authorization of preferred equity to be privately placed with a group that would be favorable to the board's vote is another board technique. A new class of security, a preferred equity with voting rights, is authorized but remains unissued until an unfriendly acquisition offer is made. At that point the board privately places the preferred stock with a group of investors who are deemed "friendly" to the board's antitakeover position. This resembles a quasi-poison pill.

Parachutes

Parachutes are employee severance agreements that are triggered when a change in control takes place. The purpose is to provide the corporation's managers and employees with peace of mind during acquisition discussions and the transition. It helps the corporation retain key employees who may feel threatened by a potential acquisition. Parachutes also help the manager to address personal concerns while acting in the best interest of the stockholder. The current board and management team establish the parachutes that become effective when a potential acquirer exceeds a specified percentage of ownership in the company. Parachutes may be put in place without the approval of stockholders and may be rescinded in the case of a friendly takeover.

Parachutes come in three varieties. First, the golden parachute is designed for the corporation's most senior management team, say, the top 10 to 30 managers. Under this type of plan, a substantial lump-sum payment (maybe multiples of the manager's annual salary and bonus) is paid to a manager who is terminated following an acquisition. A silver parachute widens the protection to a much larger number of employees and may include middle managers. The terms of a silver parachute often cover severance equal to 6 months or 1 year of salary. Finally, a tin parachute may be implemented that covers an even wider circle of employees or even all employees. This program provides limited severance pay and may be structured as severance pay equal to 1 or 2 weeks of pay for every year of service.

Negotiated Contracts

The final antitakeover technique that can be implemented by management or the board is to negotiate contracts for labor, rent, or whatever with specific clauses that rescind the existing terms of the contract and increase the costs if a management change occurs. For example, a lease may contain a provision that increases the original lease payment in the event that an unfriendly takeover occurs.

POSTACQUISITION BID TECHNIQUES

The antitakeover measures discussed above generally should be in place before unwanted acquisition threats arise. This section discusses techniques that are applicable after an acquisition bid has been received. See Table 10.7.

Just Say No

The just-say-no defense comes into play when a target board does not yield to the potential acquirer's demands. The board cannot arbitrarily decide to ignore an acquirer's overtures. Only reasonable defensive measures can be used, and the board must be able to demonstrate that the bid is inadequate and disrupts the long-term strategy of the firm.

T A B L E   1 0 . 7

Postacquisition Bid Techniques

Just say no

Greenmail

Standstill agreements

Pac-Man defense

Implement other acquisition plans

White knight or white squire

Divest "crown jewels"

Litigation
  • Antitrust effect of acquisition
  • Material information missing from SEC filing

Create antitrust incompatibility

Trigger the application of state antitakeover laws

Greenmail

As discussed above, greenmail is a practice of "paying off" anyone who acquires a large block of the company's stock and raises threats of acquisition. To alleviate those threats, a company can simply pay that individual a premium over what he or she paid when accumulating the company's stock. It is a technique that can be used in a hostile takeover situation. However, paying greenmail may be counterproductive with less than desired effects, and it could result in other potential acquirers stepping in to receive their greenmail as well.

Standstill Agreement

A standstill agreement is an understanding between a company and a large block of stockholders. It is voluntary on the part of the potential acquirer and provides a specified period of time that the acquirer will not purchase any more shares of the target company. A standstill agreement often is enacted with a greenmail payment.

Pac-Man Defense

A Pac-Man defense is an extremely aggressive (and rarely used) defense where the target company counteroffers and launches its own acquisition attempt on the potential acquirer. For example, company A launches an unfriendly takeover attempt of company T. To thwart these advances, company T launches its own acquisition attempt of company A. This technique is also effective when the original acquirer is smaller than the original target company, thus providing the original target the opportunity to finance a potential deal.

This defense is extremely risky. It mitigates the antitrust defenses that could be offered by the original target company. The Pac-Man defense essentially suggests that the target company's board and management are in favor of the acquisition, but that they disagree about which company should be in control.

Implement Other Acquisition Plans

Many large, public corporations have a list of potential acquisition candidates that could fit into their strategic plans. Some companies may build "war chests" (cash and unused debt capacity) in anticipation of an acquisition. This war chest is also a catalyst that can turn a potential acquirer into the target. With the threat of a hostile takeover looming, a target company may quicken its own acquisition plan. If the target company successfully acquires other companies, its war chest is greatly reduced, and it may be too large for the hostile acquirer to afford or it may be too complicated for the hostile acquirer to assimilate and manage.

White Knight or White Squire

In a white knight defense, the target company seeks a "friendly" acquirer for the business. The target might prefer another acquirer because it believes there is greater compatibility between the two firms. Another bidder might be sought because that bidder promises not to break up the target or to dismiss employees en masse.

During the 1980s and early 1990s, Hershey Foods had the reputation of acquiring companies at reasonable prices and transforming the businesses either by enhancing the efficiency of operations or providing a wider distribution profile. Hershey was also known for not disrupting the culture of an acquired business while respecting the traditions acquired. During that period of time, Hershey Foods was called upon as a white knight on several occasions. None of those potential deals were eventually consummated. Hershey found that its bid did not reach the level of bid originally offered by the first bidder. This shortfall may in part be due to the fact that without the business streamlining "rationalizations" enjoyed by the original bidder, Hershey's bid fell short. In those cases, eventually the money won out.

A white squire is similar to a white knight, but the white squire does not take control of the target firm. Instead, the target sells a block of stock to a white squire who is considered friendly and who will vote her or his shares with the target's management. Other stipulations may be imposed, such as requiring the white squire to vote for management, a standstill agreement that the white squire cannot acquire more of the target's shares for a specified period of time, and a restriction on the sale of that block of stock. The restriction on the sale of that block of stock usually includes that the target company has the right of first refusal. The white squire may receive a discount on the shares, a seat on the target's board, and extraordinary dividends.

Previously, we discussed another board and management defensive tactic of authorizing preferred equity that is subsequently privately placed with favorable vote. Issuing this preferred equity to a white squire allows both the target and the white squire to customize the instrument to the specific needs.

Divest "Crown Jewels"

A company may also consider selling its most valuable line of business or division. This line of business or division is referred to as the *crown jewels*. Once this business has been divested, the proceeds can be used to repurchase stock or to pay an extraordinary dividend. Additionally, once the crown jewels have been divested, the hostile acquirer may withdraw its bid.

Litigation

After a hostile takeover bid has been received, the target company can challenge the acquisition through litigation. Litigation is initiated by the target company based on the antitrust effects of the acquisition, inadequate disclosure (missing material information) in SEC filings, or other securities law violations. The target sues for a temporary injunction to prohibit the bidder from purchasing any additional shares of the target's stock until the court has an opportunity to rule on the case.

Create Antitrust Incompatibility

Through an acquisition of its own, a target company can create an antitrust situation for a potential acquirer. After receiving the initial acquisition proposal, a target can itself determine to expand vertically or horizontally. Often, through such expansion by the target, the potential acquirer is put in a less desirable antitrust situation by virtue of the newly positioned organization. For example, in the late 1970s, Marshall Field received an unfriendly acquisition bid from Carter Hawley Hale (CHH). Field's response included geographical expansion into a Houston mall through Field's own internal growth and into the northwest via the acquisition of a small chain of Liberty House stores. CHH withdrew its offer because of the antitrust position of owning two stores in the same mall in Houston and what CCH deemed a less than desirable expansion into the northwest that conflicted with CCH's own northwest expansion plans.

State Antitakeover Laws

Some states have adopted a set of antitakeover laws. Most of these laws are designed to eliminate two-tier offers. As discussed above, a company can also eliminate the effects of a two-tier offer by adopting a fair price amendment to the corporation's charter. Additional common protection offered by state laws includes an extension of the waiting period from 20 days (per the federal Williams Act). This may be particularly important in large, complicated transactions where other potential bidders may need the extra time to prepare a competing offer.

IMPACT OF DEFENSIVE TACTICS

The antitakeover literature is quite extensive. Our purpose continues to be a sampling of the literature results without providing an exhaustive list of all the studies. The studies cited below look at the impact of specific antitrust provisions. The impact is measured as the *cumulative abnormal return* (CAR) on the stock price. That is, over a specified period of time (the event period) how did the stock perform compared to its expected performance as projected by the capital asset pricing model? As an example, if a 6-month event study were conducted (3 months before the event and 3 months after the event), the company had an expected 6-month stock price return of 5.0 percent, and actually provided an 8.0 percent return, that stock would have yielded a +3.0 percent cumulative abnormal return.

A positive CAR indicates that a defensive tactic enhances shareholder value. A negative CAR indicates that the technique is detrimental to shareholders. A defensive tactic with a negative CAR raises the question of why a firm would adopt such a position and leads to speculation of management entrenchment.

Leveraged Buyouts and Leveraged Recapitalization

Bae and Simet (1998) studied the shareholder effects of leveraged buyouts (LBOs) and leveraged recapitalization (LR). The event was the announcement of either an LBO or LR, and the periods that they studied were 1 day before the event and 20 days before the event. Over both time periods, the stockholders of both LBO and LR received positive CARs.

Event Period CARs	LBO	LR
−1 day to 0	+12.0%	+5.7%
−20 days to 0	+15.5%	+11.7%

Notice, in both cases, LBOs outperformed LRs. This clearly indicates that the board and management can implement reorganization strategies that enhance shareholder value.

Greenmail and Antigreenmail Amendments

Mikkelson and Ruback (1985, 1991) found that abnormal returns are earned during the initial stock accumulation phase by a potential acquirer through the purchase-to-repurchase period. However, beyond this period, a negative abnormal return of 2 to 3 percent accompanies the announcement of greenmail payment (Dann and DeAngelo, 1983). Further, Mikkelson and Ruback (1991) found that the negative CARs are even more negative if a standstill agreement is enacted at the same time. The standstill agreement may signal a reduced probability of a subsequent takeover, and thus the price retreats. Consequently, greenmail payments reduce the value of the firm.

Eckbo (1990) found slightly negative (but insignificant) CARs related to the adoption of antigreenmail amendments. Examining a subsample of firms that had experienced an abnormal run-up over the 3 months prior to the mailing of proxy that contained an antigreenmail, Eckbo found a strong positive market reaction. He argued that removing the possibility of greenmail would remove a barrier to the takeover of the firm with positive gains to shareholders.

Antitakeover Amendments

Different studies find different shareholder impacts when antitakeover amendments are adopted. Some studies find slightly (although insignificantly) negative results, while other studies find no shareholder effects when antitakeover amendments are adopted. However, two studies examined stock ownership and board composition. These studies found conclusive results.

Malekzadeh, McWilliams, and Sen (1998) found significantly larger negative CARs when antitakeover amendments are adopted in a firm with a CEO or with a board that held only a small percentage of the total outstanding stock, than when firms' CEOs or boards hold a more substantial portion of the outstanding stock. Additionally, the results were more significantly negative when the CEO was also the chair of the board. McWilliams and Sen (1997) found that the reaction was more significantly negative if inside and affiliated outside directors dominated the board.

In a variation of the prior studies, Karpoff, Malatesta, and Walking (1996) studied the repeal of antitakeover amendments and found no significant effects of the amendment repeal. Their results support the findings of limited effects when the amendments were first announced.

Poison Pill

The evidence is very mixed on the effect of poison pills. Comment and Schwert (1995) found that only early (pre-1985) poison pill plans were associated with large declines in stockholder value and that takeover premiums were higher when a target firm had a poison pill in place. Johnson and Meade (1996) studied the topic by reviewing the market impact of an announcement of a poison pill. They found that the announcement impact was insignificant whether or not there were other poison pills already in place. Cook and Easterwood (1994) examined poison puts and concluded that poison puts created negative returns to shareholders.

Golden Parachutes

Once again, the impact of a golden parachute on shareholders' wealth is an unsettled issue. The evidence is mixed. Lambert and Larcker (1985) found the adoption of golden parachutes resulted in positive CARs for shareholders. Hall and Anderson (1997) focused on the announcement of the adoption of a golden parachute plan for firms that did not experience any takeover bids for a period of 3 years prior to the announcement. In general and over a range of event periods, they found insignificant results. Mogavero and Toyne (1995) studied adoption dates and for their full sample found insignificant results; but as they focused their attention to the later period of their study (1986 to 1990), they found significantly negative CARs of –2.7 percent.

State Antitakeover Legislation

A study by Swartz (1996) examined the impact of Pennsylvania Antitakeover Law on April 27, 1990. The act limited hostile takeover activities, and firms were allowed to opt out of coverage, which approximately 70 percent of the firms did. The firms that opted out of coverage of this act experienced an 18.1 percent higher CAR than the firms that did not opt out over a study period of 190 days (-130 days before the act and +60 days after the act). For a more narrow period (-60 days before to +30 days after), a 5.4 percent higher CAR was experienced for firms opting out of coverage by this act. State antitakeover legislation provides the incumbent board with a protection that the market views as detrimental to shareholder value.

Summary of the Defensive Tactic Impact

Of the literature presented above, three defensive tactics have clear impact. LBOs and leveraged recapitalization are significantly positively received by the stockholders. Greenmail payments have a negative impact, while antigreenmail provisions are viewed as positive steps that remove an acquisition barrier. Finally, state antitakeover legislation is negatively viewed by the stock market since acquisitions above prevailing market prices may be blocked.

Poison pills, golden parachutes, and adoption of antitakeover amendments have little significant effect on shareholder returns. With regard to the adoption of antitakeover amendments, more significantly negative returns are found when the company's CEO and board hold minimal shares, the CEO is also the chair of the board, and the board is dominated by inside and affiliated directors.

SUMMARY AND CONCLUSION

This chapter covered numerous antitakeover defensive strategies. In general, these strategies included

- Operating performance
- Financial techniques

- Restructuring and financial engineering
- Antitakeover charter amendments
- Other board or management methods
- Postacquisition bid techniques

Most companies employ many of these techniques.

Operating performance and financial techniques are aligned with strong business practices and strategies that create value for the shareholders. Restructuring and financial engineering were more fully covered in Chap. 8. This chapter served as a reminder that the incumbent board and management must also keep a keen eye on unlocking additional value from the business via self-restructuring and self-reorganization.

Antitakeover charter amendments or shark repellents include provisions to strengthen the board's position, such as staggering the board members' terms and for-cause removal provisions. Fair price provisions eliminate a two-tier offer and ensure that all stockholders receive the same acquisition price per share. Other techniques include supermajority votes, super voting stock, antigreenmail amendment, and the ability to limit shareholder actions.

Poison pills and golden parachutes are popular techniques that can be instituted by the board and management without a change in the corporation's charter. A poison pill is a right issued by the target company to allow favorable conversion into either the target or the acquirer's stock. A golden parachute is an employment contract that protects senior managers if they are terminated following an acquisition.

A number of postacquisition bid defensive tactics include paying greenmail to the bidder, initiating acquisition activity on the potential acquirer (Pac-Man defense) or others, finding a friendly acquirer (white knight), or instituting litigation or the protection offered by certain states.

In summary, two alternative possibilities of motives for takeover defenses need to be taken into account. One possibility is that managers use takeover defenses to entrench and protect their executive positions, which might be lost in a takeover. The opposite possibility is that managers use takeover defenses to improve the bargaining position of the target firm so that a higher price could be obtained for the target shareholders.

REFERENCES

Bae, S. C., and D. P. Simet, "A Comparative Analysis of Leveraged Recapitalization versus Leveraged Buyout as a Takeover Defense," *Review of Financial Economics*, 7, 1998, pp. 157–172.

Comment, Robert, and G. William Schwert, "Poison or Placebo? Evidence on the Deterrence and Wealth Effects of Modern Antitakeover Measures," *Journal of Financial Economics*, 39, 1995, pp. 3–43.

Cook, Douglas, and John C. Easterwood, "Poison Put Bonds: An Analysis of Their Economic Role," *Journal of Finance*, 49, December 1994, pp. 1905–1920.

Dann, Larry Y., and Harry DeAngelo, "Standstill Agreements, Privately Negotiated Stock Repurchases, and the Market for Corporate Control," *Journal of Financial Economics*, 11, 1983, pp. 275–300.

Eckbo, B. Espen, "Valuation Effects of Greenmail Prohibitions," *Journal of Financial and Quantitative Analysis*, 25, December 1990, pp. 491-505.

Hall, P. L., and D. C. Anderson, "The Effect of Golden Parachutes on Shareholder Wealth and Takeover Probabilities," *Journal of Business Finance and Accounting*, 23, April 1997, pp. 445–463.

Johnson, D. J., and N. L. Meade, "Shareholder Wealth Effects of Poison Pills in the Presence of Anti-Takeover Amendments," *Journal of Applied Business Research*, 12, Fall 1996, pp. 10–19.

Karpoff, Jonathan M., Paul H. Malatesta, and Ralph A. Walkling, "Corporate Governance and Shareholder Initiatives: Empirical Evidence," *Journal of Financial Economics*, 42, 1996, pp. 365–395.

Lambert, R., and D. Larcker, "Golden Parachutes, Executive Decision Making, and Shareholder Wealth," *Journal of Accounting and Economics*, 7, April 1985, pp. 179–204.

Malekzadeh, A. R., V. B. McWilliams, and N. Sen, "Implications of CEO Structural and Ownership Powers, Board Ownership and Composition on the Market's Reaction to Antitakeover Charter Amendments," *Journal of Applied Business Research*, 14, Summer 1998, pp. 53–62.

McWilliams, V. B., and N. Sen, "Board Monitoring and Antitakeover Amendments," *Journal of Financial and Quantitative Analysis*, 32, 1997, pp. 491–505.

Mikkelson, W. H., and R. S. Ruback, "An Empirical Analysis of the Interfirm Equity Investment Process," *Journal of Financial Economics*, 14, 1985, pp. 523–553.

_____, "Targeted Repurchases and Common Stock Returns," *The RAND Journal of Economics*, 22, Winter 1991, pp. 544–561.

Mogavero, Damian J., and Michael F. Toyne, "The Impact of Golden Parachutes on Fortune 500 Stock Returns: A Reexamination of the Evidence," *Quarterly Journal of Business and Economics*, 34, 1995, pp. 30–38.

Swartz, L. M., "The 1990 Pennsylvania Antitakeover Law: Should Firms Opt Out of Antitakeover Legislation?" *Journal of Accounting, Auditing, and Finance*, 11, Spring 1996, pp. 223–245.

QUESTIONS AND PROBLEMS

10.1 *a.* How many shares of stock must a stockholder own to elect four out of nine board members? Assume 10,000 shares outstanding and cumulative voting.

  b. If the stockholder owns the same number of shares as determined in part *a* and the board is staggered over 3 years (i.e., three directors elected each year), in total, how many directors can that stockholder elect and how long does it take?

  c. If the stockholder owns the same number of shares as determined in part *a* and there is no cumulative voting, how many directors can that stockholder elect?

10.2 Explain the difference between a flip-in and a flip-over poison pill.

10.3 Why are operating performance, financial techniques, and restructuring and financial engineering considered antitakeover defenses and good business practice?

10.4 General studies about adoption of antitakeover amendments provide mixed results. However, the two studies noted here found more significantly negative returns when the company's CEO and board hold minimal shares, the CEO is also the chairman of the board, and the board is dominated by inside and affiliated directors. Discuss these results.

SOLUTIONS TO QUESTIONS AND PROBLEMS

10.1 *a.* In order to elect 4 out of 9 board members, 4001 votes are required, or only 40.01 percent of the outstanding 10,000 votes with cumulative voting.

$$R = [(4 \times 10,000) / (9+1)] + 1 = 4001$$

  b. With 4001 votes, a stockholder can elect one out of three board members each year if the board was staggered over 3 years. In order for that stockholder to elect two out of three, he or she would need a majority of votes:

$$R = [(2 \times 10{,}000) / (3+1)] +1 = 5001$$

In 3 years, with a staggered board, the stockholder would capture only three seats on the board.

c. With 4001 votes and no cumulative voting, the other 5999 votes can always outvote that stockholder for any particular board seat. Therefore, that stockholder cannot elect any members of the board.

10.2 A flip-over plan provides for a bargain purchase price of the acquirer's shares; a flip-in program provides a bargain purchase price of the target company.

10.3 Operating performance, financial techniques, and restructuring and financial engineering are antitakeover defenses and good business practice. Improving current business operations (growth, margins, and capital investment), returning cash to stockholders, reducing the cost of capital, and selling off underachieving assets or businesses are all good business practices that unlock the value of the firm and enhance shareholder value.

10.4. Adoption of antitakeover amendments is viewed as board or management entrenchment when the CEO and board own a minimal number of shares, the CEO is also the chair, and the board is dominated by insiders or affiliated directors. Consider the converse—the CEO and board own a large number of shares, the CEO is not the chair, and outsiders dominate the board. In this case, clearly the best interests of the shareholders (including the CEO and board) will be served.

INDEX

ABOUT THE AUTHORS

J. Fred Weston, Ph.D., is Professor Emeritus Recalled of Managerial Economics and Finance at the John E. Anderson Graduate School of Management at UCLA, where, since 1968, he has been Director of the UCLA Research Program on Takeovers and Restructuring. He received his Ph.D. degree from the University of Chicago in 1948. Dr. Weston has served as president of the American Finance Association, president of the Western Economic Association, president of the Financial Management Association, and member of the American Economic U.S. Census Advisory Committee. He has been selected as a fellow of the American Finance Association, of the Financial Management Association, and of the National Association of Business Economists, and published 147 journal articles and 31 books, including *Managerial Finance, Public Policy Toward Mergers* and *The Art of M&A Financing and Refinancing.*

Samuel C. Weaver, Ph.D., is associate professor of finance at Lehigh University, where he formerly served as the Theodore A. Lauer Adjunct Professor of Finance. Dr. Weaver spent 20 years as an executive with Hershey Foods Corporation, serving in various capacities, including director, financial planning and analysis, and is a veteran of over 100 acquisition valuations and numerous other restructuring activities. The coauthor of *Finance and Accounting for Nonfinancial Managers,* he serves on the Board of Trustees of the Financial Management Association and the Board of Directors of the Eastern Finance Association. In 1999, he received the Lehigh MBA Excellence in Teaching award.

Shelbyville/Shelby County Public Library

Mon-Thu 9-9, Fri 9-7, Sat 9-5, Sun closed
Call (317) 398-7121or (317) 835-2653 to renew most material.
Bookdrops at front door and in alley behind library and at Morristown school.

http://www.sscpl.lib.in.us

Name: CONOVER, PHILLIP C
Address: 1109 S MERIDIAN

Materials Checked Out As Of 8/22/2007

Barcode	Title	Date Due	Call Number
159435	How to run seminars and workshops: presentation skills for consultants, trainers, and teachers	9/4/2007	658.456 Jol
114788	Franchise opportunities handbook	9/4/2007	650
100331	Creating & delivering winning advertising & marketing..	9/4/2007	658.8
400082	Mergers and acquisitions	9/5/2007	658.162 Wes

Fines Due As Of 8/22/2007

Barcode	Title	Date Due	Date Returned	Fine